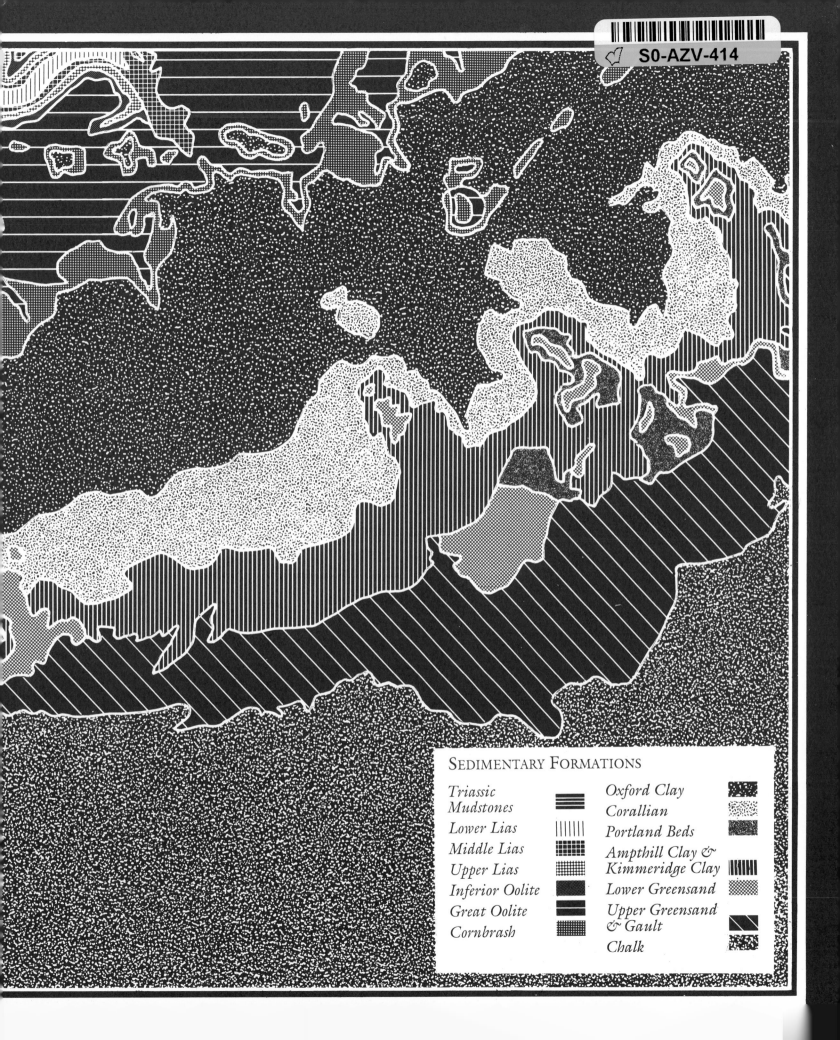

SEDIMENTARY FORMATIONS

Triassic Mudstones

Lower Lias

Middle Lias

Upper Lias

Inferior Oolite

Great Oolite

Cornbrash

Oxford Clay

Corallian

Portland Beds

Ampthill Clay & Kimmeridge Clay

Lower Greensand

Upper Greensand & Gault

Chalk

HIGHGROVE

An Experiment in
Organic Gardening and Farming

HIGHGROVE

AN EXPERIMENT IN

ORGANIC GARDENING AND FARMING

HRH The Prince of Wales and Charles Clover

SIMON & SCHUSTER

NEW YORK · LONDON · TORONTO · SYDNEY · TOKYO · SINGAPORE

SIMON & SCHUSTER
Simon & Schuster Building
Rockefeller Center
1230 Avenue of the Americas
New York, NY 10020

First Published by Chapmans 1993

All photographs by Andrew Lawson except those on pages:
131, 247 Environmental Picture Library
36, 229 Farmers Weekly
63, 81 bottom, 206, 211 Tim Graham
230 Intervention Board
19 bottom, 20, 24, 27, 52, 62, 66, 98, 108, 118, 120, 124, 129 left and right, 138, 139, 141, 142, 150, 157, 158, 160, 161, 163, 164, 170, 172, 173, 174 top and bottom, 176, 180, 182, 248, 252, 261, 268, 278 by Maurice and Carroll Tibbles
130 Royal Society for the Protection of Birds
207 Matt White
11, 12, 70 Alan Maxwell

The engraving of Highgrove House on page 68 from *Storers' Views of Gloucestershire* and the pen and wash drawing by F. Peake on page 59 are reproduced by kind permission of The Gloucestershire Collection, Gloucestershire County Library, Arts and Museums Service. The illustration on page 113 is by Peter Berry.

The authors and publisher gratefully acknowledge permission to reproduce copyright material.
Lyrics from '(Nothing But) Flowers' by David Byrne (ASCAP) © 1988 Index Music Inc. Reprinted in the UK by permission of Warner Chappell Music Ltd.
W.G. Hoskins from *The Making of the English Landscape*, 1955. Reprinted by permission of Hodder & Stoughton Ltd.
Extract from the *BBC Wildlife Magazine* article by Miriam Rothschild is reprinted by permission of Miriam Rothschild.
Laurie Lee from *Cider With Rosie*. Reprinted by permission of The Hogarth Press.
Extract from *Nature Conservation and Agricultural Change*, Nature Conservancy Council, 1990 is reprinted by permission of English Nature.
Extract from *Our Common Future*, World Commission on Environment and Development, 1987. Reprinted by permission of Oxford University Press.
Extract from *the State of Agriculture in the United Kingdom*, RASE 1991, is reprinted by permission of the Royal Agricultural Society of England.
Extract from *Alternative Agriculture* reprinted with permission. Copyright © 1989 by the National Academy of Sciences. Published by the National Academy Press, Washington DC.
Extracts from the *Farmers Weekly* article by John Burns are reproduced by permission of *Farmers Weekly*

Designed by Robert Updegraff
Production by Geoff Barlow
Printed in Great Britain by Butler & Tanner Ltd

2 4 6 8 10 9 7 5 3 1

Charles, Prince of Wales, 1948-
   Highgrove: an Experiment in organic gardening and farming / H.R.H. Prince of Wales and Charles Clover
   p.288   cm.27.6 x 23
   Includes bibliographical references and index.
   ISBN 0-671-79177-X
   1. Organic farming – England – Gloucestershire. 2. Highgrove (England) 3. Organic gardening – England – Gloucestershire. 4. Charles, Prince of Wales, 1948- – Homes and haunts – England – Gloucestershire.
   I. Clover, Charles. II. Title.
   S605.5.C43 1993
   635.0484'094241 – dc20   92 – 43341 CIP

ISBN: 0-671-79177-X

Title page: *Highgrove in December.*

Contents

Acknowledgements

The authors would like to thank all those who have helped them assemble the many elements of the story of Highgrove and those who have read it to ensure the facts are correct. Particular thanks must go to David Wilson, who was persuaded to write a chapter himself, and to Andrew Lawson and Carroll Tibbles who provided wonderful photographs to bring the text to life. The book could never have been written without Richard Aylard, Terry Summers, Lady Salisbury, Rosemary Verey, Miriam Rothschild, John Hughes, Nick Mould and Richard Young. It would not have been published in such lavish form without the considerable efforts of Marjory and Ian Chapman, Lord Buxton, Robert Updegraff, Geoff Barlow and Julia Martin. We also owe great thanks to the following who have contributed invaluable expertise, encouragement or advice: Alan and Jackie Gear, Dr Dick Potts, Dr Nick Sotherton, Patrick Holden, Lawrence Woodward, Mark Measures, Christopher Stopes, John Lister, Peter Falconer, Tim Gray, Sir Roy Strong, Lord Stockton, Willie Bertram, David Magson, Paddy Whiteland, Dennis Brown, Uwe Burka, Maurice and Carroll Tibbles, Jill Hutchinson Smith, Giles Gordon, Xandra Hardie, Sonia Holland, Jemima Parry-Jones, Rosamund and Mary Young, Barry Wookey, Helen Browning, John Gummer, Richard McIvor, John Byng, Richard Sandbrook, Richard Snook, Bob Foxwell, Richard Stainer, Tim Church, Robin Maynard, Andy Wilson, Jonathon Porritt, Professor Tim O'Riordan, Dr Ted Collins and Dr Jules Pretty. Thanks must go to David Langdale, Kevin Knott and Tom McCaw at the Duchy of Cornwall. We are indebted to Max Hastings of the *Daily Telegraph* for doing without his Environment Editor for over four months and to Clare Wood, Amanda Yaxley and Sarah Ward for invaluable assistance and keeping lines of communication open. The greatest thanks must go to the person who lived with much of this book for a year, provided constant support and ran a stern appraising eye over the results, Pamela Clover.

An Introduction to Highgrove

THERE HAVE BEEN numerous requests to film and write books about Highgrove during the last eleven years, but I have always declined, preferring to regard my activities there as a purely private passion; for gardening, for farming, and for doing both in a way which accords with my own particular beliefs. It was only when Survival Anglia, makers of some of the best nature programmes for television, asked if they could film the wildlife which appears to do quite well on the farm and in the garden, under a regime which manages without artificial fertilisers or pesticides, that my resistance weakened. Apart from anything else, I was rather keen myself to see what they would find, and to have a record of what will no doubt eventually be seen as 'the early days'. As a result, Maurice and Carroll Tibbles have spent the last eighteen months filming everything that creeps, crawls, flies or swims throughout the entire place.

I should have known that what started with a request to make a film would very soon develop into a suggestion to produce a book. I began to feel that to describe what had hitherto been a largely private enthusiasm to a nation of gardeners and lovers of the countryside might not prove to be too dangerous a pastime. The only problem was that I could never find the time to write an entire book, and besides I was far from objective about the subject matter. I therefore asked Charles Clover, Environment Editor of the *Daily Telegraph* and a self-declared agnostic about organic methods, to write the bulk of the book, describing and analysing what goes on at Highgrove and, where necessary, putting things into a broader context. He agreed, but on condition that he would have free access to the land, the people and the records which would allow him to produce an honest and balanced account. It ought to go without saying (but probably won't) that we have not sought to influence each other's contributions and that the views expressed are entirely our own.

The walled garden in spring with the prunus *blossom out and polyanthus and daffodils in flower.*

9

I realise that in writing about alternatives to accepted methods of farming I risk being accused of attacking the farmers themselves. But this is not the case. On the contrary I have every sympathy, knowing only too well that conventional farming has provided a far from easy living in the past few years, and that many farmers have found themselves in a serious financial position. In 1991 real farm incomes were fractionally over half what they were between 1979 and 1984. During that time many thousands of farmers have been going out of business each year – at the same time as surpluses have grown and parts of the countryside have become more derelict and more intensively farmed, with all the well-known and unfortunate consequences. This is not, in my view, an indictment of farmers; they have simply responded (with rare exceptions) to economic inducements offered by successive governments. The problem, it seems to me, is that we have increasingly been paying for the wrong things, including massive sums spent simply on storing and disposing of surpluses. The truth is that, in many respects, we have become the victims of our own short-term success and the whole system needs to redefine its objectives.

I do not, for one moment, pretend to have a grand solution to these very complex problems, but I am convinced that we need to look beyond minor and short-term adjustments to ever more complicated subsidies and take a fundamental look at our relationship with the land and, indeed, the whole of the natural world. In describing my experiences at Highgrove, I hope this book will put across my own views as a contribution to that process. I do not expect everyone to agree with me or to do the same as me. I appreciate only too well how fortunate I am to be able to develop my ideas at Highgrove but, even so, it will be many years before any firm conclusions can be drawn – although, of course, some minor successes and failures will no doubt become apparent along the way.

I have put my heart and soul into Highgrove – and I will continue to do so while I can. I have also put my back into Highgrove and, as a result, have probably rendered myself prematurely decrepit in the process. . . All the things I have tried to do in this small corner of Gloucestershire have been the physical expression of a personal philosophy. When I was younger I recall the nascent stirrings of such a philosophy; I felt a strong attachment to the soil of those places I loved best – Balmoral, in Scotland, and Sandringham, in Norfolk. As far as I was concerned, every tree, every hedgerow, every wet place, every mountain and river had a special, almost sacred, character of its own.

In some strange way, when I took on Highgrove, I knew what I wanted to do even though I had absolutely no experience of gardening or farming and the only trees I had planted had been official ones in very official holes! I experienced no sudden conversion to a new way of thinking, but merely developed an almost unconscious train of thought that seemed, now that I reflect upon it, like some powerful echo that arose, inexplicably, from within.

I knew I wanted to take care of the place in a very personal way and to leave it, one day, in a far better condition than I had found it. This was unlikely to be very difficult because everything was pretty dishevelled and run-down anyway!

As far as the garden was concerned, there was not a sign of one. Amazingly, there was absolutely nothing around the house. It sat, stark and exposed, without

a trace of any shelter and without a single flowerbed beside the house. On the south side an old, rusty iron fence ran alongside the large lawn, separating it from the meadow, with, here and there, a scruffy thorn bush or two. A wide, uncompromising path ran round the south and west sides of the house and, dividing the lawn in two, was a long central path, flanked by what probably must have been Edwardian clumps of golden yew and leading to a pretty dreadful square pond with an equally dreadful fluted stone pot in the middle of it. Beyond the house on the north side was an overgrown and unkempt shrubbery full of laurels, yews and holly. If you followed the path through this damp thicket you came to the only indication of a garden, consisting of a long, semicircular border, bounded at the back by a stone wall. Behind that curving stone wall lay the decrepit remains of a rather terrible rockery, surrounded by an even scruffier bit of shrubbery. Beyond the semicircular border the path continued through what must once have been a rather nicer shrubbery with bits of clipped yew and box, but it had become neglected, dark and messy and dwindled into a tangled jungle of huge laurels on one side of the square pond.

From this description you may well wonder why on earth I decided I wanted to live there. I have wondered too, from time to time. In many ways, I have often thought it would have been so much easier, and nicer, to have found somewhere with an existing and attractive garden, but I loved the trees and the parkland around the house. They had a particularly English feel. I also developed an

The house and garden in 1983: more lawn than garden, with little shelter from the prevailing winds.

11

The house from the end of the garden in 1983, showing the magnificent cedar on the lawn and the gravel path lined with golden yews, which still survive but have changed shape.

Paddy Whiteland, horseman, survivor and influence at Highgrove for forty-seven years.

instant passion for the 200-year-old cedar tree on the west side of the house. Then there was the kitchen garden. . . When I first saw it in its rather dissolute state, with its weather-beaten eighteenth-century brick walls glowing in the afternoon sun, I instantly began to see the possibilities for creating something that had been in the back of my mind for several years – a walled garden containing flowers, fruit and vegetables and clipped box hedges.

I was beginning to get carried away with visions of what I could do to the place and finally I was taken to see the stables. . . They had the kind of atmosphere which made me feel at home. They were old, worn and smelt right, and yet they had definite distinction. They were not grand, just plain elegant and full of character. There was just the right kind of hay loft above them which had played host to generations of swallows and swifts, and there was a tack room that smelt as tack rooms should – of years of saddle soap. The die was cast.

But perhaps an equally crucial and persuasive factor in the whole equation was the presence at Highgrove of one of the most inimitable Irishmen I have ever come across. 'Paddy' Whiteland had already been at Highgrove for very nearly forty years by the time I met him, but during that time he had become a kind of legend in the local area. A former prisoner of war of the Japanese, he can only be described as one of 'Nature's Gentlemen'. Meeting him for the first time, you invariably come away (a considerable time later!) feeling infinitely better. Once met he is never forgotten. His rugged features and twinkling eyes are one of the most welcoming features of Highgrove and his Irish stories are famous. . .

I soon discovered that I could not survive without Paddy and his truly remarkable organisational abilities. Everything I have done at Highgrove could not have been achieved without Paddy. He is one of those rare characters who can get things done 'by yesterday', and he is one of the most loyal people I have ever met. He is also one of the best and truest of individuals and I am forever indebted to him.

To call Highgrove an estate is, I think, stretching a point a bit too far! When I set foot on the place it consisted of just over 300 acres which, as far as I am concerned, is a farm, not an estate. And those 300 acres were divided up, most inconveniently, into three separate parcels of land – one of them a mile away from the house and the other about a quarter of a mile away. So the easiest thing to do, at the start, seemed to be a share-farming arrangement with two neighbouring farmers until we could decide a long-term policy for the future.

In those first years I concentrated on tackling the garden. It was difficult to know where to begin and I knew nothing about the practical aspects of gardening, but now that I had somewhere of my own I could attempt to translate the inner vision into an outer reality in terms of the landscape. As I greatly admired the taste and the consummate skill of Lady Salisbury, I asked her if she would come and help me. She subsequently taught me what little I know about gardening and ensured that I have become a lifelong admirer of the great seventeenth-century gardeners, the Tradescants.

The first thing to be done was to create some shelter on the windswept, 500-foot plain around the house and, as a matter of urgency, to provide a screen from the persistently prying eyes of pressmen armed with binoculars and obscenely large telephoto lenses to their cameras. There was nowhere to sit in the garden without being overlooked in those early days and because there was a strategically-placed public footpath in the vicinity you could be photographed the moment you stepped out of the front door! So Lady Salisbury helped me design a small rose garden on the south side of the house with a yew hedge surrounding it. We moved some paving stones from the back entrance and made a terrace under the house with the expert assistance of a wonderfully skilled stonemason and bricklayer (in fact, he can turn his hand to anything!) called Fred Ind. He has been responsible, together with another very special man, called Cecil Gardiner, for all the construction work in the garden and I am eternally grateful to them.

I looked at the pathetic little yew plants when they arrived and thought it would take a very long time before they were able to cut down the windspeed or obscure us from the camera lenses. But I had reckoned without good old, well-rotted manure! Lady Salisbury assured me that with generous applications of this glorious stuff the yews would grow over a foot a year – and they did, together with the help of a hurdle fence to reduce the effect of the wind. Witnessing the efficiency of muck was a very important lesson in my gardening education and I can safely say now that whatever has been achieved at Highgrove has been done through well-rotted manure. . .

At this stage, I should point out that I never had an overall master plan for the development of the garden. It grew in a rather haphazard, eccentric way as a result of ideas that would come to me after endless walks round the garden, or after sitting and reflecting on a summer evening. I also derived inspiration from books and from looking at one or two other gardens. Sometimes I wish I had made many more garden tours before beginning on my own because other people's ideas – like other people's cups of tea – always seem more interesting than your own! But I was in a hurry. I felt like a man with a mission and I was driven on by a sense of

The walled kitchen garden in July showing the simple geometrical shapes edged with box chosen by Prince Charles and Lady Salisbury. In the foreground is a tunnel of trained apple trees; around the pond is the herb garden; behind the hedges of rosemary are semi-circles of Golden Hornet crab-apples.

urgency. This was mainly because I was keen to see some of the fruits of my botanical activities if the good Lord should spare me into reasonable old age.

Redeveloping the kitchen garden proved to be a major task and Lady Salisbury and I spent several hours poring over plans at Cranborne or at Highgrove. Our original ideas were madly ambitious – a kind of miniature Villandry (a château in the Loire Valley) – but I soon found I had to moderate such ambitions in the interests of practicality and economy! The original plan incorporated elaborate box-bordered beds, rather like at Villandry, but I soon realised that I would have had to employ a one-legged gardener to hop from one small compartment to another, each of which would only have accommodated six cauliflowers or ten leeks!

Lady Salisbury knew a very competent retired architect who drew out the plans to scale and then the fateful moment came when the bulldozer moved in and cleared the whole walled garden. I remember looking at it, completely empty and flat, and wondering what on earth I had done. It then took very nearly two years to make all the brick paths, and the brick edges to the gravel paths, during which time some of the kind organisations which had given wedding presents to go in

the kitchen garden became increasingly agitated about the delay in delivering their plants. Gradually, however, we were able to plant the fruit trees and erect the iron arbours in the four quarters of the garden. The apple tunnels went in and finally the Sussex branch of the Women's Institute were able to deliver the long-delayed herbs for the herb garden around the fountain.

Once again, well-rotted manure proved its worth and everything in the garden has grown remarkably well, making it look more mature than it is. I have been extremely fortunate that one of the most brilliant vegetable growers in Gloucestershire, who also happens to be one of the nicest men I have ever met, Dennis Brown, looks after the kitchen garden in an immaculate, chemical-free way. There are certainly problems with pests and diseases. Several of the apple varieties seem to develop canker and the greenfly can be dreadful, but I find that each year is different and I decided to adopt the approach of 'taking the rough with the smooth' in order to have vegetables and fruit in their natural state. As a result, I think they taste better, but the real secret is to pick the vegetables when they are small and cook them only lightly.

Among the many wonderful things Lady Salisbury did was to introduce me to Miriam Rothschild, that remarkable exponent of the art of growing wild flowers. To me, one of the essential features of a garden is to have a contrast between the formal and the wild and so I was particularly enthusiastic to discover how to introduce wild flowers into the meadow area at Highgrove. The first attempt to slot-seed a wildflower mixture into the sward was not a success. The only things that managed to compete with the energetic grasses were yellow rattle and a few ox-eye daisies. I have since noticed, some nine years later, that the number of ox-eye daisies has grown each year, but that the yellow rattle has remained the same.

We then decided to sow a strip of wild flowers along one side of the front drive and having created a seedbed, a surprisingly expensive wildflower mixture was broadcast by hand! The resulting display that summer was dazzling – a veritable carpet of corn marigolds, ox-eye daisies, corn cockles and cornflowers. It was, as Miriam Rothschild said, like a Flemish tapestry. After this success I had visions of planting the whole meadow with such a mixture, but I could not face looking at a ploughed field for most of the spring and summer, so I decided to plant a variety of bulbs in the grass with the aim of creating, over the years, drifts of flowers in the long grass that would imitate the foreground in Botticelli's great painting, *Primavera*.

Wildflower gardening is not easy. To be successful the area has to be very carefully managed each year and cut at the right time. The great problem in England is that if you are growing arable wild flowers, or weeds as many farmers think of them, you have a constant battle with invasive and dominating grasses in our damp climate. In the Mediterranean countries such as Italy their hot summers dry up all the grass, thus providing a good seedbed for the wildflower seeds.

We have lost such a vast proportion of our wildflower and herb-rich meadows in this country, as a result of what is called 'improvement', that not only is it vital to preserve what little remains, but it is essential to try to recreate such valuable features in our landscape. This is another reason for my pursuit of an organic system of farming at Highgrove.

Having planted an enclosed rose garden and redesigned the kitchen garden it was time, I felt, to do something about the unfriendly area of lawn on the west side of the house. It was all too open and I suspected it needed enclosing by another yew hedge in order to give further privacy because, at that time, the press were even secreting themselves in various parts of the shrubbery and taking photographs onto the lawn. Lady Salisbury fortunately agreed with this idea and we spent further hours tramping up and down the lawn with measuring tapes, trying to mark out where the hedge would go around it. Maths has never been my strong point and, with hindsight, we should have had the line of the hedge properly surveyed! I have since discovered or, rather, Sir Roy Strong discovered, when I asked him to come and talk about topiarising the hedge, that everything about it is wrong. It is not laid out straight and one side is seventeen feet out from the other (I still maintain there is something very odd about the alignment of the house with the path that runs up the centre of the lawn!) but I feel this only serves to give the garden more character. . .

The borders of the front drive in July with corn marigolds and poppies flowering; both were once common in arable fields but are now removed by sprays and modern seed-dressing techniques.

16

OPPOSITE: _The hay meadow beside the house at buttercup time: a dramatic contrast with the wild flowers has been created by planting cultivated tulips. The darker ones are 'The Bishop', the medium red are 'Burgundy Lace'. The blue spikes are camassias._

LEFT: _A tawny owl, a resident of Duchy Home Farm._

BELOW: _Seeing whether anything has nested in one of over eighty bird boxes in the grounds of Highgrove._

One of the most satisfying aspects of this hedge-planting operation has been to see the increasing number of birds nesting in it as it grows bigger and thicker. It is a noticeable feature of Highgrove that there is a great variety of bird life in the garden and we are incredibly fortunate to have a considerable number of wood-peckers, both green and lesser-spotted, which seem to have taken up residence in the locality. To me, there are few sounds so redolent of an English country garden as that made by a woodpecker boring into a tree or making its peculiarly haunting cry as it flies across the garden. We now have something in the region of eighty nesting boxes in the grounds, all inspected and the nests recorded by an enthusiastic volunteer who is a member of the British Trust for Ornithology.

The next item on the gardening agenda was to make a terrace on the west side of the house so that when you walked out of the house there was an interesting and welcoming area to sit in. Once again Lady Salisbury found an architect, a young one this time, who could draw up the plan, which included a small foun-tain as the central feature and a low Cotswold stone wall enclosing it on three sides. Lady Salisbury proposed that the terrace should be cobbled with different sorts of large pebbles in patterns, rather as at Cranborne Manor in Dorset, but the pebbles were unobtainable so I had the idea to pave it with a mixture of stone slabs and granite sets with gaps in between that could be planted with a variety of interesting things that would form clumps throughout the terrace.

Planting the cottage garden.

PREVIOUS PAGES: *The terrace on the west side of the house which catches the evening sun. At the top is the new thyme path which has replaced the gravel shown in the older pictures. The terrace is made from stone slabs and granite sets, and the low walls from Cotswold stone, as are the mock-Gothic pavilions at the corners. Note the pagoda-shaped bird table hanging from a bough of the cedar tree.*

I decided to be enterprising and study a series of gardening books so that I could choose the plants to go in the beds against the low wall. I tried to select as many scented varieties as I could because, as far as I am concerned, a garden has to appeal to the olfactory senses as much as to the visual. My choice was amateur in the extreme and my planting plan ensured that half the taller plants ended up at the front of the beds and the small ones have long since been swallowed up by other shrubs at the back! There is only one way of learning and that is by your own mistakes. However, having chosen and planted everything myself, the terrace has a rather special meaning for me.

Gradually, each year, the garden grew in various directions. I had a new project each season and when, after eight years, I was able to tackle a particularly overgrown and neglected small copse bordering the meadow, which I had always planned to turn into a little woodland garden, I asked a landscape gardener, Vernon Russell-Smith, to help me with the initial layout and planting plan. When it came to clearing out the copse I very soon discovered that the trees were in a terrible state. Nothing had been touched for years and, as a consequence, the trees were misshapen, mangy, with broken-off tops and stag-headed. What big trees there were, were in poor condition and leaning at crazy angles. I took out as many of the really big trees as I could spare and then spent an entire weekend directing a man with a JCB in an earth-moving exercise in order to create a sunken area in a clearing of the copse. After a great deal of gesticulating we ended up with the topsoil on the bottom of the earthworks and the horrid, heavy clay on the top. I have never been able to grow anything worthwhile there since! As always, you learn by your mistakes. . . During the next three years I gradually completed the woodland garden, but I will have to wait some considerable time before it grows up into the form I want it to be.

As far as I am concerned, there is enormous satisfaction in growing things; in witnessing their development each year and in trying to imagine what they will eventually look like. Long after you are dead and gone, trees, in particular, will hopefully give pleasure and peace of mind to others yet unborn. To me, one of the great privileges of being lucky enough to be involved in the management of land, or in the development of a garden, is to invest in the future; to create features in the landscape which in due course may strike a chord in the hearts of our descendants. At Highgrove we have planted hedgerows, small copses, and belts of trees. At one point I asked John Makepeace, the renowned craftsman in wooden furniture and design, to help me plan a small copse which would consist of the types of trees best suited to furniture-making. We have since planted such a copse, consisting of trees like sycamore, wild cherry, holly and ash, and all that remains is to hope that someone will be around in seventy years' time who actually wants to use this timber. At least, if nothing else, there will be one tiny source of indigenous furniture wood available if the tropical timber sources dry up.

In the last few years I have been lucky enough to pick the fertile brain of one of this country's most notable plantswomen who, very conveniently, lives close by in Gloucestershire. Rosemary Verey has written a whole series of fascinating books on gardening and has created a memorable garden of her own at Barnsley. Her advice, and her genius for finding the right plant to go in the right place, and to provide interest and colour at different times in the year, has proved invaluable. When I wanted to make a small cottage garden out of an awkward area created by the planting of the yew hedge, Rosemary Verey ensured that the result lived up to the picture I had had in my mind. She has also trained my present gardeners which means that the garden is benefiting from two people who actually know what they are doing. The only trouble is that they bombard me with new ideas.

One of my ideas which I have developed recently has been the planting of a thyme 'tapestry carpet' on either side of the path that runs from the house up the centre of the lawn. Using a whole variety of different types of thyme, which I planted in random clumps during each weekend from April to July 1991, the result has been rather spectacular. In fact, it has been so spectacular that it has forced those experts, who initially tended to deride my idea, to revise their opinions! The smell is the best feature, but I also hope it will attract whole squadrons of butterflies and divisions of bees to feed upon the nectar and to rise up, like mobile flowers, as people pass by.

I am now gradually reaching the stage when I can begin to sit and appreciate some of my handiwork and that of all those kind, enthusiastic and skilled people who have given me, and still give, such invaluable advice and practical help.

Ever since I began the garden I have planted a very large proportion of the trees and plants myself which means that you at once develop a proprietary interest in all of them, and they become remarkably like children whom you watch growing up year by year. It is now a question of filling in the details with various features like gates, seats, statues and pots.

The door to the kitchen garden in autumn. Over the door is a purple-leafed vine and through the door, on the way to the fountain, are rugosa *roses turning an autumnal yellow. The pink paint was inspired by Royal Lodge, one of the Queen Mother's houses in Windsor Great Park.*

The seats are important, I have discovered, for the groups of visitors who come round the garden in the summer, in particular for the parties of elderly people from a variety of homes in Gloucestershire. Their exhausted members frequently had to be rescued by a Landrover halfway round the garden owing to the lack of resting places. Having created a garden, albeit an adolescent one, it is wonderful to be able to share it with other people and enormously heart-warming to learn of the apparent pleasure it gives the visitor. The garden at Highgrove really does spring from my heart, and strange as it may seem to some, creating it has been rather like a form of worship.

While all this gardening activity was taking place, the farming operations were also developing. After I had been at Highgrove for about three years, the decision was taken to move the Duchy of Cornwall Home Farm from faraway Cornwall to Highgrove. Additional land was purchased, unfortunately about a mile away and on the other side of the local town, and the rest of the Highgrove land taken back in hand.

In farming, as in gardening, I happen to believe that if you treat the land with love and respect (in particular, respect for the idea that it has an almost living soul, bound up in the mysterious, everlasting cycles of nature) then it will repay you in kind. But if you fail to respect the complex, universal laws to which every living creature is ultimately subject, and if you discard that essential humility which recognises the subtle balance that has to be struck between Man's ambition and the finite nature of the physical world, in the end the consequences could be painful and deeply destructive. Such ideas would once have been dismissed as alarmist nonsense, but increasing numbers of scientists are reporting mounting evidence of the catastrophic problems

The thyme walk in summer with Tigga, one of the two Jack Russells, and one of the seats which elderly visitors find useful on garden walks. The handsome bench was designed by Willie Bertram and was made to fit against the circular clump of golden yew.

we are creating for ourselves at an ever faster rate. They are beginning to see that if we play at being gods, however 'economic' and 'efficient' our activities may appear on a superficial level, we will eventually reap what we sow.

In the 1960's I remember the feeling of despair as I saw the remaining untouched, wild places being progressively grubbed up and converted to agricultural production on an almost industrial basis. Nowadays, of course, these marginal areas are the first candidates for what is known as 'set-aside', but it will be a long time, if ever, before some of these sites (such as chalk downland) revert to their original form of habitat.

What I found so difficult to understand about those heady days of 'modernist' farming (don't worry, I know all about the national requirement to be self-sufficient in food and all the other, apparently valid, reasons for doing what was done!) was the extent to which so many people seemed to lose touch with their instinct, let alone their sense of proportion, leading them to convert parts of the surrounding country-side into a virtually treeless, hedgeless desert. What was it that led seemingly sensible country people to abandon, overnight, all the accumulated wisdom and experience of their predecessors and to adopt with alacrity the novel idea that agriculture was first and foremost an industrial process?

The cynical, if not the practical, would say it was financial incentives (and the wider policy environment in which they were offered) that effected such a transformation in farmers' attitudes and there is, of course, a lot of truth in that. However, I do believe there was a more deep-seated reason; one that had its roots in the surge of so-called progressive thinking after the Second World War. The central feature of this thinking appeared to be that the past no longer had any relevance to the way we did things. The developments engendered by science would set us free from the shackles of the past, from the dead hand of tradition, and from outmoded concepts which prevented progress. In this scenario everything was possible; there could be no limit to what mankind could achieve now that the magic fire had been stolen from the gods.

This whole belief system wasn't confined to agriculture. It pervaded every aspect of life. Suddenly the avant-garde became the Establishment; the worlds of art, music, literature, architecture, education all fell under the spell of this revolutionary and, to many of its proponents, exciting philosophy of the future. Everything was carried before it and anyone who had serious doubts about the wisdom of adopting such a radical approach to life itself was instantly labelled a reactionary, or worse.

A central feature of this scientific philosophy, which has taken such a powerful hold over men's minds in the course of the last 200 years, but which received an immense boost after the last war, has been the almost religious belief in the machine and in its role as the chief engine of constant progress. This, in its turn, has encouraged us to view our existence on this Earth in an entirely different way from our ancestors. You may say this is hardly surprising (and a jolly good thing) if you believe that those who came before us and who helped to shape our landscape were pretty primitive, superstitious people who suffered severely from the lack of a scientifically-structured education. On the contrary, I believe that the way that our education has inculcated in us an almost instinctive acceptance of the concept of progress – as a linear function – has blinded us to the important fact, which our ancestors understood, that the whole pattern of nature rests on a circular function, driven by highly complex, interrelated systems. I believe this with absolute conviction and it is axiomatic to all my activities at Highgrove.

Before I am instantly accused of being a latter-day Luddite, I must emphasise that I am not unaware of the immense benefits that the development of the machine has brought. Properly harnessed, and used with restraint and wisdom, modern technology is an immense force for good. However, I am also conscious that in many ways we have allowed our fascination with the machine to enslave us and thus to distort our perception of the great truths enshrined in the laws of nature.

The perceptive contemporary American essayist Wendell Berry describes the destructive repercussions of our rather headstrong, immoderate love affair with the power of technology: 'Let loose from any moral standard or limit', he writes, 'the machine was also let loose in another way: it replaced the Wheel of Life, as the governing cultural metaphor. Life came to be seen as a road, to be travelled as far as possible, never to return. Or, to put it another way, the Wheel of Life became an industrial metaphor; rather than turning in place, revolving in order to dwell, it began to roll on the highways of progress toward an ever-receding horizon.'

This linear approach to the way we lead our lives, to the way in which we treat the whole of nature – flora, fauna and precious resources, not to mention waste products – has become an incredibly seductive one. It has been fascinating, if rather worrying, to see the extent to which the majority of 'conventional' farmers in this country are dependent upon multinational companies and their representatives for advice on which expensive compound to put on which crop at which time. The farmer almost loses the skill of being able to decide what he should be doing without a consultation. At present prices a farmer needs nearly a tonne of grain per acre to pay for his seeds, sprays and fertiliser before he even starts to pay for his fixed costs – labour, machinery, buildings, rent, etc. So once the treadmill is entered it is difficult to leave. The farmer has to produce higher yields to obtain the return to support his increasingly unsustainable system.

As far as the farmers are concerned, all the advice they have been given – and, in many cases, are still being given – is to continue with the same habit. All the agricultural education they have received has been based on the same linear approach, despite the obvious warning signs. Rachel Carson, in her book *Silent Spring*, written in the early 1960s, drew attention to the terrible dangers of proceeding along such a reckless course without listening to the promptings of the imagination or heeding the Laws of Nature. But with so much expert advice and encouragement, frequently offered free of charge, who can blame farmers for following it? Most people do not like to be thought of as old-fashioned, so we tend to opt for what the majority of others are doing. But I can't believe that many farmers didn't have some misgivings about what they were being encouraged and educated to do. However, I do believe they were badly advised and that agricultural colleges – in common with architectural colleges, medical schools, art colleges, music colleges and teacher-training colleges – have developed unbalanced teaching programmes which deliberately exclude positive references to the accumulated and traditional wisdom of the past.

It is perhaps just worth recalling what farming students were, and still are, being taught and encouraged to do in the pursuit of agriculture. Over and over

A newborn lamb in April.

again you hear references to the 'Agricultural Industry', as if farming were an industry like any other factory-based commercial operation. But farming is not just like any other industry. It has a cultural significance in the life and ethos of a country which distinguishes it from any other activity. It is a way of life that is, or should be, intimately associated with the long-term health of the soil through an almost sacred relationship with the miraculous living cycle of birth, growth, maturity, death and decay.

As Wendell Berry explains better than I can: 'the word "agriculture", after all, does not mean "agriscience", much less "agribusiness". It means "cultivation of land". And cultivation is at the root of the sense both of *culture* and of *cult*. The ideas of tillage and worship are thus joined in *culture*. And these words all come from an Indo-European root meaning both "to revolve" and "to dwell". To live, to survive on the earth, to care for the soil, and to worship, are all bound at the root to the idea of a cycle.' But we have broken the cycle and by our arrogant denial of the almost mystical relationship between tillage and worship (as if we were too sophisticated and clever for such a primitive and irrelevant concept) we have very nearly destroyed the cultural element of farming in Britain.

In a country like France, or Switzerland, they have not fallen prey to such short-sighted arrogance. The way the French manage to support their farmers – 'inefficient peasant farmers' as they are referred to derogatorily by official agencies and agricultural bodies in this country – has helped to maintain the essential rural culture of the country, precisely because the French, and, indeed, the Swiss, know only too well that the small farmer is the backbone of the country. Without support to enable the Swiss mountain farmer to farm in a traditional way, conforming to the natural cycle and foregoing short-term increases in production for the sake of the long-term health of the local environment, the entire economy and ecology of the mountain valleys would ultimately collapse.

The Swiss seem to understand the balance that has to be struck, and the *apparent* benefits that have to be foregone in order to live within the constraints that Nature imposes. And yet the Swiss have one of the most sophisticated economies and one of the highest standards of living in Europe. We are constantly being told that Britain has the most efficient farming system in Europe, or even in the world, unlike the poor, benighted, 'inefficient' French peasant. But what price efficiency when we have a £5$^1/_2$ billion trading gap with the Continent in food and drink, and if an unhealthy obsession with 'agriscience' leads to the sacrifice of the long-term health of the countryside and a great deal of public anxiety?

All these factors increasingly convinced me that what is euphemistically called 'conventional' farming is inherently unsustainable in the long term. Instead, I profoundly believe that many aspects of traditional farming systems are the most sustainable and appropriate in terms of mankind and his environment.

Perhaps you can imagine, after reading everything I have said so far, what the reaction was when, in 1985, I said I wanted to farm a part of the Home Farm on an organic basis. The 'experts' were very nice to me in my presence, but what they were saying about this latest demonstration of insanity once they were out of earshot can only be surmised! In the event eighty-five acres went through the conversion process and it was a most intriguing voyage of discovery for several people.

Some interesting changes were quickly noticed after conversion to an organic regime, such as an increased worm population, indicated by higher numbers of worm-casts. This is really a visual sign that the soil microbiology (soil bacteria and fungi) is in a healthy state and is breaking down and utilising organic matter to improve soil structure and fertility. This was borne out by two fields in particular. When they were last under a conventional arable crop they appeared to be 'dead', structureless soils that were difficult to work and produced, without doubt, the worst yields on the farm. After three years of a clover/grass ley under an organic regime the land ploughed like a different soil – full of worms, with a good structure, as was noticed immediately by the ploughman who had ploughed both before and after conversion.

I have been enormously lucky at Highgrove to have a truly remarkable farm manager, David Wilson, who by some extraordinary coincidence shared all my concerns about conventional farming and is carrying out the organic conversion with energy and enthusiasm. Our experiences on eighty-five acres were sufficient to convince me that I should have the courage of my convictions. I therefore urged the Duchy of Cornwall to convert the whole of the Home Farm to an organic system, rather than just a small part. More than 1,000 acres are now undergoing conversion and the Home Farm should be fully organic by 1997.

The term 'organic farming' is, I think, an unfortunate one. It presumably conjures up images of agricultural hocus-pocus; of some weird pseudo-scientific, 'alternative' farming system carried on by well-meaning, but essentially deeply eccentric, doom-mongers hankering after a pre-industrial, Arcadian past. On the contrary,

Rosamund Young with her fully-organic beef suckler herd at Kite's Nest Farm, near Broadway. Prince Charles visited Kite's Nest in 1989, the year he decided to convert the whole of Duchy Home Farm to organic production.

I see it as a means by which we can rediscover the rashly abandoned, but nevertheless entirely relevant, traditional principles which for thousands of years have helped to preserve the health and fertility of the soil for each successive generation. Not only have they preserved the health and fertility of the soil, but they have also preserved the essential diversity of species, on which we ultimately depend as a part of the complex pattern of life on this planet.

If we think we have outgrown such principles because we live in an age of ever-more-sophisticated technology, then I contend that we delude ourselves. What is the point of tripling the production of food with intensive systems of agriculture only to find that in the long run you have damaged the foundations on which the future well-being of our successors depends? The answer, as far as I am concerned, is to take the best of hard-won traditional knowledge and apply it with the best of modern technology, used sensitively.

It is interesting to note that this was the approach which produced the Agricultural Revolution of 200 years ago. It was farmers' own experiments which drove that revolution, bringing great increases in yield based solely on internal, or on-farm, resources. It was only later, in the 1830s–40s, with the development of various 'learned' agricultural institutions that the innovators were increasingly no longer seen as farmers but as non-farming 'scientists'. Once farmers became merely the recipients of new technologies and practices, the soul began to go out of farming.

Nowadays the situation has developed to the point where it is the vast majority of the people in the core agricultural institutions who are least willing or able to change their attitudes and accept innovative approaches based on farmers' knowledge. They are the people who lead the chorus which says that low external input, alternative and organic farming is backward.

This is an approach which we have exported to the Third World, despite all the evidence that modern farming methods are totally inappropriate to environmental and social conditions in the tropics and that traditional techniques can produce high yields of varied crops, while maintaining soil fertility and reducing farmers' reliance on expensive chemical inputs and unstable markets.

One of the great advantages of many traditional Third World agro-ecosystems is that they are genetically diverse, containing numerous varieties of domesticated crop species as well as their wild relatives. It has been shown that the great diversity of crops grown simultaneously in these polycultures helps prevent the build-up of pests on the comparatively isolated plants of each species.

In not seeking to maximise yields through the use of external inputs, but rather to achieve long-term stability through diversity, traditional farming systems exemplify the careful management of soil, water, nutrients and biological resources. That is why it is so vital to strengthen such systems – through village-based initiatives that actively involve local people. There are some remarkably successful grassroots rural development programmes in the so-called developing countries, proving that it is possible to achieve increases in yields, diversity of produce, land prices and labour rates, as well as, most importantly, greater social cohesion. Organisations like the International Institute for Environment and Development recognise that the key element is to rebuild communities first, by involving local people in planning and decision making. The technology follows, and is rarely a limiting factor. However, these successes are still chiefly parochial and limited to isolated communities. For such success to spread, wider policy factors must be brought into play. This rarely happens because, in common with many of the richer countries, there is almost invariably powerful official opposition to such an approach – and it is often associated with the enormous influence wielded by multinational chemical companies.

I have seen the results of agricultural industrialism all over the world, often encouraged by such agencies as the Food and Agriculture Organisation of the United Nations, and it makes you weep. It is such a waste of human potential and, whatever the official line is, it invariably results in ever-greater numbers of the urban dispossessed, the rootless, the unemployed and those without a stake in anything. Unfortunately, there is an unstoppable fascination and belief in the ultimate value of Western industrial models.

Despite the valiant efforts of far-sighted non-governmental organisations, in parts of the world like Ladakh (a Tibetan Buddhist enclave in the Indian state of Jammu and Kashmir) small, local systems of farming which, as a matter of principle, sacrifice immediate gains for the sake of long-term sustainability, are dying out because of an official bias towards large-scale systems and the replacement of local control by centralised bureaucracies. Likewise, in Northern Thailand and Bali, lowland rice-growing villages have, for centuries, depended on a type of locally-controlled water management adapted to a landscape dominated by forested highlands and swiftly flowing streams. The systems they have developed are now under threat from modern patterns of resource management promoted by international and state agencies. Such systems are regarded in official circles as being 'behind the times', and yet their destruction is already leading to increasingly severe environmental problems.

It may be considered in official circles to be 'behind the times' and embarrassingly superstitious for the local people to believe that if certain boundaries are overstepped and nature is damaged, then the spirits will punish humans. However, contrary to the attitude of such official agencies, it seems to me that seeking solutions to environmental problems requires a belief in the abilities of villagers who have consistently struggled to preserve their local resources.

It may be entirely unfashionable to say this, but I can't help feeling that the only prospect for a sustainable future in which our grandchildren have some hope of long-term survival is if we regain our respect for the human scale and if we ensure that machines serve people rather than subjugate them. We also need to recognise the essential dignity and worth of traditional systems of agriculture and the role that they play in the overall health of the environment and in the cultural well-being of mankind.

Here and there we see some encouraging signs on the horizon. In this country, the Environmentally Sensitive Areas scheme is an indication that there is some awareness of the problem, and additional areas have recently been announced. One of the essential features of an ESA is that farmers must operate in those traditional ways which provide the environmental benefits – the 'sentimental' bits perhaps – that people long for, deep down in their souls. There are, of course, those who see the principle of an ESA as a 'backward' step into the past. But I

LEFT: *The ultimate in sustainable farming: landscape protection, farming for wildlife and farming organically. Woodland and permanent pasture at Kite's Nest Farm, on the Cotswold escarpment.*

OVERLEAF: *Leaving a margin for wildlife: wide headlands beside a stone wall on Duchy Home Farm; hawthorn, cow parsley and hogweed in flower. Rough grass beside a stone wall will provide overwintering habitat for predatory insects – which help to control aphids – and a home for voles, which form the barn owl's diet.*

Black Aberdeen Angus beef cattle at Highgrove.

am far from being alone in hoping that, on the contrary, the ESA principles might be further extended to cover the whole country.

The ESA scheme is run by the Ministry of Agriculture. The Department of the Environment (through the Countryside Commission) operates the Countryside Stewardship scheme which, although currently a much smaller operation, seeks to achieve many of the same aims. Quite why we need two such schemes, with two sets of regulations, and two sets of people to administer them, is not clear to me – and nor I suspect to the majority of the recipients. Is it too much to hope that they might one day be combined?

In the Netherlands a feeling of unease has led to the re-appraisal of some conventional attitudes. The Dutch Government is now aiming for pesticide use to be cut by one-third by 1995 and to one-half of the 1990 levels by the end of the century. Apparently scientists at the Institute for Research in Arable Crops and Field Vegetables at Lelystad reached the conclusion that their present system is a dead-end road. An integrated systems research programme in arable farming was therefore established which concentrated on an intermediate system of farming between organic and conventional.

Perhaps the most interesting feature of the trials has been the comments of the farmers who took part, many of whom began to feel 'in control' again once they had successfully grown crops with few or no pesticides. Significantly they said they felt like farmers again, leading scientists at the Institute to appreciate how many skills have been lost from farming since 'modern' methods took over and how much younger farmers will have to learn from scratch if they are to break their dependence on pesticides.

We have had similar experiences in rediscovering traditional practices at Highgrove. It may be that to embrace sustainability in the fullest sense we shall have to start to think about maintaining and recycling, for the benefit of future generations, not only our physical resources but also the cultural aspects of sustainability. Just as topsoil erodes so too does human knowledge and so do husbandry skills. A generation or two of techno-fixing agribusiness is all that is needed to break an ancient chain.

However unlikely such a scenario may appear today, I feel sure that the time will come when people will ask why we didn't do more in this day and age to preserve those wise traditions which form mankind's lifeline with the profoundly mysterious laws of the universe.

NOTHING
BUT FLOWERS

From the age of the dinosaurs
Cars have run on gasoline
Where, where have they gone?
Now there's nothing but flowers.
There was a factory
Now there are mountains and rivers.

David Byrne, 1988.

I FIRST VISITED the Prince of Wales's estate on a still midsummer's evening and fell headlong into the dreamlike state of suspended judgement that has been known to overcome Government ministers, newspaper editors and even cereal farmers on first seeing Highgrove. Driving through Tetbury, the evening sun brought out the ochre in the limestone of the town's seventeenth-century market-house balanced on its stumpy stone pillars. Around Highgrove, a mile or so further on, sheep were grazing behind the neat dry-stone walls of the royal estate. The car swept through large gates and up the drive. And suddenly and surprisingly on either side of the car was an explosion of wild flowers: poppies, cornflowers, corn marigolds, corn cockles, melilot and chicory in an impressionist picture of pinks, whites, yellows and blues.

With time to get out and look at these drive borders and the hay meadow beyond, one might have discovered that this was no triumph of nature but a work of wildflower gardening. Here were flowers of different natural habitats, of hay meadows and wayside verges and arable fields cleverly persuaded to grow together. But the first impression was more captivating. It appeared as if all the lost wild flowers of Britain had returned in a dream. Here in one small corner of England the landscape had been healed of all the damage caused to it in the name of progress and modern farming since the war.

That, of course, was the intention. The wild flowers were the estate's advertisement. They were Prince Charles's idea and the work of the naturalist and wildflower gardener, Miriam Rothschild. Driving through the park you could tell at a glance, without mustering the social skills to ask him direct, exactly what the owner of Highgrove had set out to do. He believed in gardening and farming in

ABOVE: *Yellow Jerusalem sage, blue delphiniums, pink roses and a haze of white* Crambe cordifolia *in the walled garden.*

OPPOSITE: *The wildflower verges beside the front drive, with ox-eye daisies and poppies in full bloom.*

Acid-loving plants in a raised bed near the study window with Narcissus 'Tête-à-Tête' *planted in between. The purple flower is* Rhododendron praecox, *the first rhododendron to flower in spring.*

a way that would reverse the biological holocaust of the past fifty years. He believed in planting trees for generations other than his own. He was saying that the job of the landowner was to leave the land richer than before. The estate wore its heart on its sleeve: it was for others to judge or be judged.

There is nothing in the landscape or the architecture of the Gloucestershire estate that the Prince of Wales bought in 1980 that could be described as grand or imposing. The rolling wold around Tetbury does not have the majestic views of the Cotswold escarpment, nor is it as dramatic as the incised valleys around Stroud, Bath or Winchcombe. The house is a comfortable family house in an understated neo-classical style. It was built, very probably, by a local mason-architect much used by the penny-wise Gloucestershire gentry in the late eighteenth century. Much altered for the worse after a fire in the 1890s, it has been transformed by imaginative alteration. Highgrove is, first and foremost, a home. What is exceptional about the place, apart from royal ownership, is the fact that it has been both a gallery and laboratory for a thoughtful patron who can afford to put his ideas into effect and who can, without great fear of refusal, pick any expert he chooses to help him do so.

Prince Charles has his contradictions. He is both a lover of formality and something of a visionary. He has stretched the Prince of Wales's conventional role beyond his predecessors in that he has views – expressed in mischievous speeches on such subjects as architecture, the teaching of English, complementary (as opposed to 'alternative') medicine, the pollution of the North Sea, the destruction of the rainforests and the evils of intensive farming. He is unafraid of lobbying on behalf of the things he believes in. Yet, despite the many palaces he moves in, Highgrove is the only home he can truly call his own and the only place where he can put his ideas directly into effect.

So at Highgrove he has reshaped the house to a new design. He has created what may prove to be the most influential garden to be built in England in the past generation. He has decided to turn his farm over to organic methods – through a conviction that modern agriculture has taken a wrong turning. He is turning the traditional conception of a Home Farm, where a landlord shows his tenants a thing or two about growing prize pigs or new varieties of wheat, into a model of sustainable development. He has even decided to process the royal sewage through a non-chemical treatment plant, based on a reed-bed which produces water clean enough at its outflow to be a dragonfly reserve.

Highgrove's successes and failures would be a source of fascination to other gardeners and farmers even if its owner were not royal, because so much of what Prince Charles has done is prompted by one of the most interesting questions of our time: how a densely-populated technological society can avoid slowly destroying the natural world it lives in. No doubt it is a luxury to be able to play

The rose garden – through one of the arched windows cut in the yew hedge by Sir Roy Strong, former Director of the Victoria and Albert Museum. Nearly everything you see is scented, from the old-fashioned roses to the purple sage. The pink rose in the left foreground is Rosa mundi.

Battalions of tulips amid buttercups and cow parsley in the meadow beyond the rose garden.

with ideas, but it is also the peculiarity of the unique position in which the Prince of Wales finds himself that he can ask more absolute questions. What sorts of standards should we as consumers expect of the purity of our food or how it is produced? What moral responsibilities do farmers and landowners have to the wildlife, the landscape and the livestock they breed?

In the wake of the pessimistic environmental visions of the 1970s and early 1980s, the idea emerged from somewhere that nature could perhaps be recreated: what was lost could be found. To put it more modestly, as environmental thinking becomes more deeply embedded in the political process, what matters are not problems but solutions. Environmentalists are becoming more careful to seek out practical examples of farming, forestry, transport and renewable sources of energy which work without depleting the earth's ecology and non-renewable resources. Yet there are, even in the wake of the Rio Earth Summit, so few working examples of the concept of sustainable development to point at. The Prince of Wales is aware that one working example of sustainable agriculture is worth a hundred speeches. At Highgrove he has backed his hunch that sooner or later scientists and farmers will have to look again at the organic tradition.

I should point out that visiting Highgrove and talking to the people who have advised on its experiments in farming and ecology was for me a voyage of discovery – not a pilgrimage of the converted. In our farmhouse in the 1960s the subject of conservation, as environmental matters were then called, was a dangerous one. My father was an intensive farmer and miller in East Anglia and my mother, who had herself farmed during the war, was an early member of the Soil Association, the founding body of the organic movement. On the question of organic farming, and its rejection of some of the advances of the past fifty years, I began writing this book a profound agnostic. I am no longer. Part of my motive for writing about the Prince's experiment with sustainable farming at Highgrove, I suspect, was a need to resolve an argument started by two people long dead.

This account aims to be realistic about alternative agriculture. The nature of an experiment is that some parts are successful, some are failures. How successful is Highgrove in meeting its objective of farming in a healthier and less environmentally destructive manner? Does organic farming bring real environmental benefits for the flora and fauna? Could it provide an answer to agricultural surpluses? Or farm pollution? Is it whimsical to think that organic food which now occupies a tiny niche-market could occupy, say, 20 per cent of the market for food in Britain? Will alternative methods of agriculture be commercial enough to satisfy the scepticism of a farming industry hard-pressed by recession and the necessities of Common Agricultural Policy reform and the General Agreement on Tariffs and Trade? These are questions which this book will examine. Yet the story of Highgrove must first be of a work in progress and a source of delight.

A HISTORY OF THE LANDSCAPE

The Wold is in itself an ugly country. The soil is what is called a stone brash
below, with a reddish earth mixed with little bits of this brash at top, and...is very
shallow; and, as fields are divided by walls made of this brash, and as there are, for
a mile or two together, no trees to be seen, and the surface is not smooth and
green like the downs, this is a sort of country having less to please the eye than any
other that I have seen, always save and except the heaths like those of Bagshot and
Hindhead. Yet even this Wold has many fertile dells in it, and sends out, from its
highest parts, several streams, each of which has its pretty valley and meadows.

Rural Rides, William Cobbett, 1822.

AT THIS POINT in histories of great estates it is usual to tell the history of
the house, the great men and women who have lived in it, and the wars,
famines and strife that passed by its gates. But this is a book about the
land, and Highgrove's owner often says that his is not a great house at all and his
estate should really be called a farm, so I feel justified in beginning with the story
of the landscape of Highgrove.

The study of landscape is a post-war phenomenon. When W.G. Hoskins wrote
his classic, *The Making of the English Landscape*, in 1955, it was a pioneer work.
Like John Betjeman, with whom he had much in common, Hoskins was impelled
onwards in his writing by a sense of the accelerating pace of post-war change, the
roads, the new buildings, the demolitions, the deep ploughing of archaeological
sites and a conviction that what was disappearing was still not valued or even
understood. He wrote that since 1914, 'every single change in the English landscape has either uglified it or destroyed its meaning or both'. I doubt whether
the Prince of Wales would disagree with that.

Hoskins's great discovery about landscape was *everything is older than we think
it is*. In the Cotswolds, everything is very ancient indeed. Stone is the dominating
influence on the Cotswold landscape; it explains the farming, the flora, the lovely

*The view towards Highgrove
from the tower of Tetbury church:
the house is on the horizon amid
trees, just to the right of centre.*

vernacular architecture, even the extortionate house prices. The Cotswolds form part of the stripe of Jurassic limestone which runs diagonally across England from Lyme Bay in Dorset to the Yorkshire coast. The top layer of rock is what is known as the Great Oolite, a fine building stone. Where this has worn away, on the north edge of the stripe, the Inferior Oolite shows through, another useful stone despite its name. Further east there are shales and sandstones, which are of less value. Most of the soils are derived from the bedrock and are therefore light and well-drained and will withstand grazing animals in the wettest weather. In modern times, until the latter half of this century, this was mostly sheep country. But millennia before Gloucestershire became a royal county, the Cotswolds were favoured by early arable farmers, who lacked the technology for cultivating heavy soils.

Highgrove itself is on a flat wold at a height of 500 feet above sea level, a little over a mile out of the lovely stone-built hill-town of Tetbury. The prevailing wind, when it blows, can be bitterly cold and comes straight from the Bristol Channel. It is a few miles from the most dramatic Cotswold scenery, which is on the north-west escarpment, in the incised valleys around Bath, Stroud and Winchcombe. The roads that drop over the edge of the escarpment, towards Gloucester and the Severn, have spectacular views, as at Wotton-under-Edge a few miles away from Tetbury. But a characteristic of the land around Tetbury is its ability to hide buildings and little secret patches of ancient survival in blind valleys or folds in the wold. It does this especially at Broadfield Farm, now part of the Highgrove estate, where two lovely farmhouses are hidden from public view.

Broadfield Farm house where David Wilson, the farm manager, lives.

There I have found, unexpectedly, unimproved limestone pasture replete with wild flowers and a patch of hawthorn scrub surrounded by bluebells. Tetbury is near the source of rivers which span the width of England. It is on the high spur which forms the watershed between the Bath Avon, which rises nearby and flows west, and the dip-slope of the Cotswolds which gives rise to the east-flowing tributaries of the Thames, the Evenlode, Windrush, Coln and Churn.

It is hard to imagine what this Cotswold landscape looked like before man, as ecologists sometimes try to do. It is generally agreed that 10,000 years ago the whole of the British Isles, excepting the north-westernmost and most windswept triangle of Scotland, would have been totally covered by wildwood. The mixed oak woods on the Cotswold escarpment and the Wychwood, near Oxford, make up some of the last vestiges of this ancient woodland. These are not primary woods, in the sense that untouched rainforest is primary. They have a long history of use. But they are primeval: the escarpment provides essentially the same habitat for trees, birds, butterflies and wild flowers as it did 10,000 years ago. These remaining managed woodlands are ten times older than Westminster

A field of buttercups near Highgrove: 95 per cent of permanent pasture like this has been lost since 1945.

OVERLEAF: *A scrap of unimproved pasture and scrub in a typical Cotswold dry valley on the other side of Tetbury, a place to look for cowslips and other survivals in spring. The hawthorn scrub marks the route of an old railway line to Tetbury – indicated by the church spire in the distance – phased out by Lord Beeching in the early 1960s.*

47

Abbey, twenty times older than St Paul's Cathedral. They have, until recently, enjoyed little of the same protection.

The antiquity of other features of the Gloucestershire landscape is often surprising. Take the sheep-walks or limestone pastures for which the Cotswolds were once famous. Many still survive, though they have been much depleted by ploughing for arable land. Where they are still grass, they have often been replaced by rye-grass leys or their wild flowers have been smothered by grasses enriched with nitrogen fertiliser. It is hard to work out exactly when these managed pastures were first brought into being, but it is fair to assume that such permanent pasture that survives, with its distinctive herbs and plants, evolved at the latest in the Middle Ages. Hoskins indicates that, as far as clearance and settlement goes, the landscape of the Cotswolds by the end of the Anglo-Saxon period was much as we know it today.

Thanks to strict planning laws and a designated Area of Outstanding Natural Beauty – which still seems to permit a few ugly infill houses in every village, made unnecessarily of composition stone – the principal influence on the Cotswold landscape remains agriculture. Three distinct agricultural revolutions shaped this part of England and a fourth revolution, born of food surpluses, is shaping it again, not necessarily for the better.

On the bonus side, the landscape destruction of the past forty-five years has slowed. There is now a variety of measures for improving features of the traditional landscape such as the proposed Cotswolds Environmentally Sensitive Area, where farmers will be paid to put back landscape features they once went to some pains to destroy. On the debit side, under the current reforms of Europe's Common Agricultural Policy, 15 per cent of the arable land of England is now required to be put down to 'set-aside', the latest intellectually- and ecologically-bankrupt scheme from the European Commission. Instead of being paid simply for their crops, or for managing or for making useful repairs to the landscape, farmers will be paid subsidy only if 15 per cent of their arable land is not farmed. These areas of one-year or rotational set-aside will grow rank with weeds such as brome, blackgrass, thistles, ragwort and docks – or be ploughed up as ecologically-worthless bare summer fallow. The European landscape is beginning to take on shades of Joseph Heller's novel *Catch 22*, in which the character Major Major's father made a fortune out of the United States Government by not growing alfalfa. The more alfalfa he didn't grow, the more land he bought not to grow alfalfa on.

To the landscape historian, the countryside is a legible record which contains traces of several agricultural revolutions before the present surrealistic one. The first arguably began when Mesolithic man found his way into the Cotswolds in the 6,000 years before Christ and began to cut down the wildwood. The great forest clearances of the Bronze Age – around 4,000 to 2,000 BC – were one of the great wonders of the prehistoric world, almost as miraculous as the raising of Stonehenge: witness the difficulty of extracting oak or beech stumps, even with the aid of explosives. Early man did it all by hand. Fire would have been little use to him. As Oliver Rackham, the woodland historian, points out: deciduous woodland burns with the ease of wet blotting paper.

In the Roman occupation the Cotswolds were heavily populated because the lighter soils were easier to work and, in the early years, the hilltops were easier to defend against warring tribes. The foundations of Roman villas of increasing lavishness have been found in the Cotswolds, some supported by estates of up to 1,000 acres, not unlike those of the eighteenth century. The lasting change the Romans brought was roads; the Fosse Way, which runs south-east of Tetbury, Ermine Street and the White Way. When the Fosse Way was built, it marked the north-westernmost line of Roman settlement in the first century AD. It was a military road driven as straight as the manpower of the Roman army could make it in time of war with the purpose of bringing up reinforcements. The success of the strategy is clear from the traces of a Roman camp built on top of an old British site at Tetbury.

Tetbury has written records older than most towns in England. A Saxon charter was in existence in 681, drawn up under the Abbess Tetta from whom the town is supposed to derive its name. By the time the surveyors of the Domesday Book passed by in 1086, most of the settlements in the area were already in existence. All but the highest of the wolds would have been under agriculture: open fields bordered by heath and scrub. In the Middle Ages the Abbots of Gloucester, Evesham and Westminster all owned manors in the Cotswolds. In the fourteenth and fifteenth centuries, the lay lords consolidated their holdings, enclosing large pastures with stone walls, a process which is often wrongly thought to have begun with the Parliamentary enclosures.

The late Middle Ages brought prosperity to the Cotswolds. This was when the wool-towns began to acquire their glorious architectural character. Tetbury was a centre for wool-stapling, buying wool and having it made up into cloth, as was Cirencester. By the end of the sixteenth century Tetbury market was one of the largest wool markets in the country, and wool and cloth was brought from as far away as Leicestershire and Kent. The merchants and traders of Tetbury built themselves houses in golden ochre-coloured local stone and the towns of Painswick, Nailsworth and Chipping Camden built fine churches in the Perpendicular style, with stone tracery and stone roof tiles.

The consolidation of the large estates, Badminton, Sherbourne Park, Dyrham Park and Cirencester Park, in the seventeenth and eighteenth centuries intensified a process of enclosure that had been going on for centuries. The advances of the second agricultural revolution – the introduction of fertility-building rotations, new machinery and the intensification of sheep pasture – made farming more profitable. But as a result of the process of enclosure, under the Parliamentary Enclosure Acts, the yeoman farmer was thrown off his land. The resulting abject rural poverty was still to be felt when Cobbett rode through Tetbury in 1822 in the depths of another agricultural recession. Tetbury, however, impressed Cobbett, a scourge of idle and unjust landowners, because of the generous-spirited attitude to the poor he found that was not evident in the industrial North or in Ireland.

Not all the changes made to the landscape in the second agricultural revolution are for the worse today, though they brought misery in their time.

A moss-encrusted fortress for rabbits, voles, weasels and small nesting birds: an ancient stone wall at Duchy Home Farm.

Many of the hedges and stone walls, now in need of repair or reinstatement, date from 200 years ago. These field boundaries, once arrogant statements of the property principle that consolidated the eighteenth-century landholdings, are now havens for voles, rabbits, weasels and nesting birds. One should not forget the sporting purposes of the made landscape. The Beaufort hunt, based at Badminton, has some of the most famous hunting country in Britain and the impeccable hedges and plentiful copses of the county today owe their state of repair to the pursuit of the uneatable. It is no coincidence that John Whyte-Melville, the novelist, dedicated fox-hunter and benefactor of the grooms and stableboys of Tetbury, is buried in Tetbury churchyard.

Tetbury's growth stopped with the Industrial Revolution, a fact which has preserved its buildings and its intimate scale. It was bypassed because the town did not have sufficient water to drive machines. The wool-processing industry moved closer to Dursley, Stroud and Chalford, where large mills were built to accommodate the looms. By 1850 competition from steam-powered mills in the North and sweated labour from the northern towns had killed off the Cotswold wool-processing industry altogether.

In the Cotswolds, agricultural life changed at a snail's pace for 150 years. Even in the 1920s and 1930s the change away from horse-powered agriculture came slowly. Much was written in the 1930s by zealous modernisers about the backwardness of agriculture compared to other industries. It was the Second World War which provided the reason for rapid change, which some now call the third agricultural revolution. With U-boats on the western approaches, a desperate need for food and for airfields to defend the country, the sheep-walks were ploughed up and cereals planted where once there was grass. The story of how the goal of self-sufficiency in food destroyed a large proportion of the ancient countryside and led to the madness of post-war surpluses has been told truthfully in the writings of Sir Richard Body, a die-hard opponent of European agricultural policy, and Marion Shoard, the unforgiven scourge of farmers.

For forty-five years, under Government goading, farmers used sprays and artificial fertilisers to produce crops from stony soils that had never produced anything but nibbling sheep. Britain's food production rose from 40 per cent of all food requirements before the war to 60 per cent and three-quarters of the goods that can be produced in the British climate today. (Ironically, in the 1980s, all the benefit to the balance of payments was undone by the British consumer's growing sophistication and pursuit of Continental foodstuffs.) The intensification of agriculture needed to bring about this expansion in production, the ploughing and draining and pushing over of stone walls, began to be noticed by a largely urban public only when farmers began to produce too much. The gain in human terms of all this efficiency was that British agriculture now employs the lowest proportion of the total workforce of any country in the world.

We all know today that the landscape paid the price, that the traditional landscape changed as a result of subsidised farm-gate prices and grants to 'improve' the land by creating larger fields, draining wet patches, and removing hedges. These grants from the 'dig for victory' era were withdrawn only in the early 1980s, forty years after the need which brought them into being. Looked at beside the slow change of previous centuries, the last forty-five years stand out as a whirlwind of change. In 1935 around 40–42 per cent of the Cotswolds was estimated to be covered by permanent pasture with its distinctive wild flowers. By 1983 the figure was only 2 per cent.

The loss of the Cotswolds' hay meadows and limestone pastures is a significant but small fraction of the greater damage caused to the British landscape by subsidised agriculture and forestry since 1945. In a famous report in 1984, the Nature Conservancy Council recorded that since the war Great Britain had lost 95 per cent of its wildflower-rich hay meadows; 80 per cent of its limestone grassland; 40 per cent of its lowland heaths; 30–50 per cent of ancient lowland woods and 150,000 miles of hedges. Each rural parish has seen its losses. Every farmer has had to answer for them to his visitors at Sunday lunch throughout the land.

Farmers like to say that the damage has stopped, but this is not quite true. Consider, for example, the 63,000 miles of hedges pulled out or badly degraded since 1985 and the unreported and continuing erosion of what little permanent pasture is left. The Royal Society for Nature Conservation estimated in 1991 that 10 per cent of the remaining unimproved grassland outside nature reserves is still being destroyed every year.

Since the early 1980s, though, something has happened to which no one has yet given a name. It may be too early yet, but it is tempting to call it the *fourth* agricultural revolution – even though it is not yet clear what the result will be and what the countryside will look like when it is over. But little by little, and on a fraction of the scale of what has gone, government has begun to make funds available to repair the countryside. And farmers have begun to plant trees and hedges again. The Cotswolds as an Environmentally Sensitive Area is soon to pay farmers to use fewer sprays and chemical fertilisers, to restore dry-stone walls and graze limestone grassland. Such schemes, so far, cover only 5 per cent of the country and, where they do, are taken up on a voluntary basis. This is a beginning of a landscape change that is generated not by the farmer or the market but by political pressures, public concern and international steps to protect the environment.

So far, public pressure for a 'greener' countryside remains peripheral to subsidised European agriculture – despite such outside influences as the Rio Earth Summit and its agreement by 180 countries to foster 'sustainable development', which presumably includes more sensible use of the countryside. Under the Common Agricultural Policy the vast bulk of subsidies remains tied to agricultural output and under the control of agricultural bureaucrats. Hence the reform package agreed by European agriculture ministers in the summer of 1992 under the chairmanship of Ray MacSharry, European Agriculture Commissioner, which aims to cut surpluses by extending the sterile principle of set-aside to 15 per cent of Europe's agricultural land. As some of the more enlightened farming writers, such as David Richardson, have observed, paying farmers to do nothing without any appreciable environmental gain is likely to be a public relations disaster for the farmer. And set-aside will not keep surpluses in check for more than a few years.

Intellectually speaking, European farming remains in crisis. The pressure is on all of us to find a way of farming which pays the farmer a living, reduces surpluses and halts the attrition of the countryside which we now believe should be handed on intact to future generations. It is hard to see how the fourth agricultural revolution will end. For most farmers, the solutions depend on the wheels of public policy which grind slowly. While they come, the attractions of getting out of farming, building a golf course or 'diversifying' into some other hybrid business are very real.

After the MacSharry reforms, sensible policies, such as the extension of the Environmentally Sensitive Area principle to the whole country, seem further away than ever. How can the individual who cares for the countryside shift the log jam? The Prince of Wales has chosen the most politically challenging route, by giving his blessing to a kind of farming which does not depend on someone else's decision. He has chosen the traditional way of cutting output and looking after the countryside – by avoiding all farm chemicals or fertilisers under the

strict rules of the organic system. Organic is the most direct, purest and most absolute of several ways which allow farmers to be paid for their environmental goods. Now even the National Farmers Union believes that something like the Environmentally Sensitive Area system should be expanded to the rest of the country. Both farming regimes allow farmers to be paid directly for the environmental goods that they produce. Both reduce surpluses. Both would also allow subsidised farm-gate prices to fall, which is what almost everyone would like to achieve.

The challenge for the policy-makers is to define a new way of farming: one that is healthier, less exhaustive of non-renewable resources, less dependent on chemicals, and which restores birds, wild flowers and butterflies to the whole countryside – instead of confining them to shrinking ghettos and tiny nature reserves. Some farmers, including the Prince of Wales, are convinced that they already have part, if not all, of the answer.

THE PRINCE MOVES IN

I
T MAY SEEM STRANGE for someone else to describe Prince Charles's arrival at Highgrove when he has already sketched in the essentials of the story himself. Yet, on reflection, there seemed to be some point to his looking out of the window and my looking in. To his first-hand recollections of taking over Highgrove and making it his own, I can add the perspective of the outsider and the previously unrecorded accounts of those who had lived at Highgrove, or worked there as he moved in.

In 1979 Prince Charles asked the Duchy of Cornwall to find him a house in Gloucestershire. The criteria, as remembered by Tim Gray, who works for Smith-Woolley, the firm of land agents which discreetly undertook the search, were that the house should be attractive, though not necessarily large – he thinks someone used the words 'a family atmosphere' – and both house and gardens should have room for improvement. The prospective buyer wanted to indulge his own tastes, for until his middle thirties he had never had the freedom of a property which was wholly his own. He also wanted sufficient land to provide the possibility of farming at some time in the future.

As Gray and his colleagues began passing the word around estate agents and inquiring of the Gloucestershire gentry if they were inclined to sell, they thought that the house they were buying was intended to serve Prince Charles for a few years as a bachelor pad for entertaining his friends. They had no inkling that Prince Charles would be decorating the house with his new bride in eighteen months' time.

The choice of county was never simple. In 1967, Prince Charles was left Chevening Manor in Kent, a sizeable Regency mansion, by the 7th Earl Stanhope. The Earl had said it was his dearest wish that the Prince of Wales would make Chevening his home. Chevening was not the most convenient of places to drive to from Buckingham Palace, where the Prince then had a suite of rooms. It required a slow bumper-to-bumper progress through built-up South London. It was even more difficult, once at Chevening, to get to Wales or the Duchy of Cornwall. For a young man who wanted to make his own impression on the world, a decisive disadvantage was that the late Earl had left the estate to be run by a board of Government-appointed trustees.

For sale: handsome Gloucestershire residence, late eighteenth century, with later additions and alterations. Two of seven colour plates from the brochure produced by Humberts, who sold the house for the Macmillan family in 1980.

By the late 1970s when he left the Navy and was thinking about house-hunting, Prince Charles had long since decided that he wanted to live in the Duchy itself, the 130,000-acre landholding in twenty-three counties which traditionally provides the male heir to the throne with his income. The title of Duke of Cornwall and a substantial estate have been vested in the first-born male heir to the throne since it was first given to Edward the Black Prince in 1337. By a quirk of history, no Duke of Cornwall has chosen to live in the Duchy since the castles of the medieval princes fell into decay. Prince Charles decided that, as Duke, he wanted to live among his tenants, to farm alongside them and to take an active part in the running of the estate. There was, at Stoke Climsland in Cornwall, a Duchy Home Farm – the farm which a landlord traditionally keeps 'in hand' and where he tries to show his tenants a thing or two about farming. But the house at Stoke Climsland was small and the Prince didn't like it. He calculated that living in Cornwall itself would have involved too much time travelling.

The decision was taken to buy a house elsewhere. A house called Orchardleigh in Somerset was considered, but that, too, failed to match the Prince's requirements. Soon the Prince narrowed his sights on Gloucestershire, partly he says for the practical reason that it was halfway between London and Cornwall and close to Bath, where the Duchy has a large regional office. The private reason, I gather, was that Prince Charles had known and loved the area around Badminton since childhood. He enjoyed hunting with hounds and the Beaufort Hunt, based at Badminton, has some of the most famous hunt country in England. His sister, Princess Anne, who knows good hunting country when she sees it, had moved in 1976 with her then husband Captain Mark Phillips into Gatcombe Park, one of the Cotswolds' loveliest houses, eight miles from Highgrove. The year after Prince Charles bought Highgrove, Prince and Princess Michael of Kent moved with their young family into Nether Lyppiat Manor near Stroud, an exquisite grand house in miniature, built 1702–5.

The Cotswolds contain so much of the best of English countryside and English architecture that, knowing the Prince's interests as we do, his choice was not so surprising. The villages and vernacular buildings of the Cotswolds are one part of the English rural idyll that is relatively unspoiled. William Morris was the first to rediscover the simple elegance of Cotswold vernacular village architecture. Whether white, honey or ochre grey, the buildings in Cotswold stone merge into the landscape under lichens and mosses as if they grew from it by some biological process. These days, however, even the most modest cottage is more likely to be owned by prosperous businessmen from the M4 corridor or weekenders from London than the farmers, farm workers and rural merchants for whom they were built.

It was Martin Argles, the Duchy's Head Steward for the Eastern District, who saw an advertisement in *The Times* for a house called Highgrove, situated a mile south-west of Tetbury in the hamlet of Doughton. This was the first house the Prince indicated he wanted to visit. It was a simple late eighteenth-century rectangular block of three storeys built in ochre-grey stone and set in parkland. The gardens had been mostly left as grass, shrubs and a few rose beds by its owner, Maurice Macmillan, son of the former Prime Minister, Harold Macmillan.

Maurice Macmillan was a busy MP who seems to have been indifferently fond of gardening; he liked to hunt and shoot at weekends. At 340 acres, and in three distinct blocks, Highgrove was not the ideal size or shape for a Home Farm, being too small to allow the economies of scale that make for very profitable farming. Yet land could always be acquired later and there were other criteria to be satisfied. The most important one was whether the Prince liked the house.

Compared with many of Gloucestershire's extravagant piles, the house was unostentatious. Built in a spare neo-classical style, its appearance had not been improved by a fire in 1894 and subsequent drastic alterations. But it had some fine airy rooms and a splendid view across the fields of Tetbury church with its handsome spire framed by trees. Behind the house, there was a beautiful eighteenth-century stone stable block, the same age as the house, which overlooked a stone courtyard and looseboxes with room for several hunters and polo ponies. Around the house there were farm buildings, including a run-down dairy and five cottages. The garden was dominated by a handsome ancient cedar which the Prince admired. Beyond the lawns was an eighteenth-century walled kitchen garden, an acre in size and until lately used as a piggery, which the Prince fell in love with on sight.

The Prince Moves in

OVERLEAF: *The view of Tetbury church from the front door of Highgrove. The handsome wooden cages in the parkland are to keep livestock away from newly-planted trees.*

A drawing-with-wash of Highgrove before the fire in 1894: on the south side, where the rose garden is now, there appear to have been three Venetian-style windows.

Alex Macmillan, now the Earl of Stockton, remembers the Prince visiting the house and leaning on a brass fender in front of the fire, and the Macmillan nanny telling the Prince that not only had his mother sat on that rail but his grandmother, too. The place looked oddly familiar and like a family home. There were too many dogs and Alex was re-whipping a fly rod on the billiard table when the Prince visited. What sold the house to the Prince, according to Alex, was Paddy Whiteland, the Macmillans' factotum and groom, who looked the Prince fearlessly in the eye and said: 'I saw yez at Chepstow, the udder day. I tort you was coming off by the way your legs was flapping.'

Humberts, the estate agents, had just published their first particulars in July 1980 when the Duchy put in their offer. There were other offers but the Duchy's was the one accepted. The Macmillans decamped with some relief to Birchgrove, as they had effectively done some time before. The changeover took place at Michaelmas, 29 September, the traditional handover day for farms.

Tim Gray remembers that he spent the first year fire-fighting: carrying out pressing repairs to the house and farm buildings, doing everything from knocking down the cowsheds – the Prince decided he did not want a dairy unit beside the house – to finding farmers to share-farm the land. Latterly, he spent his time preparing for the Prince's wedding. The Prince came down frequently from London and camped in the builders' dust, made comfortable by Paddy Whiteland and his wife Nesta whom everyone, including the Prince, called Mrs Paddy.

Paddy Whiteland leading a foal to its mother by the stables while Fred Ind looks on.

A view of parkland near Highgrove.

At the beginning, when his engagement had yet to be announced, the Prince gave mysteriously vague instructions to strip the house and to paint everything white or magnolia. Gray says with hindsight: 'He obviously didn't know what he wanted at that time. He wanted to keep his options open. Clearly he was thinking that there might be someone else who had an opinion. His decision to hold everything was exactly right as we didn't waste a penny.' In the end it was the Princess of Wales who made most of the decisions indoors, recruiting Dudley Poplak, the interior designer, to draw up a decorative scheme. The Prince contented himself with the design of his own study and library.

Outdoors, he took stock of the garden, its minimal plantings, and, most important for a gardener with ambitions, its soil. The soils at Highgrove were of mixed quality, mostly brash derived from the limestone bedrock but within the gardens there were deposits of loam. The division between the loamy and the poorer soils was found to follow almost exactly the line of the ha-ha which formed the boundary of the gardens and the parkland. Clearly those who had laid out the parkland at the end of the eighteenth century had taken pains over what they were doing. There were also patches of clay: Tim Gray augered solid blue clay to a depth of seven feet just behind the farm buildings. The only soil type the gardens lacked was sand, ruling out the growing of rhododendrons which grow so well on the acid soil at Westonbirt, the arboretum now owned by the Forestry Commission, only two miles to the west.

The parkland contained some fine trees: a Lucombe oak, walnut and copper beech and in front of the house a Spanish oak. Many of the Prince and Princess's wedding presents came in the form of trees, including a Boscobel oak and a pair of black mulberry trees. Meanwhile, Tim Gray fretted about the safety of the huge cedar in the garden and said that the tree was a danger to the royal person.

The rose walk beyond the walled garden at Highgrove. The wooden uprights of the pergola are painted a greeny-blue, inspired by a pergola Prince Charles saw in Italy. The nearest rose is 'Elegance', the honeysuckle is Lonicera serotina and the red rose in the middle of the walk, 'Dublin Bay'. In the centre is a decorative terracotta pot from Assisi large enough to bathe in.

The Prince would not hear of its being cut down. Instead he allowed some unsafe boughs to be cut off and planted a young cedar himself as a replacement in case the existing one fell. Estate workers were warned expressly not to do anything to the house or grounds without first asking him.

The Army gave as their wedding present to the royal couple a swimming-pool which was hidden on the garden side of the stableyard wall and paved with York stone, another wedding present. A major tree-planting exercise began along the footpath in front of the house – shortly to be re-routed to give the household privacy from the world's paparazzi. The dry-stone walls around the house, which were originally shoulder-high, have since been raised to keep out prying eyes and lenses. The Duchy then began planting the parkland. The Prince stood on the front doorstep with a megaphone directing the planters like a film director, so that an oak or tulip tree when full grown would grow in exactly the right place. Megaphone or no, whoever planted the parkland originally took as much trouble the first time round.

The photographs from the Macmillan era show just how much has changed in thirteen years. The house has a new profile. It has been transformed from a solid rectangular block with solid parapets to a lighter, more Italian shape with open balustrades, a new pediment and Ionic columns. The young trees along the back drive, newly planted, are, one might be forgiven for not noticing, the national collection of beeches. In the parkland, the trees the Prince planted soon after he moved are now protected by elaborate stock-proof cages of unique design. The garden has been transformed. There is now a rose garden, a formal Italian garden, a woodland garden, and the hay meadow I saw on first coming to the house, planted with a mass of spring bulbs. The kitchen garden, with its tunnels and pagodas trained with roses and sweet peas, is now so well established that it flouts the rule of thumb I was taught that a garden takes twenty-five years to establish. All down to manure, I'm told.

The farm, too, has grown. In 1985, the Duchy added on Broadfield Farm, a 420-acre mixed farm the other side of Tetbury. Since then 160 acres have been added at Upton Grove and 80 acres of permanent pasture and a few farm houses at Happylands. The Duchy now owns a total of 1,112 acres and farms around 1,700 acres with the addition of share-farmed land.

In the fields in front of the house grazes a flock of 400 Mule and Masham sheep and a few dozen Aberdeen Angus beef cattle, the suckling cows fitted with clonking Swiss cowbells which the Prince acquired a taste for in the Alps. This beef is the first to qualify for its Soil Association symbol for being reared on pasture untreated by chemicals or fertilisers. The new Duchy Home Farm is now over halfway through its ten-year conversion to organic farming. The Prince has changed almost every aspect of the estate to accord with his own ideas.

THE HOUSE THAT KECK BUILT

Now, Penshurst, they that will proportion thee
With other edifices, when they see
Those proud ambitious heaps, and nothing else,
May say, their lords have built, but thy lord dwells.

Ben Jonson.

H IGH GROVE – as it was known during the Regency – was built between 1796 and 1798 for John Paul Paul, a local landowner. Most accounts say the architect is unknown. Certainly there is no conclusive proof of the hand that shaped the house, nor are there signed copies of the plans, but some of those who have studied the house, including Peter Falconer, the architect who carried out the changes to it in 1987, have become convinced that the design bears the signature of Anthony Keck, a busy local mason-architect with an eccentric grasp of classical form.

The Paul family were Huguenots who arrived in England in the late seventeenth century and settled in Tetbury, Woodchester and King's Stanley in the first half of the eighteenth. There they prospered in the cloth trade and enhanced their fortune assiduously by marriage. Josiah Paul, John Paul's father, married the daughter of Robert Clark who owned land in the hamlet of Doughton. In 1793, John Paul himself married Mary, the daughter and sole heiress of one Walter Matthews of Battersea. Almost certainly as a result of this marriage he became wealthy enough to build a substantial house on the land at Doughton that he had inherited from his mother's family. Highgrove House, finished in 1798, was built to command the best view on the property: the church and outlying houses of Tetbury just over a mile away.

The house is described by J.N. Brewer in *Delineations of Gloucestershire* (1825–7), a popular guide to the country houses of the time, as 'a substantial and spacious family residence'. Brewer describes a workmanlike house, probably built for a gentleman of modest tastes:

Highgrove today: note the new pediment, balustrade and pilasters added by the Prince of Wales.

67

The design is entirely free from ostentation, although some ornamental particulars are introduced. The principal efforts of the architect have been directed towards the interior, which presents many good apartments, of accurate proportions, will suited to the domestic and hospitable purposes of a family of high respectability. The situation is fine, and excellent views are obtained from the house and various parts of the attached grounds.

Brewer's text is accompanied by engravings by J. and H.S. Storer, which are often referred to in their own right as Storers' Views. Their plate of Highgrove shows a pleasant house, elegant but understated, with considerable differences from the house that stands there today. The original building had a Venetian window – a feature of which the architect Keck was particularly fond – above the front door. This window was removed after the house was almost destroyed by fire in 1893. The Storers' picture shows a far lower parapet around the top of the house than has survived and an open porch supported by four spindly columns. The original lodge built in 1798 survives at the beginning of the front drive. It also has a Venetian window.

The Pauls lived on at Highgrove until 1860. *Royal Homes in Gloucestershire* by Geoffrey Sanders and David Verey tells us that John Paul became in 1807 High Sheriff of Wiltshire, for which he apparently qualified, having formerly lived at

The engraving of the house from Delineations of Gloucestershire (1825-7), *showing almost certainly the Paul family who lived in it at the time.*

Ashton Keynes in that county. He bought Doughton Manor, the house and land across the main road, in 1818. When John Paul died in 1828, his estate was inherited by his son, Walter Matthews Paul, a magistrate and captain of the Tetbury troop of the Royal Gloucestershire Yeomanry.

Highgrove and Doughton Manor were sold to one Colonel E.J. Strachey in 1860. They were sold again four years later to William Yatman, a barrister. Yatman bore the cost of rehanging the bells in Tetbury church tower, when the medieval tower was taken down and rebuilt in 1891, in memory of his son. The view of the spire from the house is said to be kept clear of trees in his honour.

Yatman's enthusiasm for the estate was broken in 1893 when Highgrove was nearly destroyed in the fire in which all the original interiors were consumed. Yatman sold up and moved to Bournemouth. The house was rebuilt for the considerable sum of £6,000 by Arthur Mitchell. His son, Lt. Col. Francis Mitchell (1888–1955), Commander of the Royal Gloucestershire Hussars, lived at Doughton Manor until after the Second World War, while his elderly mother lived on at Highgrove.

After the war the house was bought by another soldier, Lt. Col. Gwyn Morgan Jones, a retired officer of the Life Guards. He took on Paddy Whiteland, the adaptable Irishman who still looks after the estate for Prince Charles as a kind of grand panjandrum. Paddy (known for his blarney and his catchphrases such as the conspiratorial 'Between you, me and the old stone wall') had survived the war by a whisker. He was captured by the Japanese in Java and spent the rest of the war in prisoner-of-war camps both in Java and Singapore. There he twice talked his way out of being drafted to his death on the Burma railway.

In 1965 the house was bought by Maurice Macmillan. He and his wife carried out several alterations to the house, and demolished a red-brick nineteenth-century wing, much to the annoyance of Paddy, who had a flat in it at one time. (Prince Charles has just built a new single-storey annex for his staff on the same site.) Mrs Macmillan added to the house two genuine Adam fireplaces. In 1979, Maurice Macmillan gave up hunting, which had held him in Gloucestershire, and moved to join his elderly father at their Birchgrove estate in Sussex. Maurice must have expected to take over the estate after Harold's death. Sadly, he died before his father, by then invested as the Earl of Stockton, in 1986.

The house that the Prince of Wales took on in 1980 was much changed from when it was built. Arthur Mitchell, who remodelled the house at such great expense in 1896, had moved the staircase from the front of the house to the side. He had built, for reasons that were not immediately apparent, a high, clumsily solid parapet round the roof and decorated it with small globes at the corners, curiously out of proportion with the rest of the house.

For the first few years what little time the Prince had was taken up with making a start on the gardens, parkland and farm. But he admits to a sense that the façade of the house was 'somewhat grim,' though he could not put his finger on what gave it this quality. Perhaps, he suggested to architectural friends, it was the windows?

A few years after moving in, the Prince decided to ask the advice of the artist Felix Kelly, who had acquired a reputation as a designer and improver of country houses. Kelly had contributed drawings for the domed Palladian-style villa built

Highgrove in 1983, showing the solid Victorian parapet, later replaced, and the withy fence which preceded the yew hedges of the rose garden.

by Sebastian de Ferranti, a friend of the Prince's, near Macclesfield in Cheshire, which is by any account one of the most ambitious country houses built since the war. Kelly produced a painting of Highgrove's present façade with a light airy balustrade; a pediment set with a round window; and the strange Egyptian-style pilasters of unique design replaced with crisply-defined Ionic ones. The Prince was delighted with the scheme.

The job of obtaining listed building consent and putting the design into effect was given to Peter Falconer, an industrial architect who lives nearby in Minchinhampton and makes a hobby of working in stone. The Duchy were pleased to find that he was still in business since he was the same man who had carried out alterations for the Macmillans in 1964.

Soon after starting work, Falconer discovered the reason for the clumsy solid parapet, part of the 1896 alterations. The Victorian builders had clearly been

Highgrove today, showing the new pediment, pilasters and open ballustrade surmounted with urns.

asked to cure an exceedingly leaky eighteenth-century roof with internal gutters. To do this they had decided to raise the roof two feet inside the parapet at one side of the house to let water drain from one side of the roof to the other. Hence the solid balustrade. In order to show daylight behind the new one, Falconer had to strip the parapet gutters and start again. At this time there was some discussion of replacing the Venetian window on the first floor, seen in Storers' Views, but this would have have entailed moving the staircase back to the front of the house so the Prince of Wales decided to leave well alone.

It was through his growing familiarity with the house that Peter Falconer became convinced that the house's unknown architect had to be the local man, in his time the leading designer of country houses in the counties of Gloucestershire, Worcestershire and Herefordshire. Keck (1726–97) is known to have lived at King's Stanley from 1768 until his death and as many as fifty houses in the three counties are, or are thought to be, by him, including Brownshill near Painswick in the Cotswolds. Yet when Keck is mentioned by architectural historians it is generally only for his most ambitious works: Moccas Court in Herefordshire, Penrice Castle in Glamorganshire and the impressive orangery at Margam Abbey in Glamorganshire, the largest in Britain.

A strong argument that Keck built Highgrove is to be found in a monograph by the Gloucestershire archivist Nicholas Kingsley published in *Country Life* in 1988. Though Keck left neither portrait nor memoir and only rarely signed his drawings, Kingsley ably pieces together Keck's career from the few facts that are known. He shows Keck to have been a well-connected local architect who was quick to copy the Adam style and tone it down to suit the tastes of his provincial clients. He made up for what he may have lacked in technical flair by combining designs of understated elegance with prices which heavily undercut the metropolitan competition.

Although it will probably never be proved absolutely that Keck built Highgrove, Kingsley argues convincingly that it has many of the hallmarks of a Keck villa, which include a Venetian window with super-arch which can also be seen at Moccas Court and Canon Frome Court, Herefordshire. Keck is known to have worked in the 1780s for John Paul Paul's cousin, Sir George Paul, at Hill House, Rodborough, so it is wholly possible that Sir George recommended him. Highgrove was Keck's last commission. He died in the autumn of 1797, before it could be finished.

Peter Falconer says that his practical knowledge of the house squares perfectly with a man of rough technical drawing skills and no known classical training. One of the remarkable things about it, particularly for a house built in a classical era, is its engaging lack of mathematical correctness. Almost no measurement from the outer walls to the centre is exactly mirrored on the other side. Keck had done his own thing, by eye, with rustic inexactness. Then there were the Keck pilasters themselves, which were of an Egyptian-looking design of a type unseen elsewhere. Falconer was surprised to find that where one would expect a base for the pilasters nine inches or so deep, Keck had left only two and a quarter inches, which gave Falconer a headache fitting their replacements. The moulding around the top of the house was again of a kind wholly unknown in the classical orders. Falconer had to improvise a mould of his own when fitting the pediment. It was, he says, pure Keck.

The facelift given to the house with the aid of Felix Kelly and Peter Falconer was not the only intervention the Prince of Wales made in the architecture of the estate. He commissioned the Bath architect Willie Bertram to build the beehive pavilions in local stone at the corners of the terrace. Bertram recalls that the commissioning process was particularly painless: the Prince of Wales got him a drink and a chair and left him to sketch for an hour or so. Bertram signed the finished pavilions with a bee inside in stone. Bee is for Bertram, like the sculpted whales by Simon Verity in the terrace pond are for Wales.

Bertram calls himself a traditionalist. He has been responsible for such projects as turning Cliveden, the former home of Nancy Astor, into a hotel, doing up the Grade I Royal Crescent Hotel in Bath, Aspinall's Club in London and

LEFT: *The gate from the swimming-pool to the cottage garden overhung with an arch of trained Golden Hornet crab-apples, which outlast the autumn leaves.*

BELOW: *The Prince of Wales and David Magson, the head gardener, in the woodland garden. The tree-house was designed by Willie Bertram.*

the ill-starred project of installing a fountain for the Queen in Parliament Square which was cancelled because of the recession. In the garden at Highgrove he has designed on a smaller scale: a bench for the walled garden with the theme of hunting (the back is a bow) and the pillar-box redoubt which forms one of the police posts on the estate. Bertram also designed a tree-house for the young princes which sits in a holly tree in the woodland garden. This is intended to echo the forms of the tree itself. The front door is a holly leaf and the red windows apparently represent berries.

When Prince Charles began to keep livestock at Highgrove, he was presented with the problem of what to keep them in. Most farmers would put up a palace of steel and corrugated tin, which is what was there before. But the Prince of Wales is not most farmers and Highgrove is not only his home and his business in the country but the Home Farm of the Duchy as well. Most people who visit Highgrove for garden parties, business or official meetings, arrive up the back drive. The farm buildings are the introduction they have to the estate. So the Prince decided that they needed to set the tone.

ABOVE: *The dovecote dedicated to the memory of Sir John Higgs.*

BELOW: *The beef unit built in the Prince's own mixture of brick, chalk, flint and Cotswold stone. The roof was built as an 'M' in section, so that it would not be as high as a single 'A'-section pitched roof.*

Accordingly, he told Bertram to design for him what is probably the only modern beef building to be built in traditional brick, chalk, and Cotswold stone. He used recycled materials that happened to be lying around on the farm. Terry Summers, the farm director, was consulted on the exact dimensions required for a modern beef-yard and Bertram designed the building to accommodate them. Tiling the barn with Cotswold limestone slates presented one of several technical problems: if the roof's angle of pitch was to be steep enough to carry off water, the roof of the beef-yard would have been too high. So Bertram hit upon two pitched roofs erected side by side in an 'M' configuration. The result has been a modern farm clothed in traditional materials. No one says that it was cheap.

At the other end of the scale, however, one of the most delightful and most economical design-changes on the estate was the improvement made to the four semi-detached cottages beyond the garden at Highgrove. These are rectangular boxes of a shape depressingly familiar from scores of housing estates built in the 1950s. They were dubbed 'the council houses' early on by the Prince. Their lifeless functionalism has been transformed by the simple expedient of painting them an ochre colour, in keeping with the local stone, and swapping their factory-

The farm cottages, as transformed by the Prince and their occupants. Dennis Brown, the gardener, lives in the one on the left. In the garden in front are Dennis's prize leeks and onions for which, in the course of one year alone, he won over fifty prizes.

made rectangular metal windows for wooden frames with glazing bars made in the shape of overlapping Regency-style arches. Their walls have been battened with simple trellising and roses and clematis trained up them. The front doors have a simple wooden trellised porch which gives their austere shapes a homely look. Altered thus, the farm cottages have an inexpensive lesson for thousands of similarly austere boxes all over the country.

GARDENING WITHOUT CHEMICALS

ARLY ON A SUMMER'S MORNING when the dew is on the grass and the mist has not yet been burned off by the sun the young garden at Highgrove is at its most spectacular. Stretching theatrically into the mist are the yew hedges of the Italian garden, already topiarised into swags, balls and pilasters. Down the avenue they enclose, towards the distant stone-tiled dovecote, all is formality. On either side of the central thyme-path, planted by the Prince himself, is an avenue of pleached hornbeams spread on metal frames which form rectangular cabinets, each containing a statue of the four seasons.

Nearer the house, the mood is less sombre and more playful. The french windows open on to the terrace with its octagonal pond in which swims Simon Verity's pun sculpture of whales. At the corners of the terrace are Willie Bertram's Gothic pepper-pot pavilions and around the french windows huge Ali Baba pots filled with scented geraniums. Turn left through a yew hedge on the south side of the house and there is the rose garden. Here the Prince has been known to have breakfast on fine summer mornings surrounded by lavender, rosemary, honeysuckle and the double blossoms of old English roses. Arched windows have been cut in the hedge of the rose garden by Sir Roy Strong, former Director of the Victoria and Albert Museum, who has discovered a new vocation in cutting the Prince's topiary. The Prince likes abrupt transitions between formality and wild nature: hence the windows. Through the hedge one can see the hay field which lies between the enclosed rose garden and the walled kitchen garden. The spring battalions of cowslips, narcissi, tulips and camassias are over and have been replaced by an impressionistic haze of buttercups, ox-eye daisies, lilium martagon and alliums in the long grass.

Sir Roy, who is never lost for an opinion, calls Highgrove the most important garden to be made in the 1980s. He says that it reflects two of the great themes of the past decade: a return to formality in design and a growing delight in wild

The hay meadow at Highgrove, early on a July morning. At the end of the path, under the house, is the rose garden. The formal garden stretches off to the left, behind its yew hedges.

ABOVE: *The kitchen garden looking towards Dennis Brown's cottage. Note the rose arbour in the middle of the diagonal path and the fruit trees growing in the middle of the vegetable beds. The trees use up many of the nutrients, so the beds have to be generously manured.*

Dennis Brown, master organic gardener.

nature. The garden looks backwards to the last time that country-house gardens were built on a grand scale, before the First World War. It looks forward in its ecological concerns, in Prince Charles's decision to garden organically and in his use of wild flowers, traditionally despised as weeds.

The place where the two themes come together is the most private: the walled *potager* or kitchen garden. There the gardener, Dennis Brown, grows his vegetables organically behind neat box hedges. The paths run in tunnels of apples, roses, broad beans and sweet peas. Walking to the centre one finds a round pond, with golden and multi-coloured carp and a fountain, surrounded by a herb garden. The eighteenth-century red brick walls of the kitchen garden are lined with rosemaries, pinks, lavender, roses, and espalier apple pear and peach trees. The mixture of flowers, fruits and vegetables is both decorative and useful, for the blossoms provide a lure for natural predators of aphids like hover-flies and ladybirds. The overall result is probably the most beautiful acre of garden I have ever seen.

When Prince Charles moved to Highgrove he already knew who he wanted to help him with his garden designs, a lady famous both as a great beauty and a great gardener. He had once asked the Marchioness of Salisbury tentatively to design a garden for him at Chevening. He had seen a garden she designed for Mary Anna Marten at Crichel in Dorset and the garden of one of her husband's family homes, Cranborne Manor, also in Dorset. Both gardens had features the Prince liked; a blend of formality and romance: old-fashioned roses and box hedges in walled kitchen gardens and the mixture of fruit, vegetables and flowers.

Lady Salisbury, now in her seventies, presides over sixty acres of garden, all farmed organically, at Hatfield House, the Cecil family's Jacobean palace in Hertfordshire. There she has made magnificent flower-filled knot-gardens, parterres, a new kitchen garden and orchards. She has been a dedicated organic gardener for over forty years and first banned chemical sprays at Cranborne, where she spent many years of her married life, in the early 1950s.

One morning at Hatfield when the butler had taken the coffee cups away Lady Salisbury showed me the plans that she had drawn up for Highgrove. Aided by a small dog, we arranged them on the floor of her study in a wing of the palace which Robert Cecil, the first Earl of Salisbury, caused to be built in 1609. His remarkable gardener, John Tradescant, filled the grounds at Hatfield with unusual plants which he collected on overseas expeditions. Lady Salisbury, who made a study of Tradescant when she took on the gardens in 1972, planted as he had done combinations of fruit, flowers and vegetables within hedges and walled enclosures.

When Prince Charles bought Highgrove, recalls Lady Salisbury, the garden had little character, consisting of trees and mown grass with here and there a few lumps of shrubbery. The first project was to get a sense of enclosure into the garden with yew hedges to give protection from the fierce west wind. There was a debate over the golden yew blobs lining the central path, then an expanse of municipal gravel. The Prince was always reluctant to do away with the golden yews – they are still there – but the gravel has been replaced by thyme. There was also the problem of the rectangular pond at the end of the garden which seemed out of scale and divorced from any coherent plan. This has now been partly enclosed by yew hedges, which Lady Salisbury says is a tremendous improvement. I take that to mean that neither she nor Prince Charles has finished with the pond just yet.

ABOVE: *Prince Charles with Lady Salisbury in the kitchen garden.*

A view of Highgrove in the early days after Prince Charles moved in. The terrace has been built and the rose garden, to the right, is still under construction.

Early on, Lady Salisbury laid out the rose garden and enclosed it with yew hedges as somewhere near the house the Prince could go to be private, away from the telephoto lenses which could reach him from the road. (At that time the walls had yet to be raised around the estate.) She and the Prince could have decided to use fast-growing conifers but Lady Salisbury was confident that yew would grow up to eighteen inches a year properly planted and properly fed. Twelve years on the yews have grown up with dense growth at the bottom as well as the top, thanks to plentiful manuring. In less than ten years they were ready to withstand Sir Roy Strong's shears.

Planting the rose garden was comparatively easy, for Lady Salisbury knew that the Prince liked scented plants and old-fashioned roses. She chose what she calls old-fashioned flowers, many highly-scented, such as pinks, violas, pansies, lilies, and standard honeysuckles. She planted something for each season; for the spring, coloured primroses, species tulips, small scented narcissus and jonquils. She surrounded his favourite Italian terracotta vases with hedges of box and lavender-cotton (*santolina*) and planted them with scented geraniums after the frost had gone. She also provided a design for the terrace and the octagonal pond.

The walled kitchen garden was suffering from acute neglect. Prince Charles recalls that a gate-sized hole had been knocked in the wall on one side to let a tractor through. Paddy Whiteland, whose memories of the estate go back to the 1940s, said

The cottage garden.

Old-fashioned sweet peas, the scented kind, growing up arches made of hazel from a coppice on Duchy Home Farm.

pigs had been kept there in the not-too-distant past. There were the remains of an orchard and a filled-in pond with no fountain. The Prince remembers a depressing day when everything in the garden was bulldozed flat. Then they started again.

The Prince had begun with a complicated geometrical plan, with box hedges laid out in the manner of a knot-garden. In the end he and Lady Salisbury simplified the design drastically, scrapping the knots because they were too impractical. It would, the Prince inferred, have taken half-a-dozen one-legged gardeners to have sown vegetables in the small spaces left. Instead he chose a different simple geometric shape for each quarter of the garden, outlined in box hedging and centred by dome-shaped metal pergolas with iron pergolas planted with roses, honeysuckles and white wisteria.

Around the fountain Lady Salisbury conceived a startling centrepiece. She had the idea of planting a circle of Golden Hornet crab-apples, with each tree's branches trained into a crown. After the leaves have fallen in autumn each tree in the circle is now topped by a living crown of golden crab-apples which glow even in the worst November and December weather. Between the crab-apple trees and the fountain she planted hedges of rosemary and thyme and other herbs for the kitchens.

The walled garden is often the most private place on the estate, far away from the bustle of horses, farm tractors, dogs, chickens and policemen that goes on at Highgrove. Behind the walls, there is seldom more than the sound of birds singing, the bees buzzing and the squeak of Dennis Brown the gardener's wheelbarrow. The Prince sometimes takes his paperwork there and sits on a bench in the sun. The outsider feels as if he has walked into a private world.

The kitchen garden at Highgrove is probably the best advertisement in the country for gardening organically. The vegetables and fruit are vigorous, healthy and delicious. Certainly the odd caterpillar hole and slug bite can be found if you stick your nose into a patch of oak-leaf lettuces or exotic purple Brussels sprouts, but the birds and insect predators seem to keep pests within bounds. If there is wastage, it is not serious: the garden produces vegetables by the ample trugful. All the evidence of one's eyes, ranging over the glorious profusion of flowers, vegetables and fruit, says that this garden is in the very bloom of health.

The genius of the kitchen garden at Highgrove is Dennis Brown, now fifty-six. Dennis was for sixteen years the whipper-in for the Duke of Beaufort's hunt. He was no novice to gardening, having won dozens of first prizes for his huge speciality leeks at shows. Having learned his gardening from his father before synthetic sprays and inorganic fertilisers were widely available, Dennis found it easier than most gardeners to adapt to organic methods when he came to Highgrove in 1984. In addition to his labours in the kitchen garden, he provides twenty-five or so scented houseplants each weekend when the Prince is at home, from stephanotis, jasmines, and paperwhites, to hyacinths and pelargoniums. The air in his greenhouse is a glorious assault on the senses.

The first principles of organic gardening are to create a favourable environment for the plants by feeding the soil. With a healthy soil, containing the right blend of humus, beneficial bacteria and trace elements, the theory goes, plants will grow strong and more resistant to disease. A malnourished plant, like a malnourished child, will catch a disease that a healthy plant will not. Control of insect pests such as aphids depends on building up a network of insect predators, such as ladybirds and hover-flies. Slugs are more difficult to kill but hedgehogs and traps filled with beer can be effective. The aim is to keep pests to a level where they can be tolerated, not to eradicate them altogether.

It would be wrong to suggest that organic gardening at this level is easy, but then no gardening of this standard ever is. The answer to nearly every gardening problem in Dennis's eyes is manure, which involves back-numbing work. Well-rotted cow manure from the farm is dropped for him by the tractorload in the adjoining wood. He digs eighty to ninety wheelbarrow loads of muck into the acre-sized kitchen garden every year; five barrowloads in each triangular vegetable plot. These quantities are necessary, he explains, because the box hedges and fruit trees planted among the vegetable plots steal lots of nourishment from the open ground. He also uses seaweed extract both as a soil supplement and as a liquid foliar feed to toughen up the leaves of plants so that they resist pests.

Home-grown fruit and vegetables for one weekend at Highgrove, as delivered to the house by Dennis Brown.

Dennis believes in cultivating the ground three times between autumn and spring, once when the last crop is pulled, once in winter and once again in spring. Late into the night in spring and autumn Dennis can be found digging or rotavating on his own vegetable garden, having spent until evening digging and double-digging the Prince's ground. The results of his labours are to be seen in the profusion of blooms and of fruits, vegetables and herbs – and in his own prize onions and leeks. A couple of years ago, Dennis's rows of parsley were as lush as a rainforest, the best he had ever grown, while my own few stalks at home had been eaten low by some nameless, often-sprayed beast.

Dennis avoids synthetic pesticides by using soot to treat carrot fly and mildew on roses and foliar feeds to persuade roses and brassicas to harden themselves against aphids and to repel mildew. He hangs yellow sticky plastic strips in the greenhouse to control whitefly. Diseases and pests of the soil he avoids by winter digging and long rotations. With sixteen plots, some cropping twice a year, rotations are a complex planning task which requires the keeping of a careful record. He plants spinach after spring cabbage followed by carrots. After early peas he plants leeks and after potatoes, lettuce.

Even the most functional plant in the vegetable garden is planted to be decorative. Dennis spends hours planting lettuces within the triangular hedges in attractively-spaced rows. He pays particular attention to setting out his decorative vegetables, such as the pink and blue cabbages beloved of modern flower arrangers. The purple Brussels sprouts he grows in the autumn are appreciated by the chefs at Highgrove for their unusual looks, but they are indifferent croppers. The chefs (who come, in rotation, from the staff at Kensington Palace) cut the eighteenth-century purple carrots into strips and serve them along with white and ordinary orange ones as crudités to accompany a drink before dinner.

Organic gardening can become an even more complex art when one enters into the refinements of companion planting to attract beneficial insects like hover-flies beside other plants vulnerable to pest species. Hover-fly larvae, for example, devour aphids. At home at Hatfield, Lady Salisbury plants *limnanthes*, yellow and white flowers known as the poached egg plant, to attract hover-flies. *Calendula* (pot marigolds) and *nemophila* (baby blue eyes) are also recommended for this. Hover-flies are also fond of the flowers of umbellifers such as fennel, dill, parsnips and carrots. There are also new biological methods of pest control. Tomato and cucumber growers in commercial greenhouses are already using biological methods to kill some pests because they are cleaner and cheaper. There are now pheromone traps for attracting the males of codling moths – the maggot of which is traditionally found in apples. The male moths are attracted by the hormones of female moths and become stuck inside the trap. While this method does not entirely eradicate codling moths it does control them to a tolerable level.

The organic experts say there is really no need to garden in any other manner. They say that farmers and horticulturalists use inorganic fertilisers and chemical sprays, rightly or wrongly, because they need to make a living by wringing the last drop of productivity out of the land. In the process they kill benevolent insects as well as harmful ones, leave residues on food, and their crops become dependent on the spraying regime. Their fields are quiet, where few birds sing. So what is the amateur gardener's excuse? He or she just wants a garden with healthy flowers and vegetables with perhaps a few birds and butterflies as well. All that is required for organic gardening is a different attitude of mind. Lady Salisbury says that all the great gardens of the past, since Adam, have been organic. She regards the chemical episode as a historical aberration.

While Dennis Brown is king of the kitchen garden, the rest of the gardens are run by the young head gardener, David Magson and his even younger team. David, who is now twenty-seven, came straight to Highgrove from Myerscough

Hall, the Lancashire college of agriculture and horticulture, after two placements at Ness Gardens, in Liverpool, and Hidcote in Gloucestershire. David soon found himself in charge of the gardens after the Prince and the previous head gardener agreed to part company. He has an awesome responsibility in keeping the flower gardens well-stocked and looking their best for the summer when the Prince is conducting much of his official business at Highgrove. Even when the Prince is not doing official business, small parties from local organisations visit every week. Magson also has to adjust his timetable to accommodate the continual programme of improvement and new planting suggested by the Prince and his advisers. David now has the enthusiastic help of James Aldridge, aged twenty-three, who studied horticulture at Wye College, London University, and Liz Mather, who is still completing a City and Guilds day-release course in horticulture.

It would not be right to give the impression that everything goes entirely uneventfully in the Prince's pursuit of a closer relationship with nature. David Magson ran into practical difficulties when Prince Charles announced his determination to stop using peat. Peat-cutting with huge machines, and the elaborate drainage schemes this requires, is undoubtedly damaging wetlands such as the Somerset Levels, Thorne Moors in Yorkshire and the Irish bogs. The difficulty for gardeners and professional horticulturists is that they have become dependent on peat. Peat is an extremely stable, largely sterile substance whose properties have been accurately known and exploited since the early 1900s. Before that gardeners got by perfectly well – even for seeds and potting mixtures – by using sifted compost, sand and loam.

Magson had the same difficulties as thousands of other gardeners have experienced when trying to adapt peat substitutes for potting in the greenhouse. Many of the substitutes for peat have wholly different properties from the original material, particularly in their water retention. Magson found that coir, or waste coconut fibre, had quite different water-absorption properties from peat when he tried to use it as a potting compost. It looked dry on the top but below the surface the coir was saturated, so it was easy to overwater. This he found out the hard way when a whole season's worth of cuttings and bedding plants, petunias, antirrhinums (snapdragons) and geraniums went rotten on him. It was little consolation to Magson at the time that other gardeners were experiencing the same problem and the letters columns of organic gardening magazines were filled with debate about how to use coir. Having developed a different watering regime, he says he is now having excellent results. He is also beginning to produce Highgrove's own peat-free compost made from compost, sand and loam. Some consolation for his early difficulties is that in giving up peat when he did he beat Kew Gardens by a year.

On technical organic gardening matters Lady Salisbury advised Prince Charles to draw on the advice offered by the Henry Doubleday Research Association, based at Ryton near Coventry. The HDRA is now the largest organic body in Britain with 18,000 members, a larger membership than that of the Soil Association, the society which began the reaction against synthetic pesticides and fertilisers in farming in 1946.

OVERLEAF: *The heart of the kitchen garden is the pond, in which swim multi-coloured and golden carp. The Prince had a fence built to stop children falling in. The pink rose in front of the fountain is 'Raubritter'. Note the Golden Hornet crab-apple trees: later in the year Dennis binds the new growth into crowns.*

The association is named after a Quaker smallholder who introduced Russian comfrey into Britain in the 1870s and spent thirty years experimenting with the plant's exceptional properties as an instant compost and soil improver. Henry Doubleday was the figurehead chosen by the late gardening writer, Lawrence D. Hills, who founded the association in 1958. His place has been taken by Alan and Jackie Gear, two scientists who joined him in 1973. The association moved in 1980 from Lawrence Hills's home of Bocking in Essex to its present 22-acre site on a former smallholding at Ryton-on-Dunsmore outside Coventry. There it has successfully ridden the environmental roller coaster of the 1980s, doubling in membership in the process.

The Gears and their colleagues have brought the organic movement into the era of the 'green consumer'. You can buy all sorts of bone, blood, hoof and sea-weed concoctions from the HDRA shop or by mail order. They also produce a series of excellent leaflets on slug and weed control without chemicals, alternatives to peat, and composting. They solve the problem of making compost in the small urban garden by advocating a worm-farm, which uses the brandling worms favoured by small boys to catch perch. These worms can digest small volumes of organic waste into usable compost in a matter of weeks provided they are kept warm in winter. A favourite of the HDRA is old carpet which it recommends for a vast range of purposes, whether cut up into square mats and used to prevent cabbage root fly, as a mulch, or as an insulating layer to keep compost heaps working at the right temperature.

Ryton Gardens provides evidence to 55,000 visitors a year, and through their Channel 4 television programme, 'All Muck and Magic', that organic gardening is practicable even in the smallest urban garden and that it can produce healthy, enjoyable food. The canteen, Jackie Gear's brainchild, is listed in the Good Food Guide. The Gears have won respect for their scientists in unpromising quarters such as the Ministry of Agriculture, which now awards them research contracts. Alan believes that one day, when the oil runs out, the whole country will be organic by necessity. Estimates of when that will be, however, are notoriously variable. In the short term, he says most farmers do not pay the full price of the pollution they cause. If they did, organic produce would look cheap by comparison.

The Prince of Wales, who became patron of HDRA in 1989, fought a celebrated campaign on their behalf to save the National Fruit Collection at Brogdale in Kent which was threatened with closure by the Ministry of Agriculture. The thirty acres at Brogdale contain the reference collection and living gene bank of British fruit, including 2,500 apple, 500 pear, 350 plum and 220 cherry varieties. The oldest was a variety of apple, Decio, which grew in the gardens of Roman villas. Old varieties of vegetables and fruit, such as Prince Charles's purple carrots, are a particular interest at Ryton where they regularly carry out trials to find the varieties of vegetables and fruit best suited to organic regimes.

The story began because the Ministry of Agriculture decided that 'near market' research, with likely commercial benefits, should be funded by the industry and not by the taxpayer. The industry proved unable or unwilling to find the considerable sums involved to save Brogdale since it was alarmed that the

Ministry would cut other vital research which they would have to fund. In the end the Duchy and the local authority solved the problem by providing a joint 100 per cent mortgage to enable the Brogdale Horticultural Trust – a new charity with the HDRA, the Duchy, and the Worshipful Company of Fruiterers, amongst others, on the board – to buy it.

Looking back on the 1980s, the decade in which the garden at Highgrove was made, we see that the practice of organic gardening made a greater breakthrough with the general public than it has done in any decade since the war. 'Organic', as an adjective, lost its cranky associations. It became used without scorn in a wide selection of newspaper gardening columns. It had a slot on Channel 4. No one can say how much of this was the hard work of the talented populists at the HDRA, how much a result of the Prince of Wales's interest in organic methods and how much the increasingly environmental mood of the times. What can be said is that it was the gardeners who made the organic movement popular.

A 'Constance Spry' rose tumbling over the garden wall.

ALL THE
THYME IN
THE WORLD

ROSEMARY VEREY REMEMBERS vividly the first time the Prince of Wales called to see her award-winning garden at Barnsley near Cirencester. The telephone started ringing as she was having breakfast. She had visitors and was in no mood to answer it in a hurry. The phone rang and rang and eventually she finished what she was doing and picked it up. A voice said: 'This is the Prince of Wales' and asked whether she was free that day. Would she have time for him to come over and see the garden?

Mrs Verey designed and built the garden at Barnsley House with her late husband David, the architect and architectural historian. It is not, at just over four acres, enormous in size but it packs in more than many gardens of five times the area. Hugh Massingberd described it knowledgeably in the *Daily Telegraph* as 'a singularly satisfying combination of seventeenth-century pattern-making, eighteenth-century picture-making and nineteenth-century-style plant-collecting'. Despite appearances to the contrary, the garden has been created almost entirely in the past thirty years.

The lovely honey-coloured stone house, where her son now lives, was built in 1697 for the local grandee Brereton Bourchier before he built Barnsley Park, one of Gloucestershire's finest houses, up the road. It later became the village rectory, and was given a Tudor-Gothic façade by the Reverend Adolphus Musgrave in 1830. David Verey's parents, the Reverend and Mrs Cecil Verey, lived there and planted the Irish yews which line the garden path like sinister green columns. Mrs Verey now lives in converted stables by the side of the house which boast a newly-added top-lit garden-room with a magnificent modern shell-and-stone grotto.

As might be expected, perhaps, from a garden built with her late husband, the garden at Barnsley House is a carefully-designed architectural creation, using a classical temple brought stone by stone from nearby Fairford Park, a Gothic summer-

ABOVE: *Rosemary Verey in her garden at Barnsley House, near Cirencester.*

OPPOSITE: *The rose garden: in the foreground is the pink geranium* endressii *'A.T. Johnson'; the roses to the left and right are* Rosa alba, *'Queen of Denmark'. The purple foliage is purple sage,* Salvia officinalis *'Purpurascens'. The field poppies are self-seeded from the wildflower verges.*

93

The laburnum walk at Barnsley in full flower: the exotic yellow of the laburnums is set off by mauve ornamental onions.

house and stone statuary as focal points. It has a knot-garden, herb borders, lime walks and other historical features which came about through the Vereys' passion for historical gardening books. The vegetable garden is, like Highgrove's, laid out as a decorative *potager* with fruit and flowers. Its paths and patterns are based on intricate seventeenth-century designs inspired by the words of the English parson, William Lawson, who wrote that a kitchen garden could have 'comely borders with herbs' and 'an abundance of roses and lavender' which would 'yield much profit and comfort to the senses'. The whole garden has the feeling that every vista has been laid out to the minutest detail, somehow without feeling fiddly or contrived. Its secret, I suspect, is a combination of classical form and Mrs Verey's inspired and romantic flair for colour.

A striking feature of her garden is an arched tunnel hung with laburnums. This looks from the classical summerhouse to a four-foot column with an inscription from John Evelyn: 'As no man be very miserable who is master of a garden here: so will no man ever be happy who is not sure of a garden hereafter.' One only has to take a few steps around here to see vistas at every turn. One leads to the summerhouse, with its pond full of water-lilies; parallel to this is the laburnum-and-lime-tree walk: if you turn there is a path towards the house, lined with yews and planted with rock roses.

The colours of the laburnum tunnel have been carefully thought out to create dramatically changing moods from season to season. In winter the architecture of the arches and decorative balls of box along the path stand out. In spring, white honesty and red tulips emerge from the beds under the green branches. The tunnel reaches its peak in June, when it bursts into a rich but devastating combination of purple and yellow. The beds beneath the yellow-flowering laburnums have been underplanted with the purple alliums, *Allium aflantunense*, which flower just as the laburnums produce their grape-like bunches of colour.

Mrs Verey's great expertise is as a plantswoman. She writes about gardens and lectures on garden design in this country, the USA and Australia. She has written the *Scented Garden, Classic Garden Design* and *The Flower Arranger's Garden*. Her book *The Garden in Winter* is now a classic account of how gardens can hold interest throughout the coldest season. Her latest, *Good Planting*, with photographs by Andrew Lawson, who took some of the photographs for this book, is a manual of how to blend the palette of colours in a garden to suit the gardener's own personality, and how to achieve magnificent effects with companion planting of similar and contrasting colours.

Among her particular virtues for Prince Charles are that, living only seventeen miles away, she can both advise on plants that do well in Gloucestershire and is often able to drive over at short notice. He writes to her enclosing a list of plants which he has read about, and she lets him know what is obtainable and what will do well on the Highgrove soil. When I visited her, she was working on a letter from Prince Charles asking for more unusual plants to give further interest to the borders. She was looking up unusual dog-toothed violets, species crocuses and exotic narcissus. She had just solved the problem of how to obtain 3,000 camassias, which have a flower like giant bluebells, to plant a bold wave of blue through the wildflower meadow. She had ordered them while on a visit to Toronto.

Mrs Verey began at Highgrove by advising Prince Charles on plants for the cottage garden, an area of beds with a winding grass path between them near the swimming-pool. Here she has advised him which plants would provide exactly the right combinations in the thick banks of colour that change from one week to another in the summer months. The garden was planted to be at its best in June and July, when the Royal household is there. By August or September every year the Prince and Princess are away and anything flowering then goes unseen. One March day, the Prince and Mrs Verey worked until dusk to plant the border, with intermittent help from Prince William. She remembers that as they finished and the light faded, it obligingly began to rain.

Mrs Verey also advised on another recent project, the woodland garden, where the young princes' tree-house is built. There were more trees in the woodland garden at the beginning but a winter gale has thinned them drastically. This has been a blessing in disguise for when Mrs Verey began helping with the garden in 1989 the shade had been lightened enough to support a wider variety of plants. Where there were shrubs and brambles, beds have been filled with species that need relatively little care: hostas, hardy geraniums, foxgloves, bulbs and violas, together with clumps of scented white tobacco plants.

OVERLEAF: *Drifts of snowdrops in the woodland garden.*

Tree casualties of the storm gouged with a chainsaw to form seats at the Prince's suggestion.

There were tree trunks left over from the storm in the woodland garden. Instead of having them towed away to be sawn into firewood, the Prince had the idea of turning them into seats in an Arts and Crafts style by gouging buckets out of them with a chainsaw. As they slowly grow fungi they are taking on lives of their own. Prince Charles was working in the winter of 1991 to enclose the woodland garden, always one of the coldest parts of the estate and the most prone to frost. On the winter's day I went there with Mrs Verey, the Prince had marked out the shape of a scalloped hedge with bamboo stakes just inside an emerging carpet of snowdrops.

Rosemary Verey brought in Sir Roy Strong when Prince Charles wanted someone to topiarise his maturing yew hedges. Sir Roy and his wife Julia have created an immensely theatrical garden out of a three-acre field in front of the house in Herefordshire which they bought in the early 1970s. There he has taught himself topiary, which he generally performs extempore to the horror of other gardeners. He remembers the first time he came to cut the hedges at Highgrove. David Magson, the head gardener, had gone to find the templates they were thinking of using. While he was away, Sir Roy attacked his first yew. Magson came back and looked at him. 'What do you call that?' Sir Roy recalls his asking. 'Free style?' Sir Roy said he didn't know what to call it. In fact he didn't call it anything. He just went at it. Orthodox or not, it seems to work.

The Prince chose pilasters, buttresses, pompoms and swags for the long yew hedges which line the Italian garden. Sir Roy pronounced that it lacked statuary, so he obtained handsome figures of the four seasons from Italy. Prince Charles liked Sir Roy's suggestion of quatrefoil Gothic windows cut into the yew hedges in the rose garden to give views out of the garden, which is like an extension to the house, and to reflect the Gothic shapes of the pepper-pot pavilions at the corners of the terrace. He claims to have begun to chop the yews at the end of the garden into the Prince of Wales's three feathers but these are, as yet, unrecognisable to anyone other than himself.

Other additions and embellishments to the garden happen all the time, and bewilder the regular visitor. The Prince is never satisfied in his gardening. The changes are not always expected by the gardeners either. Prince Charles regularly returns with a new idea from some foreign trip or a piece of sculpture that he has commissioned arrives and must be accommodated. Giant Ali Baba pots for the Prince's already large collection arrive in a steady trickle, from undisclosed sources.

In the end one gets the impression that Prince Charles likes nothing better than an idea without fuss that he can follow through without expert advice. He will call the experts in to get the colour of a plant or the flowering season right or exactly the right kind of plant for the Gloucestershire brash. But he prefers things that he can do himself, such as the thyme walk he planted in 1991.

Formerly a path of municipal gravel, fifty yards long and lined with blobs of golden yew, led from the house to the raised lily pond. The Prince had never been fond of the gravel. He also had a load of bricks, stone and cobbles left over from the new beef unit and was anxious to use them up. So he had the idea of a green path, formed of stone and brick but planted with cuttings of every different kind of thyme, which would eventually fill every crevice and spill out over the bricks. It would be dry in winter, since thyme is tough and heathery, yet be fragrant to walk on in summer.

Despite the evident disapproval of Sir Roy Strong, who clucked about it, the Prince duly planted his thyme walk, doing all of the work himself over four months. The result, composed of thousands of cuttings, is unique in England. It can truthfully be said to contain all the thyme in the world. Recently, Prince Charles reports, Sir Roy is having second thoughts.

The thyme walk: spreading healthily but no butterflies yet.

WILDFLOWER GARDENING

Solitude in the presence of natural beauty and grandeur is the cradle of thoughts
and aspirations which are not only good for the individual, but which society
could ill do without. Nor is there much satisfaction in contemplating the world
with nothing left to the spontaneous activity of nature; with every foot of land
brought into cultivation, which is capable of growing food for human beings;
every flowery waste or natural pasture ploughed up, all quadrupeds or birds which
are not domesticated for man's use exterminated as his rivals for food, every
hedgerow or superfluous tree rooted out, and scarcely a place left where a wild
shrub or tree could grow without being eradicated as a weed in the name of
improved agriculture.

Principles of Political Economy, John Stuart Mill, 1848.

T HE EARLY 1980S when Prince Charles began planning the garden at Highgrove was a time of dawning public awareness of the awesome damage that
subsidised farming had caused to the flora and fauna of Britain since the war.
Marion Shoard's book, *The Theft of the Countryside*, published in 1980, irritates
farmers to this day because it brought them great unpopularity (though Miss Shoard
placed most of the blame on government policy). Reading it again, however, it is no
real surprise to find that her book has become the orthodox version of the story of
agriculture's greedy consumption of the ancient landscape since 1945. The Nature
Conservancy Council, the state conservation body, at last got around to publishing
the official scientific version of the country's losses of natural habitat in 1984 –
which showed that 95 per cent of herb-rich grassland had been destroyed since the
Second World War.

This focus on the countryside in the British newspapers and media in the early
1980s was sharpened by the passage of the Wildlife and Countryside Act 1981,
the first legislative attempt to halt the unfolding destruction. This new and cum-
bersome Act provoked a number of confrontations with farmers who did not see
why they should be forced to stop draining or ploughing their own acres. Two
celebrated showdowns took place: on Halvergate Marshes, in Norfolk, and on
the Somerset Levels, where farmers burned effigies of senior conservationists.

*The door into the garden at
Ashton Wold, the home of
Miriam Rothschild.*

101

By the time he was working on the garden at Highgrove, Prince Charles had heard that a counter-movement had begun which aimed at using the millions of acres of garden in Britain as a sanctuary for the wild flowers that had once grown in cultivated farmland. These flowers had been suppressed by farming practices such as the growing of silage instead of hay, the reseeding of permanent pasture, and seed-dressing techniques which, over the last century, have filtered out the seeds of plants such as the corn cockle and cornflower which in Shakespeare's day grew in profusion and each year were resown with the corn.

Prince Charles asked Lady Salisbury to recommend a list of suitable wildflower species for his garden and someone who would be able to advise him on how to plant them at Highgrove. She replied by sending him on a pilgrimage to see an extraordinary old lady in an overgrown house on the other side of England.

Anyone following in his footsteps to Ashton Wold in Northamptonshire could be forgiven for missing it altogether. The house where Miriam Rothschild lives could have been imagined by Edgar Allan Poe. Creeping clematis, honeysuckle and ivy have already successfully colonised the walls and are well on the way to engulfing the gables and the roof of the substantial Edwardian building. On my visit, in the depths of winter, the house was dark and forbidding and appeared to have been abandoned to nature several decades before. I drove into an empty courtyard, over gravel that I later learned was planted with wildflower seed waiting for summer. Silence. I backed out thinking I had taken a wrong turning, consulted a map, then returned.

A rap on a huge oak door gained admission to a house lined with books like a university college library. The house was built in a solid Arts and Crafts style in the early 1900s by Miriam Rothschild's father Charles, a partner in N.M. Rothschild, the family merchant bank. He also constructed the handsome stone-built village on the estate which includes a pub that his daughter Miriam has renamed The Chequered Skipper, after the butterfly now extinct in Britain.

Miriam's father could justifiably claim to have been the father of nature conservation in Britain. He founded in 1912 the Society for the Promotion of Nature Reserves which changed its name to the Royal Society for Nature Conservation as recently as the 1970s. In the way wholly characteristic of his exceptional family, he practised his hobbies at the level some people practise their careers. While a partner at the bank Charles Rothschild was also an entomologist and collector who made expeditions to the corners of the Empire in pursuit of his collections. On one of these, to the Sudan, he made his greatest scientific discovery: the plague flea which had devastated medieval Europe, still living comfortably on African rats and mice.

Miriam, aged eighty-three at the time of my visit, was still a lady of prodigious energy, a fact sworn to by her housekeeper. When I arrived the housekeeper explained that Mrs Lane (her married name; she divorced in the 1950s) was in the garden conducting an experiment (this was January) apparently into a chemical which increases memory in birds. On her return to her study-cum-drawing-room, strewn with some of the latest scientific books, Miriam Rothschild handed me a copy of a seventeen-page article she had just finished for an ecological magazine on the importance of maintaining biological diversity.

Like her late brother Victor, Lord Rothschild, described in his obituaries as one of the most variously-gifted men of his time, Miriam has turned her hand to a wide variety of disciplines, from biology to biography as well as bringing up five children. Though educated at home, she became a Fellow of the Royal Society and has published 300 scientific papers; including a quarter of a million words on fleas on which she is a world expert. She discovered that the acceleration of a flea jumping is twenty times that of a moon-rocket re-entering the Earth's atmosphere. The flea jumps off its knees, she explains, for if it jumped off its feet they would be shattered by the force.

Miriam Rothschild has also bred domestic livestock and written several books. Among them, *The Butterfly Gardener*, as its title suggests, is a manual on the plants that attract butterflies, and *Dear Lord Rothschild...*, is a biography of her uncle Walter, the banker, zoologist and collector of the largest number of natural history specimens ever made by one man. *Dear Lord Rothschild...* are the words which began the letter now known as the Balfour Declaration, in which in 1916 the Prime Minister, Arthur Balfour, promised the Jews a return to their scriptural home in Palestine.

When Prince Charles visited Mrs Lane at Ashton, she had abandoned formal gardening for nearly thirty years. She had grassed over the flowerbeds and seeded them with wild flowers and encouraged old man's beard (wild clematis) and ivy to grow on the walls of the house for birds to nest in. In the early 1970s she had begun to grow wild flowers for seed. She seems to have become convinced decades earlier than most of the scientific establishment that the flora of the British Isles was either

Miriam Rothschild, shown here, stopped gardening in a formal sense in the mid-1950s.

103

disappearing or being forced into tiny ghettos in which it could not ultimately survive. So in the 1970s she turned over the decrepit greenhouses in the vast walled garden built by her father to the cultivation of the wildflower species of England, Israel and North America. In 1979 she put on her first show of wild flowers at the Royal Horticultural Society. In 1981 she won a gold medal for her exhibit. And in 1991 she was given the Victoria Medal of Honour, the Society's highest award, in recognition of her visionary role in bringing wild flowers into horticulture.

There have always been those who disagreed or argued with Miriam Rothschild. She tells the story of how she asked Professor Kenneth Mellanby, Director of the Monks Wood research station near Huntingdon, if he thought she could recreate one of the Gothic cathedrals of English flora, a medieval hay meadow. 'Certainly,' he said. 'It will take a thousand years.' Mrs Lane retorted she could make a passable imitation in fifteen.

To prove it she planted the lawn in front of her house. It now holds ninety-six native species. Not all the flowers that emerge in summer are those she has planted. Of the five species of orchid in the wildflower lawn, four came in from the cold. This is the more remarkable since orchids, whose seed is as fine as face powder, are often dependent for their growing medium on exactly the right fungi in the soil. She attributes their arrival to creating the right habitat, withholding artificial nitrogen and mowing after the third week in July when the flowers have had time to seed. Wildflower gardening is essentially helping nature to create effects that it would itself create naturally over time, and with the right management. There is no real substitute for letting nature do what it wants to do by itself. Her hay meadow also attracts butterflies. Professor Ghillian Prance, Director of the Royal Botanic

A plot in the enormous kitchen garden where Miriam Rothschild grows the wildflower mixtures she sells commercially. This is 'The Farmer's Nightmare': corn cockle (the pink one), cornflower, corn marigold and ox-eye daisy, with barley and oats, some of the cereals they traditionally grow beside. Andrew Lawson, who took this photograph, says that the bed was swarming with insects, particularly hover-flies – a reminder of the natural predators of aphids that once existed in unsprayed cornfields.

Gardens at Kew, told her that he had not seen such clouds of butterflies since child-hood as those which rise from her hay meadow.

Prince Charles sought her help in creating a traditional hay meadow in the field beside the house at Highgrove. The species chosen were all known to occur locally in Gloucestershire, although the source was a Site of Special Scientific Interest in Northamptonshire. She provided plants that would flower from May to high summer: yellow rattle, ox-eye daisies, lady's smock, cowslips, self-heal, meadowsweet, bird's-foot trefoil, and timothy among them. The seed was drilled direct into the pasture but, as Prince Charles has said, the project was not vastly successful, with only yellow rattle, ox-eye daisies, lady's smock and buttercups surviving after the first year. It is possible that the ground was too fertile, making the grasses too competitive.

The second project was spectacularly successful, particularly in its first four seasons. This involved flanking the drive with belts of the wild flowers normally associated with cornfields: cornflower, corn cockle, scentless mayweed, field poppy and corn marigold; rare species known as the arable weeds. The seed mixture was a special version of what Mrs Lane calls 'The Farmer's Nightmare'. The Prince had asked for some meadow perennials like those already drilled into the meadow to be included, together with a few plants characteristic of road verges, such as chicory and melilot. This mixture was much more successful in competing with the existing grasses and provided in its first seasons a dazzling wave of impressionistic colour.

The hay meadow at Highgrove, showing the success of the ox-eye daisies.

OVERLEAF: *Poppies and corn marigolds beside the drive: the survivors of a spectacular mixture which originally included cornflowers – not all of this mixture competed well with grasses.*

105

Peacock butterfly on a thistle.

Wildflower gardeners cannot break the rules for long and get away with it. Arable weeds depend upon cultivation to germinate, so gardening with them is made complicated if they are mixed with competitive meadow grasses. Either the meadow plants predominate, or the sward has to be cultivated each spring to allow the arable weeds to germinate. This has led to some tricky decisions. Prince Charles has compromised by asking his gardeners to rotavate selected strips along the drive verges to ensure the germination of the cornfield flowers. This has been mostly successful. His gardeners have also been harvesting the seeds for reseeding the next spring.

Mrs Lane and her friend Lady Salisbury also advised Prince Charles on planting a butterfly garden. She recommended several species of the shrub buddleia, the all-purpose butterfly and moth attractor, together with old varieties of Michaelmas daisies, verbena, cherry-pie and valerian. Butterflies being butterflies, they often prefer other parts of the garden, such as the Prince's thyme walk.

Prince Charles recently asked her to suggest plants for a flowering hedge of traditional English species beside the drive which would provide a wall of blossom in spring. She has recommended two species of dog rose, field rose and sweet briar, together with wild pear, crab-apple (wild apple), bullace (wild plum), blackthorn, hawthorn and honeysuckle. The question posed by Paddy – how to prevent the new plants being eaten by the horses in the field behind – has now been overcome by a discreet electric fence.

Miriam Rothschild has also advised Prince Charles on recreating natural habitats. At Ashton Wold, Mrs Lane has turned a 25-acre lake into a dragonfly reserve. Dragonfly larvae feed on acquatic vegetation and by planting appropriate species that attract female dragonflies to lay their eggs she has increased the number of species there from two to fifteen. More such reserves need to be created, she believes, because of the forty-one British dragonfly species, three have become extinct since the 1930s, and many are still declining. She has planted the same varieties on a small scale in the clear-water outfall from the reed-bed sewage-treatment system which the Prince has chosen to replace Highgrove's overflowing septic tank. The dragonfly reserve at Highgrove will be tiny by comparison, but it will be lush and colourful with yellow flags, ranunculus, marsh marigold, pink water rush and other bog-loving species planted round the edge. Water-lilies, bog arrowhead and water soldier have been planted in the water.

Dedicated as she is to building new habitats to replace those that have been lost, there is nothing that makes Miriam Rothschild angrier or more passionate than the continued erosion of Britain's flora and fauna, especially by roads. There are, she says, only 130 national nature reserves in England. Why then is there no sacrosanct status for such reserves? How is it that there are conservation societies with more members than political parties yet 590 important wildlife sites are threatened by the current road-building programme? She advises people to protest to their MPs, local council, local paper and the Government at every such absurdity, believing that sooner or later such voices will be heard.

The prospect of mass extinctions of species worldwide as a result of the inevitable development that will accompany a doubling of the world's population in the next century fills her with dread. She thinks that, in the event of such losses, people will be left with rats, bluebottles, grasses and bacteria as the only wonders of nature – but she finds the prospect profoundly depressing. She observes sadly that someone said 'Pollution is people.' She believes, as did John Stuart Mill, in a stationary world population and that there is a social value in leaving some parts of the world for the activity of nature alone.

Meanwhile Miriam Rothschild takes every opportunity she can, in her energetic eighties, to hand in petitions and to repair what damage she can by planting native wild flowers on every barren habitat she can find – she has sowed her mixtures in places as varied as the new Oundle bypass and around the runways at Stansted airport. After my visit to Ashton, I glanced at the article she had written, which later appeared in BBC *Wildlife* magazine. It was written in the same clear voice and with the same practical solutions:

There are over a million and a quarter acres of gardens in the United Kingdom – a larger acreage than all our nature reserves combined. It provides quite a sizeable space for the conservation of wild flowers. If each back garden planted a buddleia bush against the fence many female butterflies would be able to lay their eggs successfully. They require nectar for nourishment and nectar is scarce along tarmac roads and in fields of mono-crops.

If we want to lay a sound and enduring foundation for biodiversity – here and elsewhere – we must imbue our children with a knowledge and true love of nature. Personally I believe naturalists are happier than the majority of mankind so it follows this procedure is of mutual benefit.

Finally, one must grit one's teeth and breach the current conspiracy of silence concerning overpopulation.

A hundred and fifty years after John Stuart Mill wrote the words at the beginning of this chapter, the outlook is considerably more depressing. Miriam Rothschild's answer is activism.

THE SEWAGE GARDEN

OWN AT THE END of the garden by the bullock-yard and Highgrove's unavoidable car-park is what Prince Charles is now fond of calling, in imitation of its serious German inventor, his 'sewage garden'. This is the reed-bed treatment system lately installed by the Duchy to process the Royal pollution, a successful example of the alternative technology which the Prince is determined to prove on the estate. That is not to say that the Royal sewage plant is something he is always able to take entirely seriously.

Drains are a favourite obsession of the English landowning classes, and Prince Charles, for once, is no exception. The Prince had every reason to think about the Royal drains in summer 1990. The ageing septic tank that deals with the waste water from the house and washings from the farmyard decided it had had enough. The combined demands of the Royal household – Royal persons plus cook, butler, several gardeners and policemen – together with the summer influx of garden-party-goers and other visitors, all with healthy bodily functions, amounted to a load ten times greater than the tank had been required to cope with before. On several nasty occasions the Royal sewage erupted and ran down the ditch in the direction of Tetbury.

No one doubted that the existing septic tank would have to go. The question was what to replace it with. The current philosophy of sewage processing in the developed world is based on mechanised treatment on site or centralised processing by sewage farms. Both are economically efficient, but ecologically less than perfect, since sewage farms tend to filter out only the solids and the actively-harmful pollutants and leave a high proportion of nitrates, phosphates and ammonia. The result is that rivers become cloudy, less oxygenated and clogged with the algal growth that the enhanced nutrients in the water stimulate, particularly in dry summers. Passing the waste water on to someone else for treatment encourages us polluters, in Prince Charles's view, to take a 'flush-and-forget' attitude to some of the unmentionable things that we put down the drain.

The reed-bed sewage-treatment system: in the foreground, Norfolk reeds; in the middle, willows; in the distance, the pond.

111

Prince Charles asked the Duchy to provide a full list of alternatives to the leaking and, by then, reeking septic tank. The conventional option, the basic legal requirement of the National Rivers Authority, was that Highgrove should install a compact primary treatment plant, a kind of two-chamber plastic tank which is dropped into a hole in the ground and extracts most of the solids and unpleasantness from the waste water before it is allowed to run off into the ditch. This would have used electricity to pump air into the effluent and move it through coils treated with micro-organisms which break down the nutrients and bugs. It would also have needed the solids emptying by a waste-disposal company from time to time.

Prince Charles had heard that a way could be found of producing almost-zero waste from a sewage plant, together with a usable compost, by using a reed-bed similar to those used in countries which do not have the electricity or the technology to install 'conventional' treatment plants. He also liked the *idea* of a reed-bed which fitted in with his philosophy of how waste should be disposed of.

The reality turned out, reassuringly, to be a little more complicated than just releasing sewage into a reed-filled lake. The sewage is passed first through concrete tanks filled with bark which trap the solids and enable them to be composted. This compost can be used, after a safe interval, on the fields. Then the waste water is pumped into a tank filled with sand, gravel and stone and planted with Norfolk reeds whose roots hold a web of micro-organisms which take up and use the nutrients. The reed-bed alone, it is claimed, is enough to treat the water to well within levels set by the National Rivers Authority. But as a final measure, the treated water can be passed through marshy ground planted with osiers or basket willows which take up more of the nutrients.

The company offering to design the reed-bed was run by Uwe Burka, a German-born member of the Camphill movement, a series of communities around the world where able-bodied people live with the mentally handicapped. The Camphill movement is based on the ideas of the Austrian writer and educationist Rudolf Steiner and practises biodynamic farming – a system one step further than organic, which makes use of natural cycles, such as phases of the moon to determine when to plant crops. Rudolf Steiner's philosophy ascribes spiritual value to natural processes and the Camphill movement believes that bodily waste should be integrated into the natural cycle, rather than treating sewage as 'septic' and in need of chemical treatment. Burka had already built two reed-bed plants at his Camphill village, at Oaklands in the Forest of Dean, which currently serve the needs of 200 people and satisfy the pollution standards of the National Rivers Authority. He had also built plants for farmers and industry, including a pilot version for treating large quantities of acidic slurry from a Beecham pharmaceutical plant.

Nick Mould, the pragmatic Duchy agent who looked into the idea, was initially sceptical. He recommended to the Prince the top-of-the-range version of Uwe Burka's basic design: what Mould calls the 'belt, braces and safety pin' model. The Highgrove design provided by Burka includes a reed-bed, a willow-bed and a landscaped pond where the water is circulated, aerated and filtered for a last time before being allowed to seep away down the ditch to the river.

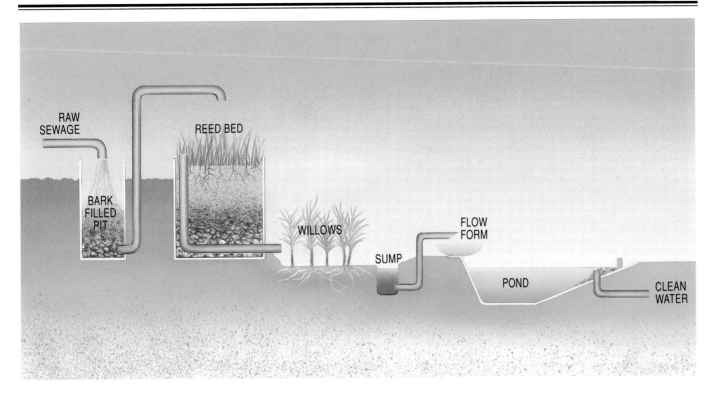

RAW SEWAGE

REED BED

BARK FILLED PIT

WILLOWS

FLOW FORM

SUMP

POND

CLEAN WATER

This more elaborate system, now in place, has several advantages: the additional treatment capacity means that the reed-bed can cope with the washings from the beef-yard and the willow-bed produces a 'crop' of osiers, which could be chipped for mulch or fuel or be used as basket-weaving material. The whole plant has been made into a landscaped feature, which Burka dubbed, to Prince Charles's amusement, the 'sewage garden'. The osiers have been planted with marsh marigolds and the pond with the water-plants Miriam Rothschild considers best for a dragonfly reserve. In its first summer the pond attracted several species of dragonfly and, to everyone's surprise, a fleeting visit from a kingfisher.

For the technically-minded, Burka explains that there is a radical difference between the kind of reed-bed design he uses and the kind which has been tried by some industries with indifferent success. His reed-bed is filled from the top, through perforated pipes, and drains downwards through the reeds, leaving the roots supplied with air all the time. In other reed-bed systems, the water passes horizontally through the reeds and so the roots, which need oxygen to break down the pathogens and nutrients, become waterlogged and are unable to do their job as effectively. Burka says that a horizontal system in which the roots are submerged will serve only to 'polish' the effluent after conventional treatment.

The clear water at the outfall now testifies that the plant is working. The result of the process is dramatically low levels of pollution and a system which meets the Prince's criteria of treating pollution locally instead of pushing it along the line to someone else. It is highly efficient. For example: a conventional treatment system for 45 permanent residents (the specification for Highgrove) would be required to bring down biological oxygen demand (BOD) to 30 mg per litre and suspended solids to 20 mg per litre. Conventional systems are not currently required

A cutaway view of the way the reed-bed system works: in an ideal world the water would flow downhill and not have to be pumped – but that would mean building the house first.

113

The willow-bed has been planted with marsh marigolds; the bank which forms the edges of the osier-bed, with one of Miriam Rothschild's wildflower mixtures.

to strip out nitrate, phosphate, or ammonia. The reed- and willow-beds reduce both BOD and suspended solids to 5 mg per litre – a sixth of the legal limit – and that is before the water has passed through the pond. They *also* reduce ammonia, nitrates and phosphates, which current sewage-treatment tanks do not treat, to the same levels.

It is an education, being responsible for one's own pollution. Uwe Burka made a close study of what people poured down the drain before the system started working. He discovered that the staff in the kitchens were using a kitchen shredder to pulp vegetables and even metal packaging, all of which went down the sink. The metal threatened to pollute the compost, and the vegetable wastes threatened to put unnecessary volumes of solid material through the bark filters. Another problem was grease, which the cooks were accustomed to pour down the drain in large quantities. This, too, was gumming up the bark filters before their time. Prince Charles now insists that the kitchen staff keep two waste buckets, one of organic waste for the compost heap, one of non-compostable material for the dustbin, and that nothing inorganic or troublesome should go down the drain.

Recently, Burka received a visit at Oaklands from Dutch government scientists who had heard of the success of his reed-beds. The Dutch Government are desperate to find something to do with the millions of tonnes of liquid slurry produced every year by intensively-reared livestock in farms in southern Holland. There is now more pig slurry from the intensively-reared pigs than the land can absorb. Piles of manure, left to rot in the open air, produce so much ammonia that it has been known to strip the leaves off the trees. The Dutch Government

114

offered Burka a substantial deal to build treatment plants for the liquid part of this slurry. He refused, saying it would have entailed bolting a 'green' form of treatment onto a form of 'crazy farming'.

The Highgrove reed-and-osier bed has many advantages, including landscaping an unattractive part of the farm. It has some disadvantages: it was more expensive than a simple conventional plant – though much of this must be put down to the landscaping. A reed-bed system should not necessarily work out more expensive. It also uses electricity (as would a conventional plant) since it requires the water to be pumped around the system several times a day. Ideally it would have been laid out down a hill and the water allowed to trickle down by gravity, but this was not feasible at Highgrove. Nick Mould is now investigating a way of pumping the water which does not use the mains, such as solar power or a windmill. The reed-bed also requires specialised maintenance, more like the skills of a gardener than those of a conventional water engineer.

If the reed-bed system works, as it shows every evidence of doing, then it must create a ripple of curiosity. It may even, as Burka hopes, appeal to large sewage plants or industries with acidic and unpleasant wastes to get rid of and sufficient land to contemplate a large-scale reed-bed. Such a system would certainly be welcome around Britain's sewage-strewn coastline. The idea is appealing; that wastes can be reintegrated in a beautiful and harmonious way into our surroundings. It also works. If the reed-bed at Highgrove consistently delivers the high level of cleaning that Uwe Burka claims for it, it may even be looked at as a standard against which other processes are judged.

The flow-form: showing the clarity of the water treated through the system.

WHY HIGHGROVE WENT ORGANIC

Farmers have ensured that the people of Europe are well fed. Now they are
successful, they are being blamed for the surpluses...I believe we also have to
face up to the fact that there is a separate crisis – a cultural crisis – facing us. It
concerns the very identity of farming itself, and it has arisen largely because we
have not made clear our dual role of providing food and looking after the
countryside. . .What makes farming different is the element of long-term
stewardship of a precious natural resource – and I don't think there is anything
soft, romantic or otherwise unrealistic about such an interpretation.

Lecture to the Royal Agricultural Society of England,
H.R.H. The Prince of Wales, March 1991.

Meadow cranesbill at Highgrove.

W HEN PRINCE CHARLES began farming at Highgrove in 1985 he told his
Duchy advisers that he was looking for a kind of farming which would
provide both a commercial return and would halt or preferably reverse the
despoliation of the countryside he witnessed as he grew up. It was a layman's
request, but the layman's question often confounds the experts and finding an
answer put the Duchy advisers, all trained in conventional farming, to the test. It is
a question which the devisers of European agricultural policy have yet to address
satisfactorily to this day.

There were good reasons why a farmer new to the business and with a bit of
spare cash might think that he could improve on the mess his forbears had made of
things. At that time a number of home truths about farming had begun to dawn
on policy makers and the public. The catastrophic damage to the countryside and
to flora and fauna was well known. The story of how farm slurry was polluting
rivers and how pesticides and fertilisers were contaminating drinking water was still
unfolding. The food scandals of the late 1980s caused by intensive farming methods – salmonella in eggs, listeria in cheese, pesticide residues on vegetables and
'Mad Cow Disease' – were over the horizon. The 'engine of destruction', as intensive farming was described at the time, was still firmly in gear.

Never mind the pollution, or the insistent ecological arguments, what worried
European agriculture ministers was that the Common Agricultural Policy was

tottering from budget crisis to budget crisis because of the price of subsidising record surpluses. In Britain, while manufacturing industry emerged devastated from recession, British farmers picked up £1.4 billion in subsidies a year. In retrospect, 1984 was a watershed: that spring European agriculture ministers agreed a reform package imposing the first milk quotas, designed to reduce the EC powdered milk mountains. There were whispers about cereal quotas – which never came into being – to tackle the mountains of grain in EC stores. (When it comes to surpluses, depressingly little has changed. By 1991, skimmed milk surpluses were 500,000 tonnes and cereal surpluses 17.5 million tonnes.) The mid-1980s were a time when many people wondered aloud why record subsidies were going to provide food we didn't need, at continued cost to J.S. Mill's 'spontaneous activity of nature'. It was a time when anyone new to farming, with a mind of his own, might be forgiven for wanting to go his own way.

A farm depends on those who run it, and those who ran Highgrove struggled with the questions that the Prince kept asking them. A close friend and adviser to Prince Charles at the time was the late Sir John Higgs, Secretary to the Duchy, and a farmer himself. Highgrove's farming consultant was Terry Summers, Director of Farming for Smith Woolley, the firm of land agents and chartered surveyors. Terry Summers had been appointed farm director when the Prince of Wales bought the farm in 1980. Summers had left school at fifteen and worked his way up the farming ladder the hard way, taking time off to attend two farming

Until 1985, the land at Highgrove was share-farmed and the Prince of Wales retained only those parts of it that were needed for grazing his horses and polo ponies.

colleges along the way. His contact with the Duchy began when his firm was brought in to maximise income from the estate for the Prince in 1977. Now, at sixty, he is a tall, upright figure known for his plain speaking and his wide farming experience. He is personally in charge of running 37,000 acres of farmland, the vast majority of which is farmed conventionally, for a variety of clients. These have included Lord 'Rab' Butler, Lord Pym and Sir Francis Dashwood, Master of West Wycombe and Premier Baronet of England, as well as a number of more ordinary landowners.

It was Terry Summers who presided over the share-farming arrangements with local farmers (usually a 60/40 deal, renewed annually) which had kept Highgrove ticking over until the Prince had time to farm it. Knowing that the Prince was increasingly anxious to begin farming, Sir John Higgs arranged the purchase of Broadfield Farm for the Duchy in 1985 to increase the acreage to a more economic size. It was at this time that the existing Duchy Home Farm at Stoke Climsland in Cornwall was handed over to the county council to become an agricultural college. Broadfield became the base for the new Duchy Home Farm, in theory a model for all the tenant farmers of the 128,000-acre estate.

Terry Summers remembers that Prince Charles had strongly-developed views about farming long before he took the farm 'in hand', but he was prepared to defer to those with practical farming experience as to how his ideas were carried out. He commissioned Terry to write him detailed reports of how the farming was going so that he could learn as much detail as he could. Terry says of the man he ususally calls 'the boss': 'I find him a very pragmatic man who does not expect things to be done if they make no sense at all. What he won't accept is the automatic rejection of an idea because someone says that it is not the way to do it today. I have to admit that on occasions he has been proved right.' One example of this, according to Terry, was the eventual shift to organic farming. 'I won't say it was pooh-poohed, but it wasn't thought of as a likely success.'

Summers recalls that there was, at first, no talk of going organic. The idea of organic farming evolved slowly as an answer to the question how to avoid mainstream farming's glaring excesses but still make a profit. Initially, Terry says, Prince Charles and Sir John Higgs described their objective as 'biologically-sustainable farming'. The idea was to find a middle way between conventional farming and organic agriculture which, at that time, like most of the farming community, the Prince's farming advisers regarded with some scepticism. The Prince set about enhancing the new acres of the estate with new trees and hedges. Meanwhile he talked in farm meetings about less intensive farming, with lower inputs of pesticide and fertiliser.

It was clear, before the discussions on how to farm less intensively were resolved, that someone on a similar wavelength to the Prince was going to be chosen as the farm's full-time manager. When Terry Summers telephoned him in late 1984, David Wilson, then aged thirty, was working as a farm manager for the merchant bank Hill Samuel. He was looking for a job as the bank was getting out of the farming business, as were a lot of institutions at the time. David had grown up outside the farming world (his father is a clergyman), perhaps the ideal credentials for an organic farmer, since farmers are a conservative breed. He was less

OVERLEAF: *Westonbirt in June: the first block of the farm to go organic. In the foreground are trial plots of barley. In the middle ground is a field seeded with a ley of cocksfoot and clover. In the distance, silage cutting is under way.*

than impressed by the prophylactic spraying and high nitrogen inputs of big-business farms. He remembers Terry telephoning and saying, mysteriously, that one of his clients was looking for a farm and would need someone to manage it. 'He was being very elusive about it. I thought it was maybe a film star,' says David. Terry went to see him farm and came clean about who his client was. David was asked for an interview with the Prince. David went thinking that at least he would get to meet the Prince of Wales. To his surprise, he got the job.

In the discussions that took place the summer David was appointed, two options presented themselves: the first was to farm with lower chemical inputs across the board. The difficulty here was one of definition. Exactly what was one trying to achieve in terms of wildlife? How would one measure it? How would it be measured in terms of the input of pesticides and fertilisers? What bothered the Duchy advisers about lower inputs was that it was like throwing money away with no appreciable wildlife gain. The only form of low-input farming all agreed worked was 'conservation headlands', ten-metre unsprayed strips around the edge of cereal fields pioneered by the Game Conservancy. These had been shown to encourage a return of rare arable weeds, partridges and hares.

The second option considered was full-blooded organic agriculture, known on the Continent as biological farming, and usually (if inaccurately) defined as farming without chemicals. The advantage of an organic approach was that it was definable. There were strict rules developed over forty years by the Soil Association, the mother organisation of the organic movement. Two big disadvantages were that farming without bag-nitrogen would mean producing radically less and that no field would qualify as organic for two years. But, on the plus side, it was clear that organic produce was beginning to command substantial premiums over conventional crops.

Coincidentally, 1985 was also the year of the advent of a more clearly defined halfway house between conventional farming and organic agriculture: conservation grade. The standards of the Guild of Conservation Food Producers are now operated by 400 British farms. This system of lower-input farming permits the use of some approved least-harmful chemicals and certain quantities of nitrogen fertilisers. The Guild has its own scheme of inspectors, labels its produce in supermarkets 'conservation grade' and commands a premium only slightly lower than organic produce. It is an honourable way of farming. However, what the Prince of Wales was looking for was a way of farming which would be seen publicly to be wholly distinct from conventional practice.

Instinctively, the Prince was keen on the organic option but he deferred to those who would have to put it into effect. His advisers were cautious because, unlike the garden which is strictly for pleasure, the farm at Highgrove is a business. It forms one part of the Duchy of Cornwall which is required by the spirit of the legislation which governs it to operate in a responsible commercial manner and thereby to produce an income for not only the current Prince of Wales, but all future Princes of Wales. Contrary to popular belief, the Prince of Wales receives nothing at all from the Civil List and, after making a voluntary contribution of 25 per cent of the Duchy's net income to the Treasury, has to pay for all the costs of the public and private lives of himself, the Princess of Wales and the two princes. The Prince cannot use the capital of the Duchy and therefore must, like all landowners and farmers, keep his eye on the bottom line of all his operations, including the farming at Highgrove.

Recollections vary slightly as to what happened next. Prince Charles recalls that he persuaded the advisers to begin an experimental organic area on part of the farm at Westonbirt. The rest of the farm would be farmed conventionally with some conservation headlands. Terry Summers and David Wilson recall that it was they who found themselves recommending a more radical route. Far better, they said, to farm flat-out conventionally or flat-out organically. Each way held a chance of making a profit. A halfway house, at that time, did not.

'It was really the people doing the farming who got into the organic side,' says Terry Summers. 'What the boss seemed to want was expressed in the term "environmentally-sensitive farming". This meant not throwing nitrogen about and generally reducing the use of chemicals. We could see that premiums on organic produce were going to be up to 100 per cent. That was better than producing less without making any money. Organic simply meant, as far as I was concerned, going back to farming as it was when I started in 1947. That was all right except that I could not remember what we did!'

In fact, as those already farming organically well knew, the ground rules of farming, the crop varieties, the manning levels and the machinery of farming had changed out of all recognition since the 1940s. Going organic would mean learning a new, dynamic and evolving way of farming. Terry wanted to advise the Prince to take up a system of farming that would be the best-quality alternative available. Organic had the advantages of being established, with an advisory service run by Elm Farm Research Centre in case one got into trouble. There was also the likelihood of high premiums on the food they sold after enduring a drop in profits during the conversion period.

It looks very much as if Prince Charles, who had already visited organic farmers and expressed interest in their methods, wanted to persuade his advisers to make their decision willingly, based on what they believed would work at Highgrove. Terry Summers's version does nothing to contradict this thesis: 'On one occasion, when we were discussing organic farming very early on, he just sat there and looked at us and said: "How long would it take you to stop organic farming?" There was a pause for thought and we said "One day." You could get your sprayer out and your fertiliser spreader and off you would go back to what you were doing before. I found that an example of his down-to-earth attitude which I find all the time.' Summers, who has been involved in every decision at the Home Farm over thirteen years, finds it no contradiction to describe himself as a 'non-royalist' of long standing. He says it is a pleasure to have worked with a client he respects enormously as a man.

Summers describes how it was agreed, with some caution, to begin organic farming on a trial area of the farm where they could make any mistakes out of public view. 'We thought we would start with a block of land of eighty-five acres at Westonbirt which is quite separate from the rest. It was well off the main road and we could start messing about with it without other people knowing what was going on – rather a good idea I would have thought.'

THE CHEMICAL LEGACY

One of the penalties of an ecological education
is that one lives in a world of wounds.

Aldo Leopold, as recalled by Jonathan Kingdon, in *Island Africa*.

T O THE LAYMAN, the number of sprays and fertilisers used on a conventional farm comes as a surprise. Few people, even today, are aware of the sheer volume of chemicals used in the fields unless they have direct experience of working on the land. The parts of Highgrove that are still farmed conventionally are no different. David Wilson, the farm manager, now finds all chemicals slightly disturbing. He says his instinctive rule of thumb is that one does not provide a benefit by chemical means without an equal and opposite disadvantage appearing somewhere else in the food chain. Economics, however, dictate that the Duchy Home Farm must be farmed partly conventionally, partly organically during its ten-year conversion to organic and so Wilson finds himself in the position of running both regimes side by side.

We compiled together a list of the pesticides likely to be used by any arable farmer in the course of the year on one field of wheat. Starting in the autumn, the conventional farmer will spray with a broad-spectrum weedkiller such as Javelin to kill emerging weeds such as grasses, chickweed, pansy, speedwell and red deadnettle. (Pesticides tend to have macho names like Missile, Rapier, Impact and Commando. Chemical companies find that they give the farmer confidence in the product.) Next the crop will receive a dose of Avadex which keeps it free of wild oats into winter. Then, in rapid succession, come methiocarb pellets (brand name Draza) to kill slugs and the first spray of insecticide, say Ripcord, to kill aphids.

In spring the farmer assesses the crop: if it is full of weeds he might spray with MCPA, one of the hormone weedkillers. In March, he would give the crop a dressing of fungicide, either Early Impact, Radar or Punch, which can radically

A young tawny owl at Duchy Home Farm. Owls, like many other birds of prey, have only recently been recovering from the effects of the first generation of synthetic pesticides, like DDT, which were concentrated in their flesh each time they ate contaminated prey.

125

improve yield. March, too, would be time for spraying with Chlormequat, a growth regulator designed to stop the wheat straw growing long and weak as a result of all the bag-nitrogen that he uses. A few weeks later he would return with a fungicide designed to kill fungus in the flag-leaf which holds the grain – this could be Tilt or Corbel, or a cocktail of the two. In May, if he still finds his crop infested with cleavers, he would spray with Starane, a highly-effective herbicide. If he still has a problem with wild oats, he may use Commando, a herbicide designed for late control of wild oats in a standing crop. If he has a problem with aphids, he will again spray with an insecticide. Many more farmers are now aware of the effect of insecticides on users and wildlife so instead of using a largely indiscriminate organophosphate compound like dimethoate, he may use a synthetic pyrethroid, an artificial version of the insecticide found naturally in chrysanthemums. This is less likely to kill ladybirds and some other natural insect predators – but it is more lethal to other insects, spiders and fish. Ripcord is one of these. Lastly our farmer will use a fungicide against mould in the ear of the wheat.

It is some list. In 1990, the average wheat crop was sprayed 4.4 times with over 9 active ingredients, according to the Ministry's figures. If the volume of chemicals needed to produce a field of wheat sounds a lot, consider then that a crop of oil-seed rape requires heavier applications of both pesticides and fertiliser. The farmer has to balance the cost of the chemicals against the potential reductions in yield if he does not catch a fungal or insect infestation in time. It is likely that as wheat prices fall farmers will try to keep their costs down by spraying as little as possible. And the new EC system of payments based on acreages rather than yield will mean that farmers are more careful about whether pesticides and nitrates are cost-effective – and therefore use less of both compared with what they might have used in the early 1980s. But as long as the farmer sticks to the 'conventional' system, the bill for treated seed, sprays and fertilisers is not likely to drop much below £80 an acre.

The extraordinary truth is that one billion gallons of pesticides are used in Britain each year. Around 3,000 brand-named pesticides are sold for use on farms, containing about 400 known ingredients. The billion-dollar question is, what harm do they do?

The older generation of farmer answers that question by saying that chemical farming has done miraculously little harm to humans but has provided a social good: quantities of food in the supermarkets at affordable prices. In the 1930s, crop yields in India, Britain and the United States were broadly the same. The breakthrough came when, to beat the U-boat blockade of food imports, artificial fertilisers began to be poured on the land. At the same time the insecticide DDT was developed in vast quantities to help armies marching in jungles infested with malaria mosquitoes. The Second World War produced the first organophosphate compounds, as a result of research into nerve gases. It also gave rise to selective herbicides. Partly thanks to pesticides and fertilisers, partly to advances in plant-breeding and partly to simple intensification of pressure on the countryside, Britain has moved from being a producer of less than 40 per cent of its food needs before the Second World War to 60 per cent of all UK food requirements in 1990. In 1946, it was normal for a farmer on the best land to grow a ton of wheat to the acre. Now he may produce over four. Another by-product of the new chemical-based system is that most young farmers know no other way of farming.

Yet most people today look at pesticides with less utilitarian eyes. For one thing, there now exists more worrying data on the toxicology of some of the hundreds of substances in general use, both the effects on humans and on flora and fauna. For another, the use of toxic substances in the environment becomes less defensible at a time when most staple foods are in surplus.

As to the effects on human health, the direct effects of pesticides on users and farm workers are the easiest to quantify. A UN committee estimated in 1983 that globally two million people were poisoned by pesticides each year, 40,000 of them fatally. The effects of involuntary exposure to small quantities of pesticide are harder to ascertain. Some pesticides have been linked to cancers, leukaemia in children and birth defects. A few have been banned. Considerable public attention in the United States has been devoted to the US servicemen exposed to Agent Orange (2,4,5-T contaminated with dioxin) used as an defoliant on the jungles of Vietnam. The 1,000 servicemen involved, known as the Ranch Hands, have been studied by the US Air Force for possible effects on their offspring. The study has found a higher number of miscarriages, a higher number of birth defects and a larger number of neonatal deaths in the period following exposure.

The two pathways by which most members of the public come into contact with pesticides is as residues on food and dissolved in drinking water. The Government maintains that current health standards are now sufficiently rigorous for there to be no risk to the general public from pesticide residues in food. Pesticides in drinking water are generally present in much smaller quantities. All pesticides have to pass Government testing procedures which require an elaborate series of experiments to be carried out on laboratory animals to find the dose at which there is 'no observable effect'. This figure is then divided by the arbitrary figure of 100 to give the acceptable daily intake for human consumption.

The British Medical Association examined the effects of thousands of pesticides used in the environment – whether dissolved in drinking water or found as residues on food such as bran and potatoes – in its 1990 report, 'Pesticides, Chemicals and Health'. It pointed out the incompleteness of existing knowledge of the effects of pesticides on human health and the lack of a national strategy for minimising their use. The report concludes: 'The BMA endorses the principle that until we have a more complete understanding of pesticide toxicity, the benefit of the doubt should be given to protecting the environment, the worker and the consumer.' Suffice it to say, this principle has yet to be incorporated into European agricultural policy.

Where there is ample evidence that pesticides cause harm is in the wider ecosystem. Pesticides, after all, are designed to kill. A general rule about pesticides, from the sulphur fumes which Homer knew as an insecticide 3,000 years ago to the latest synthetic pyrethroid, is that most of them kill more than the pests at which they are targeted. Modern testing procedures still fail to consider many of these ecological effects.

After harvest: an overgrown headland by a stone wall on Broadfield Farm. The hedge is a rich larder for birds, full of sloes and thistle seedheads. Bramble and columbine climb over everything.

As a simple case history, it is worth returning to the example of a Highgrove cereal field. For 10,000 years, unsprayed cereal fields have provided an alternative habitat for wildlife which would originally have lived in natural dry grassland or steppe. Much of this grassland would have existed within or around the natural forest cover. These dry grasslands were rich in plant, butterfly and other insect species but were the first habitats which came under severe pressure from agriculture from the earliest times. In the European Community less than 5 per cent of dry grassland remains.

Over the 10,000 years that man has been growing the modified grasses we call cereals, a community of wildlife species has evolved which is peculiar to cereal fields. Indeed, some birds such as the grey partridge, stone curlew, great and little bustard and demoiselle crane actually prefer unsprayed cereals to natural grasslands, as do quail, larks and buntings.

In an address he delivered to the British Association for the Advancement of Science in 1992, Dr Dick Potts, Director General of the Game Conservancy, the independent research foundation, painted a startling picture of the damage that modern intensive farming has done to the healthy semi-natural habitat that cereal fields provided until the advent of chemical sprays.

The full richness of the non-sprayed cereal faunas may never be known but, using methods perhaps more appropriate to archaeology than ecology, I have calculated that the cereal ecosystem prior to the use of herbicides in the UK contained 250 species of plants, 1800 species of insects and 180 species of spiders. The comparable numbers in Europe as a whole would in each case be more than twice as high. . .

The overall effects of pesticides on the cereal ecosystem are difficult to assess but they must have been immense. There are records of partridges being killed by wheat seed dressings in 1804, with other cases in 1844 and of course in the 1950s and 1960s. Most of the effect occurred before 1968, when the Game Conservancy began its monitoring of the cereal crop flora and fauna, so we will never know the full picture. Meanwhile it is astonishing that probably the best indicator of the ecological impact of herbicides on wildlife is the calculation that it reduced the food supply for partridge chicks to about half the pre-herbicide level.

The casualties of the herbicides that began to be used in the 1960s and 1970s were the arable weeds which nurtured the insects that birds like the partridge depend on in their first months of life. (Dr Potts points out that there was another dramatic, but unremarked ecological change at this time: the decline of undersowing cereals with clover or grass, a technique still practised by organic farmers as a way of establishing the next crop in the rotation. The increase in straw burning may also have wiped out millions of insects that birds depended on for food.)

ABOVE: *A grey partridge at Highgrove: fewer agrochemicals mean more insects for birds to eat.*

LEFT: *A badger drinking: the Home Farm has a healthy badger population.*

A dead sparrowhawk: in the 1960s when organo-chlorine pesticides were in use, sparrowhawks virtually died out of the south-eastern counties of England. Usually, DDT and other organo-chlorines caused infertility, but accumulated doses from the birds' prey were sometimes high enough to kill adult birds.

Fungicides were introduced in the mid-1970s. An unintended effect of these was to kill off vast numbers of the predators of cereal aphids. The next, highly-damaging, development came in the early 1980s, with the use of aphicides on winter wheat. The Game Conservancy has shown that the effects of organophosphate insecticides on the food supply of farmland birds, the most important being the sawfly larvae, has been catastrophic. All but the most selective, and expensive, insecticides kill these insects and a single application may reduce sawfly numbers for up to six years.

The decline in the insect population of cereal fields has been reflected in the steep decline of birds formerly common on farmland such as the skylark, the corn bunting and of course the grey or English partridge. The lapwing is also on the decline, though this may be more to do with herbicides and the increase in continuous cropping, according to Dr Potts.

The most frequently cited examples of pesticides damaging wildlife are the reductions in numbers of birds of prey such as the peregrine falcon, sparrowhawk and owls during the 1960s. The cause was the use of persistent organo-chlorine pesticides such as dieldrin and DDT which accumulated in the small mammals and birds which made up their food. Foxes and badgers also died slow, painful deaths through the build-up of organo-chlorines in their food. Today many of the organo-chlorines, like DDT, have been banned. The modern generation of pesticides break down much more readily in contact with the soil or the air. But, as Dr Potts's research shows, the ecological effects of continuing use of pesticides and herbicides are probably as great as ever and, certainly, are far from ecologically sustainable.

It would be wrong to suggest that the spiral of farm intensification applied only to cereal farmers. Livestock farmers are even bigger scatterers of artificial fertilisers. According to David Wilson's rule of thumb the arable farmer will use 150 units of nitrogen per acre in a year for barley, 175 units for wheat and 190 units for oil-seed rape. The dairy farmer, however, will use as much as 300 units of nitrogen on an acre of grassland in the course of a year to obtain two, even three cuts of silage to feed to his animals. Given the high price of bought-in concentrated feed, the amount of forage a farmer can produce on the farm is a critical factor in a dairy farmer's profits.

Inevitably, whoever is spreading it, a proportion of this nitrogen will be washed off by the rain into rivers and aquifers and will eventually trickle down into drinking-water supplies. Drinking water in the arable East of England, the Midlands and part of the South of England now has to be treated, at great expense, to remove nitrates which in high doses are supposed to be the cause of blue baby syndrome.

Until recently, the only pesticides livestock farmers used were to kill parasites on cattle and sheep. That was until the manufacturers of fungicides began targeting their advertising at the dairy farmer. Ciba-Geigy now advertise their fungicide Tilt, used hitherto on arable crops, as a remedy for the mildew to which fertilised grassland is prone. They claim that Tilt improves silage yields by up to two tonnes to the

Spraying grassland with fungicide to improve silage yields.

acre. What only an organic farmer would point out is that mildew attacks are exacerbated by using quantities of nitrogen fertiliser on a modern grass ley comprising only one or two species. A cycle of dependency frequently builds up in intensive agriculture, where the use of one chemical makes necessary the use of another. The farmer is caught on what environmentalists call 'the chemical treadmill'.

It is not only pesticides and nitrates, of course, which cause anxieties about livestock farming. It is absurd that we talk about millions of acres of land coming out of production while, at the same time, factory-farming methods are actually preventing the use of many acres of the land and causing cruelty in the process. In intensive pig-rearing, for instance, sows have been confined throughout their fourteen-week pregnancy in stalls in which they are unable to turn around and have no contact with other pigs. No wonder that pigs, which are highly intelligent animals, develop mindless repetitive 'tics' in factory farms which Cambridge University has identified as the symptoms of delinquency.

There are dangers in treating animals simply as converters of protein. The great scare over Bovine Spongiform Encephalopathy (BSE) or 'Mad Cow Disease' came about because someone had the idea of feeding animal protein to cattle. Cattle are wonderfully adapted converters of grass but do not have the elaborate system of intestinal blocks that carnivores have to prevent them absorbing toxins or malign bacteria from meat. Feeding animal offal to cattle sounded like an efficient use of waste protein. In fact it broke one of nature's fundamental laws. Cattle fed proteins infected with the sheep disease 'scrapie' developed BSE, an entirely new disease, unknown until 1985. At its peak, 600 cases a month have been detected. More than 55,000 animals have so far been destroyed. The great question still remaining is whether BSE can jump the species barrier to humans. So far it has been found to have been transmitted to a cat, an antelope and a monkey. We may not have heard the last of it yet.

The arrival of bio-technology has brought a whole new generation of possibilities for accidental pollution and disease – and pest control – stretching far beyond the pesticide era. An example of one of the more beneficial of the multifold products that genetic engineering might offer is the insecticidal cotton plant, which does not need to be sprayed – an example of how genetic engineering might, conceivably, benefit the countryside if tightly controlled. A counter-example, however, is a frightening idea perfected by the same company: the sugar beet which has been genetically 'improved' to have a high tolerance to herbicides. The farmer simply sprays his field with an indiscriminate herbicide such as glyphosate, which the manipulated plant has been designed to resist, and everything else dies. Ecologically speaking, the prospect is disturbing to say the least.

It would be comforting to think that tough regulation will eventually embrace all forms of pesticide and genetically-engineered organism. What the British Medical Association would like to see is a national strategy for reducing the use of existing pesticides, on the lines of the national plans that already exist in the Netherlands, West Germany and Scandinavia. 'It is desirable,' said the BMA, 'that we should continue to decrease the use of conventional pesticides where alternatives are available.' One alternative is known as Integrated Pest Management, a system of using rotations and varying cultivation times to keep fields free of weeds and natural predators sheltered in 'beetle banks' – unsprayed grass hedges – to reduce the need for the application of chemicals.

Farmers have to live with the system of incentives that politicians give them to work with. While the 'conventional' farmer still avoids paying the price for the pollution he causes, it is hard to see how the present system of chemical farming will change. At present the farmer is able to pass on to someone else the cost of cleaning up most of the pollution he causes. The atmosphere – and future generations – pay for the farmers' enthusiastic use of fossil fuels, whether as chemicals, fertilisers or diesel. The taxpayer pays the National Rivers Authority to police rivers soaked with slurry. The water customer pays for cleaning up the contamination of drinking water by pesticides and nitrates. Yet many conventional farmers still will not face the uncomfortable facts about a system in which they have been brought up – and, some would say, brainwashed.

There are some signs that the chemical farmer is not going to get away with it for ever. The spiralling cost of water bills has provoked influential people to talk of taxes or pollution charges for nitrates and pesticides. Not before time, many would say. While industry is expected to pay higher and higher pollution charges, can farmers continue to get off so lightly for the damage they cause by spraying or scattering chemicals on the land? Until the chemical farmer faces real disincentives to pollute, organic farmers, who pollute dramatically less, will be forever struggling to catch up.

THE ORGANIC TRADITION

I remain astonished at just how many other farmers still look at organic farming
as some kind of drop-out option for superannuated hippies....To me, organic
farming combines the traditional wisdom of sound rotational farming practice
with much of the best that modern technology can provide. There are, I believe,
greater advantages in improved soil management, maintaining a diversified flora
and fauna, reduced pollution and increased energy self-reliance than many
commentators have so far been prepared to acknowledge.

Lecture to the Royal Agricultural Society of England,
H.R.H. The Prince of Wales, March 1991.

T HE DUCHY HOME FARM at Highgrove, like most farms in the middle of
England, is a mixed farm, divided into grass for livestock and arable crops.
The Cotswolds farmer, with his dry but not very fertile soils, has traditionally spread his risks by growing some arable crops and keeping an area of his farm
in grass. Arable crops would do better one year, beef or sheep another, dairying
the next. The East of England with its lower rainfall and better soils will always
grow the big tonnages of wheat. It is now rare to see a mixed farm on the arable
'prairies' of Norfolk, and Cambridgeshire. In the western counties of England,
Wales and Scotland, the rainfall is higher and the lush grass means that farmers
have traditionally been able to produce higher milk yields. These farms are often
specialist dairy farms which grow no crops other than grass.

An organically-run farm is necessarily based on a traditional mix of enterprises.
The simplest, most widely-known definition of organic farming is farming without the use of pesticides or synthetic fertilisers; but this definition overlooks the
importance to organic farming of using farmyard manure and break crops to
maintain the fertility of the soil. Livestock are vital to the organic system: this
often comes as a surprise to those who imagine that organic farmers inhabit the
same cultural niche as vegetarians. Yet organic farmers shun the overcrowded,
drug-dependent methods of livestock farming which account for many people's
concern about the meat they eat. ('Stockless' systems, using green fallows, which
might enable the East of the country's arable farmers to make the transition to

*Headland on a field of organic
wheat at Westonbirt: blackberries,
poppies, wildlife habitat and a
crop which is worth 80 per cent
more per ton than conventional
wheat.*

135

organic more readily, are being worked on by the Elm Farm Research Centre, but these need more time and money to develop.)

Crop rotations are integral to the organic system of farming. In the absence of bought-in fertilisers, the soil's fertility has to be maintained by growing fertility-building plants before nutrient-hungry arable crops. The key to this system is the legume family of plants such as clover and lucerne which have the ability to fix nitrogen from the atmosphere and turn it into available nitrate which is stored in the roots. A field will, typically, be sown with a mixture of clover and grass for three years before arable crops such as wheat, barley or oats are sown. The clover not only provides a good crop of forage for the livestock but when it is ploughed in, the nitrates are released into the soil ready for use by the next crop. The organic farmer's aim is to grow healthy plants by creating a healthy soil, full of microbes and earthworms. He tries to discourage pests by providing natural habitats such as hedges as homes for birds and insect predators. The essence of the organic system is expressed in the phrase 'work with natural systems rather than seeking to dominate them'.

There remains much confusion about the term 'organic', particularly among consumers browsing the supermarket shelves. 'Organic', when applied to farming or farm produce, is not simply a general term meaning produced without pesticides, as many believe. It is a system of producing food with a strict legal definition. The rules of organic farming were largely devised by the founding body of organic farming, the Soil Association, and since 1989 have been enshrined in the Government's United Kingdom Register of Organic Food Standards (UKROFS). To fly the Soil Association's Kite mark, a farmer must use animal and green manures, shun synthetic pesticides and fertilisers, eschew factory farming and straw burning and promise not to destroy recognised conservation features such as permanent pasture. (The one controversial difference between the Soil Association and UKROFS standards is that specific environmental criteria are not included in UKROFS standards, an omission which has provoked criticism from other environmentalists.) Under an incoming EC regulation organic food is now required to be grown in the same way throughout the European Community.

A small number of plant-based natural insecticides *are* permitted under Soil Association rules, including pyrethrum, based on chrysanthemums, and derris which contains rotenone, a potent insecticide. These are non-persistent in the environment and have low toxicity to mammals but their use is discouraged except in extreme circumstances since they destroy the natural pest-control system that organic farmers try to build. Bought-in animal feeds and concentrates are also discouraged, for the virtue of organic is that it is a 'closed' system supposed to return all the goodness to the soil and receive a harvest in return. But, for practical reasons (such as the high price of feeding organic cereals to livestock), organic farmers are allowed to buy in a ration containing a small percentage of non-organic grains. No farming system which exports crops or livestock from the land can be 100 per cent a 'closed' cycle, so organic farmers are allowed to use some fertilisers to replace some of the nutrients that are taken out of the soil. Seaweed and rock phosphate are permitted because they are retained in the soil and do not leach into water supplies. More controversially, the Soil Association discourages the use of conventional drugs such as antibiotics in livestock. It insists on long withdrawal periods before animals can be slaughtered for meat or their milk used if antibiotics have been administered. This rule encourages the use of homeopathic remedies, with which many organic farmers, including the Prince of Wales, treat ailments in livestock.

A feature of the organic tradition and the whole-food market to which it is related has been to choose traditional breeds and unusual varieties. The Prince of Wales has chosen Ayrshires for his dairy herd, instead of the ubiquitous Friesians which are slightly heavier milk producers. He says that he likes his farm to look like a Gainsborough, rather than a Dutch landscape. Aesthetics apart, he is following in the footsteps of a number of organic farmers who claim that Ayrshires are unusually well adapted to producing high milk yields from a diet high in forage – that is, grass, hay and silage – instead of concentrated 'high-protein' feeds.

The Ayrshire dairy herd in summer: a brief six weeks of peace before the business of calving and milking starts again.

Harvesting organic thatching straw – with an old binder – one of the few tasks on an organic farm for which efficient modern machinery does not exist. The thatch lasts twice as long as straw grown with nitrogen fertiliser and can be extremely profitable, if also very labour-intensive.

Modern organic farmers do use sophisticated machinery, as big and as energy-intensive as that used by conventional farmers if they can afford it. Specialist harrows, and muck-spreaders which spread this valuable resource as thinly as Marmite, usually turn out to have been designed and built in Austria, Switzerland or Germany. (Finding comparable machinery designed and made in Britain has proved both difficult and expensive for the Prince of Wales.) The use of fossil fuels to pull this elaborate machinery around is the one not-very-sustainable part of the organic system. Few organic farmers speak of returning to draft horses or oxen; but they can justifiably claim that they use up to 60 per cent less fossil fuel than conventional chemical farmers per unit of food they produce, if you take into account the manufacture and transportation of pesticides and fertilisers which depend on petrochemicals and coal-fired power stations.

Organic farming has changed dramatically since the organic movement was born in the 1930s and 1940s amid the first stirrings of concern over the effects of modern agriculture. Then the prime cause of anxiety was what bad farming practice was doing to the soil. The dangers of soil erosion were all too clear following the dust bowls of the United States in the 1930s. This environmental disaster, which became the social disaster of the Okie Trail, is captured vividly by John Steinbeck in his novel *The Grapes of Wrath* and in the photographs of Dorothea Lange. In 1943, one of the darkest and hungriest years of the war, and with – ironically – the desperately necessary intensification of farming going on all around her, Lady Eve Balfour published *The Living Soil*, a manifesto of her concerns about modern agriculture.

The ideas she set out in the preface to the first edition of *The Living Soil* constitute an agenda for health and the environment which still underlies a wide range of environmental concerns. 'My subject is food,' she wrote, 'which concerns everyone; it is health, which concerns everyone; it is the soil which concerns everyone – even if they do not realise it – and it is the history of certain recent scientific research linking these three vital subjects.'

The book struck such a chord with the public that it led in 1946 to the foundation of the Soil Association. The declared purpose of the Association was to investigate the relationship between soil, plant, animal and man. This infinitely difficult mission strikes less of a chord today than the remarkable fact that the pioneers of the organic movement accurately foresaw the negative aspects of a technological system of farming at its outset. Many environmental ideas are a lot older than we think. The idea of the earth as a self-regulating system made up from all living things, dubbed in the early 1970s the Gaia hypothesis by the scientist James Lovelock, is a close cousin of the ideas under discussion in the late 1940s by Soil Association pioneers.

One of the ponds on the farm restored on the advice of the Gloucestershire Farming and Wildlife Advisory Group.

The Soil Association was, in its way, a forerunner of environmental groups such as Friends of the Earth and Greenpeace. But its brief was wider, some would say impossibly wide. In its early days the Soil Association was the focus of concern about continuous-cropping practices, inorganic fertilisers, synthetic pesticides, the rights and wrongs of veterinary medicine and medicated animal feeds, about the loss of the traditional countryside and, by the 1960s, about the long-term wisdom of using up the earth's fossil fuels.

In what is known as the Haughley Experiment, a 25-year research project on a Suffolk farm, Lady Eve Balfour attempted to prove that organically-produced food was inherently more wholesome than that produced by other means. The results were inconclusive and the massive research project proved more than the finances of a small charity could withstand. Many believe that she would have been more successful scientifically and politically if she had asked simpler questions, such as whether organic farming methods were better for the wildlife of the farmed countryside, something that only fragmentary research exists on to this day.

Most of the problems the Soil Association highlighted in 1946 have now got dramatically worse. Soil erosion has become a growing threat to human survival in large parts of the world. In the tropics, bad farming practices and the removal of forest cover lead quickly to the sight of bright-red soils being washed down rivers and out to sea. Estimates by the World Resources Institute in 1992 showed that more than 10 per cent of the earth's vegetation-bearing soil, an area larger than India and China combined, has suffered moderate to extreme degradation since the Second World War. The land on which a doubling world population will have to grow its food in the next century has just blown or washed away.

Soil erosion is a less dramatic affair in temperate climates but it remains a very real phenomenon even in Britain. Most people who have lived in the arable prairies of East Anglia remember brown soil-storms. I have also seen wind-blown soil in drifts two feet deep against stone walls in the Borders after fierce winds in autumn. Studies by the Soil Association have shown that rates of soil-loss in Britain greatly exceed the rate of soil renewal from the ploughing-in of organic material. There may be a change of some sort now straw burning is to be banned and more straw will be ploughed in.

It is interesting to reflect that many if not all of the concerns addressed by the Soil Association in earlier decades have become mainstream today. The Association decided in 1974, for example, to ban the feeding of animal proteins to cattle, which turned out in the 1980s to cause 'Mad Cow Disease'. It raised concern about the implications for the food chain of mercury-based seed dressings when they were introduced in the 1960s. Mercurial seed dressings were banned by the Ministry of Agriculture in 1992. The Soil Association raised questions, too, about the organophosphate dips used to treat sheep for 'scab'. These substances, developed originally as nerve agents, have been blamed increasingly for health problems in farm workers. The Ministry has just decided that these dips should no longer be compulsory.

Many of the questions raised by the organic movement's founders are still unanswered by science. Is there an interrelationship between a healthy soil and

LEFT: *Testing soil for worms and insects: part of a comparison of conventional and organic farming systems and their benefits for wildlife being undertaken by the British Trust for Ornithology and Rothamsted laboratories. This was one of the conventionally-grown crops.*

healthy food? How big are the gains for wildlife from an organic system? How important are the hundreds of different soil microbes and invertebrates and does it really matter if we kill some of them off? Ten tons of soil microbes, after all, are estimated to exist in every acre of healthy soil (more than the livestock walking about on top of it!) Little research seems to have been conducted into understanding the micro-ecology of the soil. It has been a continuing source of complaint in the organic movement that, until recently, no government money was spent on research into organic or environmentally-friendly farming methods while hundreds of millions of pounds were spent each year developing chemical systems.

Where the tiny band of purists in the Soil Association have been successful is in keeping the flame of organic farming burning through nearly fifty years of chemical farming – into an era where the long-term 'sustainability' of the life style of the West has become a mainstream concern. In the past decade the organic farming movement has been transformed by self-sacrifice and the dedication of some

OVERLEAF: *Harvesting organic crops on the Home Farm. In the distance, combining organic barley. In the foreground, a minor disaster: wheat-sheaves, cut and stooked by hand for thatching straw, have been blown over by a strong wind.*

141

extremely able people – Patrick Holden, Director of British Organic Farmers, the Soil Association's sister organisation, Richard Young, Development Director of the Soil Association and Lawrence Woodward, co-ordinator of Elm Farm Research Centre. They have battled to establish a set of standards in food production which take in strict environmental and welfare concerns. They have introduced inspections to make sure that these standards are enforced. They have successfully lobbied for a national standard and an EC standard for organic agriculture – a first step in securing the take-off in organic farming that they want to achieve. There are many more organic farmers than there were, but it is still a tiny proportion of the market. There were at the end of the 1980s around 1,000 organic farmers out of 250,000 farmers in Britain, a total of around 10,000 in Europe and small groups of organic farmers in nearly every country in the world.

Criticisms of the Soil Association are not difficult to frame. Despite the great upsurge of popular environmental interest in the 1980s, it has been less successful in capturing the public imagination through the media as other organisations have done. The Soil Association remains known only to a minority. Environmental millionaires are more likely to leave their money to Greenpeace, Friends of the Earth or even a cats' home. When it comes to public relations, the Soil Association has a lot to learn from the organic gardeners.

There are other serious criticisms. For instance, since its beginnings the organic movement has been prone to internecine arguments which are almost incomprehensible to the outsider. It remains riven by factions to this day, broadly between 'deep' greens and 'light' greens. It is absolute about standards to a degree that some people find irritating. Not everyone would go along with the Association's enthusiasm for homeopathic medicine (though these have now been removed from the standards as a requirement), which non-enthusiasts consider a cruel way to treat animals, or its opposition to vaccinating livestock.

Organic farmers consider themselves environmentalists, yet there has been bad blood here, too. The Soil Association has now made environmental standards mandatory: for example, they ban hedge-trimming between March and September to protect nesting birds, the ploughing of medieval ridge-and-furrow field-systems and say approval should be sought for ploughing up unimproved pasture 'said to be of conservation interest'. But organisations like the Royal Society for Nature Conservation say these standards still leave something to be desired. Environmental standards are not yet part of the legal standards set by the government quango, UKROFS, either. It would certainly help if they were. On the other hand organic farmers are the only ones to impose environmental standards on themselves at no cost to the taxpayer. And there is something baffling about the scepticism shown to organic farming by certain influential environmental organisations – for instance the Royal Society for the Protection of Birds and the National Trust – when all the empirical evidence is that organic farming is good for habitat creation, particularly for farmland birds. Could this opposition be something to do with influential conventional farmers among their members?

The organic movement is certainly far from perfect. It has preoccupied itself with defining a system of 'sustainable' farming, and has often failed to demonstrate to a wider public why that system might be part of the solution to many contemporary environmental problems. But the fact remains that the system of farming that organic farmers have successfully established, and doggedly pursue, is almost without doubt the most 'sustainable' kind of agriculture – in the sense that one could go on doing it indefinitely – whether in terms of the landscape, flora and fauna, the use of fossil fuels, and in terms of the reduced pollution it creates. Organic agriculture has evolved over thousands of years, while high-input chemical agriculture has been with us only for a matter of decades. Organic agriculture also produces the most risk-free food in terms of human health. That much is common sense.

TROUBLE WITH COUCH GRASS

'THERE IS NO DOUBT we started in 1986 in some fear and trepidation,' Terry Summers recalled in a recent letter to Prince Charles in which he reflected on the lessons to be learned from converting the Duchy Home Farm to an organic regime. The questions which troubled him then were the same as he is accustomed to hearing from visiting farmers now. How well would they be able to cope with weeds, insects and fungal attacks in the absence of chemicals? Would the premiums for organic crops be enough to compensate for lower yields?

What also worried Terry was the initial drop in soil fertility when inorganic fertilisers were stopped, which has been described by many farmers who have converted. The use of bag-nitrogen fertilisers bypasses the microbes and bacteria on which plants have depended for their nutrients over millions of years. The living part of the soil also tends to be suppressed by the use of artificial fertilisers. Most important to this soil ecology are the rhizobia bacteria (which live in nodules attached to the roots of legume crops and fix nitrogen from the air) and the mycorrhizae (fungal threads which intersect with roots and allow the plant to draw nutrients from the soil). On some conventionally-run farms, the soil suffers a dramatic loss in its natural fertility and time is required to build this up again by growing leguminous plants and spreading farmyard manure. This can take a few years on some farms. Some mixed farms which have spread manure on the land and practised crop rotations before they converted to organic, however, have been known to escape this 'fertility-drop' completely.

Working out their first rotations, Terry Summers and David Wilson took advice from the organic farming advisory service run by the Elm Farm Research Centre. They chose then to follow their own instincts, which they felt was probably the best way to learn. The seven-year rotation they devised for most of the fields at Westonbirt was red clover and grass for three years followed by winter wheat, spring oats and spring beans. In the seventh year, winter wheat, spring barley or oats would be undersown with clover to begin restoring the soil's fertility again.

A field seeded with a grass and red clover mixture: the fertility-building part of the rotation on an organic farm. Clover fixes nitrogen from the air, ruling out the need for synthetic nitrogen fertilisers.

147

For their first two years all went well on the block of eighty-five acres at Westonbirt; indeed, there were some notable discoveries. The unfertilised cereal crops, planted after grass, grew up astonishingly free of weeds. The annual weeds such as cleavers and chickweed, which grow as tall as the crop under multiple applications of bag-nitrogen, grew only a few inches high under a low-nitrogen regime. The weeds were present in some numbers but once a wheat crop was established, it grew up and smothered them. Summers and Wilson observed that without nitrogen plants proved remarkably resistant to disease. Seven years on, Terry Summers says that they have simply given up worrying about the problems of diseases and annual weeds in organic arable crops.

This is still something that conventional farmers find hard to believe when they come on visits to the farm. David Wilson has evolved a technique of taking the group into the middle of a field of organic wheat, explaining what variety it is and then asking for any questions. The first, almost inevitably, is: 'How do you deal with annual weeds?' David Wilson usually replies by inviting them to look around. From May or June onwards there are weeds present but you have to look hard to find them. They simply are not of a size to compete with the crop. Organic crops are clearly recognisable because they are thinner than their conventional equivalents. But David Wilson is convinced that many conventional farmers think that before they arrive he has quietly been round with a sprayer to kill the weeds.

Organic farmers carry out their main weed strike before the crop is sown. A seedbed is prepared, whether autumn or spring, then left for the weeds to germinate before the seed is drilled. The operation of drilling is usually enough to dislodge the weeds to the extent that they do not pose a problem. Unlike the 'conventional' system, which depends on using herbicides early on in the season to kill the weeds altogether, the weeds in an organic cereal field are still present but in quantities which do not affect the crop. This system demonstrably benefits the plants which have evolved over thousands of years to live in cereal fields. Many of these cereal weeds are now very rare. The unsprayed cereal fields also benefit the insects and hence the bird life of the farm.

Cereal yields on the new block at Westonbirt were lower, at just over half what might be expected for conventionally-grown wheat. But prices for organic cereals began to rise, as the 'green consumer' boom got under way after 1985. The premiums for organic wheat for bread-making and oats for muesli and breakfast cereals soon reached 80–100 per cent more than conventional crops. So low yields were compensated by a rising premium for organic goods.

There was only one disaster, and this overtook the first field to go organic. The Fourteen Acre Field taken over in 1985 had had no nitrogen fertiliser on it for a year, so it was a year ahead in its two-year conversion required by the Soil Association. For the first year of conversion it was just grazed by sheep. For the second it grew a respectable wheat crop, given the lack of fertilisers, which went for the higher than average price of £170 a ton to an organic farmer. This was classed as a crop 'in conversion'. The Soil Association permits farmers to mix some crops in conversion with their organic crops to feed livestock and this crop went for mixing in this way. With growing confidence they then planted their

David Wilson drilling barley at Broadfield.

first wholly organic crop of beans, a variety called Troy. Beans, like clover, are from the legume family, which means that they are able to fix nitrogen from the atmosphere and therefore work well as a booster-crop to top up the fertility of the soil. From the time it was sown, things started to go wrong with the field of beans. The rooks enjoyed the field more than usual when it was newly sown and cleared it completely. It was drilled again, but this had unforeseen effects. The beans grew beautifully at first although they had to be hoed a couple of times with a tractor-mounted hoe to tackle weeds. Then problems began: soon it became clear that the weeding was having no effect. The crop was becoming smothered with couch grass, the rough-stemmed perennial weed, which had been spread around further by the second drilling. Perennial weeds are the organic farmer's greatest dread since the Soil Association rules permit no herbicides and only cultivation may be used to tackle them. This is one of the rare occasions when organic farming can become energy-intensive.

The Prince and his advisers were faced with an expensive and difficult decision. Option one was to sacrifice the crop, fallow the field, and destroy the couch grass the only way permissible under the Soil Association's rules – by dragging it onto the surface with tines and leaving it to dry in the sun. This would preserve their organic status, which would otherwise take two years to win back, but it would entail an expensive loss of fourteen acres of crop that year. Option two (the panic option) was take out the sprayer and give the crop a dose of Roundup, or

Sainfoin: another nitrogen-fixing crop planted at Westonbirt.

glyphosate, a cheap and effective chemical herbicide which kills all weeds to their roots. It was still early enough in the year to plant another cash-crop, such as spring barley, and keep the Fourteen Acre Field in production that summer albeit with a non-organic crop. The Prince of Wales was consulted. He told them to fallow the field and retain their organic status.

Since then, each field that is badly afflicted with perennial weeds is given a dose of Roundup just before it goes into conversion, which buys a few years of clean ground. This, Terry claims, is allowable within the Soil Association's rules and gives a breathing space to the converting farmer in which he can learn how to avoid perennial weeds. The loss of that first bean crop demonstrates the potentially expensive and heartbreaking decisions which sometimes face the organic farmer in the course of conversion.

Organic farming, Terry points out, demands a standard of management and a degree of foresight that has become unnecessary on conventional farms. The timing of rotations has to be planned to *avoid* problems whereas the coventional farmer can wait to treat problems when they arise. Weed prevention is done by cultivating crops at a different time each year so that no one weed becomes dominant because its life cycle exactly fits, say, regular autumn planting of crops. Many traditional skills have been lost and have to be relearned.

After fallowing, the Fourteen Acre Field was sown with wheat in the following autumn and proceeded to produce a low-yielding but very valuable crop of wheat the next year. This was sold for the astonishing price of £275 a ton, compared with around £120 for conventional wheat, a premium of well over 100 per cent. This was in 1989, the first year that all the supermarket chains went into the marketplace and deliberately began buying up organic products. Given a crop of wheat at around 1.5 tons to the acre instead of the 3 grown using chemical methods this meant that the field was *more* profitable that year than with a conventional crop. It had also cost a whole crop of beans ploughed-in the year before. But there were also great savings: at least £60 an acre from the nitrogen, pesticides and seed dressings that did not need to be used.

The first years of organic farming at Duchy Home Farm brought other discoveries. One of these was that the high yields that modern farmers routinely expect were less connected to high nitrogen and pesticide use than might be thought. Where yields are concerned, organic farming has moved on since 1945. Manuals of farming written then said routinely that Cotswold land might expect to yield a ton of wheat to an acre. Yields of *conventionally-grown* wheat on the same land today now reach around 3 tons to the acre. One might expect organic yields to be the same as before the chemical era, but they are, in fact, routinely higher than in 1945, ranging from 1.5 tons to 2.25 tons to the acre today. The difference can be explained by newer varieties of wheat and by more efficient harvesting. A combine harvester does not drop as much of the crop as did the laborious procedure of cutting with a binder, stooking and threshing.

The favourite wheat variety at Highgrove, Maris Widgeon, is relatively modern, developed as it was in the 1960s. It has an exceptionally long straw which grows even longer with nitrogen, which means that conventional farmers have stopped using this variety. The long straw is a positive advantage on an organic farm where the crop needs to form a canopy to smother weeds. Straw is also a necessary commodity on organic farms as bedding for livestock – and it can also be harvested as thatching straw (see Thatching and Bread-Making). Maris Widgeon yields well, resists disease, and produces a wheat which is well suited to bread-making. It has been superseded many times over in conventional farming by newer higher-yielding varieties, but many of these do not tend to work so well in a low-input system. (Mercia, for instance, does yield more than Maris Widgeon and is used by many organic farmers, but it does not have the same disease resistance or grain quality.) Modern wheats are often short-strawed varieties which respond well to chemical fertilisers. What yields might have been achieved if the seed industry had ploughed their millions into researching disease-resistant varieties suited to organic methods as well as conventional ones can only be guessed.

Three years after the original discussions on starting the organic experiment began, the Duchy farming committee (chaired by the Prince of Wales and comprising David Landale, Secretary to the Duchy; Kevin Knott, his deputy; Tom Macaw, Duchy Land Steward for the Eastern District; Nick Mould, his deputy, Terry Summers, David Wilson, and John Pugsley, a tenant farmer on Exmoor) reviewed the progress made. Terry Summers reflected that it had made sense to start gradually and on a small scale allowing the rest of the farm's production

A close-up of a grass/clover ley.

to support the experiment. There was no doubting, however, that the experiment had been a success.

As a result, they decided to expand the acreage under organic cultivation. That year, 1988, the organic scheme was extended to two other 85-acre blocks, Troublehouse (behind the old pub of that name on the Cirencester road) and Beverston. Then, in spring 1990, with the acquisition of another block of 160 acres at Upton Grove, the decision was taken to turn the whole farm organic.

These two decisions, close on each other's heels and prompted by the acquisition of new blocks of land, meant a number of new headaches for Terry Summers and David Wilson. Each time the plan was speeded up and new land was taken in, this meant the complicated scheme of rotations had to be designed again. And from 1990, there was the further complication of the conversion of the dairy herd, which meant ensuring there was enough converted organic pasture to feed the cattle. Another complication was that organic livestock husbandry requires cattle to be given up to a third more space, both indoors (which can be expensive) and in terms of pasture. This can have very real health benefits since the animals are less prone to stress and its related disorders. It does mean longer hours burning the midnight oil designing the conversions.

If it had been most other farmers, Terry Summers says he would have advised a more gradual conversion for economic reasons. But full conversion, by the quickest route, was seven years away and the Prince of Wales felt he needed to get on with it. He was anxious to use what time he had to explore the benefits of organic for the wildlife of his estate and to test markets for organic produce. And a lot could happen, even in seven years, to distract him from this task. For him, the fast-track approach to conversion appeared to be the right one. The organic regime was set up, well staffed and working. Prince Charles was unwilling to listen to cautious advice any longer. In the end, he says, he took the decision that turning the whole farm over to organic was the right thing to do morally and was in the long-term interests of the soil, the flora and fauna and the landscape.

DAVID WILSON'S DIARY

TODAY ONLY A FIFTH of the British population lives in the countryside. Fewer of those who do are intimately connected with the cycles of the land than in previous centuries; with ploughing and sowing, the birth of lambs and calves, and the harvest of the seasons. So I asked David Wilson to write a diary which would explain exactly what happens when, and why. He has captured, as I could not hope to do, the chores, anxieties and satisfactions of the farming year. This traditionally begins at Michaelmas, 29 September, a time of ploughing and sowing, but now that the fashion in farming has moved heavily towards autumn-sown crops, the period of cultivation goes on from August until late in October.

SEPTEMBER

This is the cultivating season, when we are working flat out to prepare the fields for the planting of winter cereals – wheat, barley and oats. Every tractor is covered in clouds of dust for twelve to fifteen hours a day. We all start to feel irritable. The haggard faces tell their own story but unless it is pouring with rain there can be no let up. We have to take the attitude that it is going to rain for a week, starting tomorrow, even if we are in the middle of a drought.

Autumn drilling starts on 18 September moving through from winter barley to winter oats and finishing with winter wheat preferably by 10 October. Winter crops, if they survive the winter, generally produce heavier yields than those planted in spring. The idea is to choose varieties that will survive the hard weather. There is a penalty in yield for conventional crops drilled after the end of October; this is much less noticeable with organic crops as one is gambling with lower stakes.

ABOVE: *The Prince with David Wilson at Westonbirt. In the background, a more successfully stooked batch of sheaves for thatching.*

OPPOSITE: *December at Highgrove.*

155

A harrow-comb: the organic farmer's main weapon against weeds.

October

There is a great sense of relief once drilling has been completed and everybody celebrates by catching their first good cold of the autumn. They are all so tired that their immune systems are low.

The organic cereals are weeded with a harrow-comb as soon as the crop is strong enough to stand it. This is a machine with springy tines that is dragged between the rows of growing crops. Those weeds it does not completely uproot it disturbs enough to delay their growth and thus allow the wheat to grow ahead and smother them. Ewes are 'flushed' on good grass. This is the process by which ewes that have deliberately been kept on less good pasture will then be turned in to a field of lush grass and clover in the month before mating. This causes a higher number of eggs to be released for fertilisation – which in turn gives higher numbers of twins and triplets.

November

Rams are turned out with the ewes on 5 November which gives a birth date of 1 April. We hope the tups (rams) live up to their reputation for fertility. Each has forty ewes to cover in three weeks. The rams lose a lot of weight as they fight each other for ovulating females, just as they would in the wild, but they do have ten months to recover after their job is done. The beef cows have been in calf since they ran with the bull in midsummer. They are fed partly on straw over the winter to allow them to lose condition in preparation for calving in spring. This means they calve more easily because the calf is small and they have little internal fat to restrict space in the birth canal. Beef calves born last April are weaned now. In December they are brought in and fed on their winter diet of silage and hay.

The cow-yard at Broadfield in snow.

DECEMBER

From the start of harvest to Christmas, time flies. During November and December the staff take much-needed leave and we do all the jobs that were put off during harvest and drilling. The Aberdeen Angus bull is turned in with the dairy heifer replacements (about a quarter of a dairy herd is replaced each year) and artificial insemination (AI) begins in the dairy herd. Dairy herds traditionally calve in the autumn and milk through the winter and into the summer, though some herds now vary this timing to take advantage of the high prices now offered for milk produced in the late summer. Artificial insemination is used in dairy herds for two reasons: first, it is simply not always practicable to run a bull with a housed dairy herd in winter; second, AI means that one can afford the semen of a much more expensive bull than one can afford to keep on the farm. Dairy farmers, whose cows are their most important asset, are always trying to improve the genetic quality of their herd.

The period between Christmas and New Year is one of the few times when the staff can relax with families and friends. Over a ten-day period the farm is run with a skeleton staff on a shift system to cope with milking, feeding and bedding of livestock. At this time of year, stock work eats into the shortened winter day, amounting to three hours daily for four of the seven staff. The cows still have to be milked on Christmas Day and everyone comes in early on Christmas morning to get the jobs done. Christmas morning, for some reason, is usually the time that the water freezes up or some such complication decides to happen.

Mule ewe lambs at Highgrove: next year's breeding stock.

JANUARY

If the ground is frozen hard then the strawed yards are cleaned out and the farm-yard manure is tipped in windrows (long heaps on field edges) to compost and break down. It is turned twice over the next eight to ten months to allow it to heat, killing weed seeds and harmful pathogens and to help it break down faster. If the weather is wet, the tractors cannot get out onto the fields without churning them up. Then the men are kept busy by cleaning the grain-handling plant, servicing equipment or winter workshop-projects such as designing and making sheep-feeders or modifying existing pieces of machinery.

The dairy cows have almost finished calving by now and the August and September calvers (the first to finish calving) are well into lactation. The calves suckle their mothers for two days to ensure they receive colostrum which provides disease immunity. They are then moved to the calf house where they are fed with milk until they are weaned at eight weeks. Dairy cows are fed their richest diet at the beginning of their lactation which encourages them to produce their best possible yield of milk. After peaking at 100 to 120 days, their milk production slowly tails off for the next 180 to 200 days. During this time we can cut the concentrated feed and rely on the home-produced grass/clover silage. The aim of all dairy farmers is to produce as much as possible from home-grown forage as it is the lowest-cost feed. As organic milk producers it is even more important because we are restricted on the quantities and types of bought-in feed we can use.

Sheep are usually still outside in January – the last of the lambs from the previous year are grazing what is left of the sparse clover leys and still managing to get

fatter. They are checked every week by a shepherd's sensitive hand to see if they are fit for the butcher. Ewes are scanned with ultrasound to determine the number of lambs they are carrying. They are then brought into the lambing yards where they are split into groups according to how many lambs they are carrying and body condition. This enables us to target our food cost-effectively. Priority is given to ewes with triplets and those with 'singles' are allowed to rough it to a certain extent. Ewe lambs which will join the breeding flock in the following autumn stay outside and scavenge round the grassland. We give them a little hay if conditions are harsh.

In organic husbandry, we try to avoid having to use chemical drenches to treat parasites. Parasites don't usually survive a full season away from their animal hosts. So to ensure their future grazing is kept free of roundworm and tapeworm eggs we have to plan a careful rotation, always thinking a year ahead to avoid any overlap. The conventional sheep farmer is able to dose the stock with the appropriate wormer when an infestation occurs. Some conventional farmers, however, are finding that worms are becoming resistant to the chemicals used to control them. This can happen when they use one kind of chemical wormer too often instead of rotating the three main chemical types. This is a case where conventional farmers can learn a lesson or two from the organic system.

Snow is not the wonderful element that one adored as a child. On the farm it means keeping the lanes and drive unblocked for the milk tanker and our farm machinery. Other time-consuming tasks are the defrosting of water-troughs for hundreds of restless animals and clearing waxing diesel from tractor fuel-lines.

P.C. Tudor Davies setting up bird boxes in winter.

FEBRUARY

This month sees a noticeable lengthening of daylight which gives us an air of optimism. If it is dry and not too frozen, we will start on whatever fencing needs to be done. More of the farm will need fencing during conversion. Apart from some roadside hedges, we try not to cut the hedges every year. We usually start after the worst of the winter weather is over to leave the berries for the birds. The cutting is better finished before the birds start nesting and before the leaves break bud. If it is wet, the silage-making machinery is serviced – silaging is only ten to twelve weeks from the end of February and looms up quicker than we expect. The wood pigeons are especially hungry now and they pay great attention to our conventionally-grown oil-seed rape crops. They must be kept at bay with shotguns and automatic bangers. The end of February and early March is the ideal time for spreading our muck-heaps on the grassland. From an environmental angle it has advantages too, since the grass is beginning to grow and takes up the nitrates without their leaching away as they would do in winter. The farmyard manure that has been stockpiled and turned in long windrows for ten months or so is now a well-composted, friable and odourless material that quickly disappears into the soil when spread onto grass.

Instead of regarding manure-handling as an unpleasant job to be got out of the way, the organic farmer regards muck as a valuable resource which he has to spread thinly over a large area. The spreading of our farmyard manure (FYM) is a way of feeding the soil microbes as well as providing small amounts of nitrogen and some phosphate and potash. Our observations show that even a small amount of FYM has beneficial effects on the fertility-building clover leys which are the backbone of our rotational system.

Rooks' nests in Tidcomb's Gorse in early spring against a wintry sky.

MARCH

This is the month when serious action begins. We run the harrow-comb through the organic crops to control weeds. Spring crops are sown now and the newly-planted seed attracts hordes of hungry end-of-winter rooks. They love our seed which has none of the unpalatable chemical dressing which puts them off the seed of our conventional neighbours. They are very intelligent birds. Old farmers say that a rook can tell the difference between a stick and a gun.

This is the last time an organic farmer can hope to improve his arable crops. After March, whether they are doing well or not, he can close the gate until harvest. Grassland is now rolled and chain-harrowed, to pull out the dead grass which impedes growth, to level molehills, and spread out the cowpats. The roller pushes the stones under the surface in preparation for silage-cutting.

The ewes are close to lambing. A special effort is paid to those carrying twins or triplets. We look for signs of twin-lamb disease, a metabolic disorder that is fatal if not caught in the early stages. Also prolapsed vaginas can be a problem – the ewes are very full of lambs and if they eat too much hay then something gives. These are very easy to pop back in, you just need a good eye and a beechwood mallet!

Beef suckler-cows are three to four weeks from calving. They are turned out to grass in March, although there isn't very much growing. They always do two or three laps of honour with tails in the air like flagpoles – a sight we never tire of. Beef cattle are calved in April to make the best use of the new season's grass. The idea is to turn them out in lean condition – a natural state for most mammals coming out of the winter. As the grass grows, the cow produces more milk and the growing calf can take more and more. The system works along natural lines and makes life easy.

Prince William and Prince Harry learning about lambing from Fred Hartles.

APRIL

Ewes lamb in the first ten days of this month and Fred Hartles, the shepherd, is working long hours. Over this period someone has to be on duty in the lambing pens twenty-four hours a day. Again, lambing at this time is natural. After three days inside 'mothering up', the ewe and her offspring are turned out onto spring pasture. The days are now much longer and summer feels closer, although we have had both heavy snow and sunshine in the seventies in one lambing period. Suddenly the lambing pens are empty and all is quiet in the yards and the contrast between the deafening bleating of ewe to lamb and the silence is staggering. The dairy cows are turned out to pasture in the first settled period of weather after mid-April. They are housed at night until May when the weather improves and they are allowed to stay out all night long.

MAY

All animals are now at grass and the work they generate drops to a minimum which allows our attention to be given to other tasks. These include the final mucking-out of all stock and lambing areas, more spanner-work on silage equipment and finishing any fencing that we didn't get around to in the winter. Now the stock are hanging their heads through the gaps or even escaping we have no alternative but to fence them in. The lambs are growing very fast now. They gather in groups of thirty to forty and charge madly round the fields just like teenagers on motorbikes roaring up and down the High Street.

Silage-cutting for the conventional farmer starts from 8 to 18 May depending on the weather. On an organic farm, without artificial fertiliser, the grass takes longer to start so we wait until late May or early June. Once the organic leys start

Lambing in April: Ewes are liable to adopt anything warm and fluffy – whoever it may belong to – a couple of hours either side of lambing. Later they become more discriminating, often turning on the lambs they have adopted. Fred Hartles uses the portable wire cages to prevent mismothering.

growing there is little difference between them and conventional ones. The clover part of the sward makes the quality of the feed higher, and more digestible for livestock than the standard fertilised rye-grass mixture.

The theory of both silaging and haymaking is to preserve grass with a minimum loss of nutrients. Silage loses a quarter of the nutrients that hay loses and is less weather dependent, so is much more cost-effective for dairy farmers. Hay is still fed to sheep, horses and sick cows. The principles of silage-making are: **1** Cut; **2** Chop; **3** Cart; **4** Compress in a clamp. Grass is cut from late morning onwards when sugar levels are high. Sugars are vital to the preservation process. They are changed to acid by the lactobacilli – bacteria which occur on grassland and in the bowels of most animals – in an airless fermentation which stabilises at about pH 3.8, when the grass is, in other words, 'pickled'. Silage is really the bovine equivalent of mixed pickle.

Mown grass for silage is left for twenty-four hours to wilt which reduces the weight to be carted, concentrates the sugars, and, more importantly, reduces the amount of effluent that seeps from the finished clamp of silage. Silage effluent has a higher biological oxygen demand – the ability to strip all the oxygen out of water – than slurry and can wipe out fish and insect life in rivers. We installed a concrete silage clamp with new effluent controls in 1986 to stop this happening. After it has wilted, the grass is picked up by a forage harvester, chopped and blown into trailers to be taken back to the farm. At the clamp, the grass is tipped up in a great heap and then rolled to remove the air. This prevents the silage oxidising and an imperfect fermentation. Then the clamp is sealed with a black polythene sheet and decorated with spent car tyres to stop this blowing away.

Contract sheep-shearers from New Zealand working at Highgrove.

JUNE

With luck the weather is more settled now enabling us to shear the sheep and make hay. The shearing needs dry weather because the wool won't cut when it's damp, and cold wet weather can shock a newly-shorn ewe into drying up her milk when she has another month until her lambs are weaned. Beef bulls are turned in with the cows for spring calving.

Before haymaking it pays to wait for a settled spell of high pressure with the wind in the east and the needle in the glass straining to reach the 'e' on fine. Mowing hay when the wind is from the west always means the hay spoils. The nearer the hay is to being ready to bale, the less rain it needs to spoil it. Hay is the main forage source for our sheep and, of course, the Prince's horses for which only the best will do. The beef cattle are fed a mixture of hay and silage.

One reason why conventional farmers grow less hay these days is that it is very difficult to make hay with new varieties of grass that have been fed with a lot of nitrogen. It looks good when it is cut but goes mouldy in the barn. A lot of country people will go out of their way to buy organic hay for cattle or horses.

Haymaking has changed little over the centuries. The grass is mown and then turned each day to let the sun dry out the green. The biggest differences in the last forty years are that instead of carting it to a haystack, we bale it mechanically, depending on the machinery, into small bales, big round bales, or big rectangular bales. Clover/grass hay takes more making because of thicker stems and so we need a week for it to dry rather than four or five days.

Newly-mown hay.

To avoid the cloverleaf shattering when the hay is turned (the leaf being highly nutritious), we turn it early in the morning before the dew has gone and while the leaf is still flexible.

Like many operations in the farming year, haymaking is a gamble and when well done gives everyone satisfaction. It is always a pleasure in the depths of winter to open a bale of hay and smell the summer – one can almost hear the larks and the hissing of the east wind through the drying swathes of grass. To be caught out by the weather means mouldy, dusty hay that smells unpleasant and is bad for the health of man and beast alike. For this reason we never have too much hay on the ground at one time which means that haymaking can go on intermittently for six or eight weeks.

Staff members are trying to take a holiday before we are locked into harvest. Seven staff, each with four weeks' paid holiday, means twenty-eight weeks' holiday which must not be taken from mid-July to mid-October because of the harvest and the autumn drilling. This means that twenty-eight weeks have to be taken in the thirty-nine available weeks, so we are a man short for quite a time.

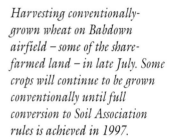

Harvesting conventionally-grown wheat on Babdown airfield – some of the share-farmed land – in late July. Some crops will continue to be grown conventionally until full conversion to Soil Association rules is achieved in 1997.

JULY

July is the month for topping thistles on grassland. Topping every year at this time is said to wear them down in the end. The old saying goes:

> Top'em in May and they're here to stay
> Top'em in June, still too soon
> Top'em in July and they're sure to die.

Docks, which root deeply and have to be dug out, are another problem. I have bought several 'dock spuds' for this and given one to the herdsman, Paul Chadwick, to take with him on his walks around the farm. It is much easier to dig out a few docks when you see them than to put someone out there for a month to get rid of them. It used to be a job they gave to 'the boy' when every farm had one. For the last two years we have been trying a new system of topping every two to three weeks through the summer which depletes the root reserves and seems to reduce the population of perennial weeds further.

Many dairy cows are now dried off and no longer milking, and so milking takes less than an hour. The dry period is an important period for cows, allowing them six weeks' holiday before they start the physically demanding business of calving and milk-producing all over again. It is also an easier time for Paul, allowing him to paint the dairy parlour and generally smarten things up. Beef suckler-calves are now growing very fast and spend more time grazing in small groups away from their dams.

Lambs are weaned and moved on to clean pasture. It is still as important as ever to keep the lambs grazing worm-free pasture to avoid chemical drenches. As the season progresses it becomes more difficult to maintain this system and it means that Fred

Hartles and other staff members put in much time moving electric fencing and transporting our 700 lambs to the cleanest field we have, which can often be on the other side of the estate. The ewes are put on to bare pasture where there is just enough to nibble at and keep them content while allowing their milk to dry up.

The harvest begins with the winter barley about 20 July, but this can vary by ten days either way depending on the season. In the last week before we start, final preparations are made: the drier is checked; the silage sides are taken off the trailers so they may carry grain; oil in the tractors is changed. It is a bit like the build-up to a big race.

Winter barley takes longer to ripen than one thinks and an old saying is 'When you think your barley is fit, take a week away.' This has to be weighed against the fear of having a heavy storm of rain which knocks the heads to the ground. Once the combine starts cutting there is noticeable relief in everybody. Now the staff know what needs to be done and it is a question of nose to the grindstone and team effort continuously for the next three months.

Once the combine, driven by John Underhill, moves out of a field, the baler, driven by Andrew Baker, moves in. Then the bale-carting team, usually Tim Longhurst and Paul Chadwick, can start. When the bales are cleared the ground can be cultivated or ploughed in preparation for the following crop. Stuart Jepps will do the cultivating, or John Underhill if he is not combining. Harvesting of our conventional oil-seed rape follows barley and then come spring oats, winter wheat and finally beans. If we grew linseed, that would be harvested last. The combine driver's dream crop is standing wheat – the combine always goes well. If it has 'lodged' or blown over, it can be more difficult.

Filling the grain store at Babdown airfield owned by Mrs Yvonne Randall.

AUGUST

Clover/grass mixtures are sown as soon as possible after the cereal crop is harvested so that they are strongly established as they go into winter. These leys will provide some sheep grazing after germinating in the autumn. Our conventional crops of oil-seed rape are usually planted by 20 August which keeps the pressure on.

The dairy cows have started calving now and although they calve outside (the healthiest place) they are brought straight in afterwards and put onto a winter ration as the goodness required for milk production has gone from the grass.

All harvested crops are brought back to the drier at Broadfield where they are tipped into a large reception pit. They are then cleaned and dried. It normally pays to hold grain at least until November or December when the price tends to improve. By now all next year's crops are planned and the land is being cultivated ready for sowing again.

*Ploughing in oil-seed rape stubble,
ready for drilling autumn crops.*

NATURE AT HIGHGROVE

The valley was narrow, steep, and almost entirely cut off; it was also a funnel
for winds, a channel for the floods and a jungly, bird-crammed, insect-hopping
sun-trap whenever there happened to be any sun. It was not high and open
like the Windrush country, but had secret origins, having been gouged from
the Escarpment by the melting ice-caps some time before we got there. The
old flood-terraces still showed on the slopes, along which the cows walked
sideways. Like an island, it was possessed of curious survivals - rare orchids and
Roman snails. . . . The sides of the valley were rich in pasture and the crests
heavily covered in beechwoods.

Cider with Rosie, Laurie Lee.

THERE IS AN ELEGIAC QUALITY about Laurie Lee's descriptions of his Cotswold
childhood in *Cider with Rosie*, for he was conscious that he was recording a
world on the edge of the abyss. It was the mid-1950s by the time he began
recording the sights, sounds and smells of a 1920s childhood in the hamlet of Slad,
near Stroud, where the long day chirped and croaked and sang with all manner of
things. By then, the changes were under way. 'I belonged to that generation,' he
wrote, 'which saw, by chance, the end of a thousand years' life.'

The end, as he saw it, was the advent of the internal combustion engine. It
brought the end of isolation, the end of horse-powered agriculture and the beginning of motor transport. It brought the end of a life in which nature provided
many of the pleasures as well as the hardships. Today, as the tractor driver ploughs
a furrow in his sound-insulated cab, he no longer has to contend with the
drudgery of walking behind shire horses, or ditching, at which a man used to wear
out a spade in a year. These are material gains. There are material losses, too. The
farm worker often lives away from the land he works, perhaps in the nearby town,
while a commuter lives in the knocked-through labourers' cottages. The result is
sometimes that a man of farming stock cannot tell an oak from an ash.

Social change meant that, at first, fewer people noticed the extent of the ecological changes which took place. Yet in hindsight, anyone who has been familiar
with the life of the countryside has noticed some evidence of wildlife being slowly

*New to freedom: a juvenile barn
owl from a clutch of three hatched
in the hay loft above the stables at
Highgrove.*

squeezed out of farmed land. Some will remember smaller fields, with hedges. Others will have memories of wild flowers in summer and more lapwings on the wet fields in winter. Others again will remember when there were more skylarks. The British Trust for Ornithology's Common Birds Census shows that many farmland species are in serious decline: for example, the skylark, the grey partridge, the turtle dove, the linnet, tree sparrow and corn bunting. There are other farmland birds such as the wyneck and cirl bunting which have all but died out. One has only to look to literature for evidence of sights and sounds that are rarer today in the South of England: flocks of goldfinches, for example, clouds of butterflies or the hedgerows full of honeysuckle, as observed by William Cobbett in *Rural Rides*. The decline in the biological diversity of the British countryside is still greater than most people realise and it is continuing.

Yet though the flora and fauna of lowland agricultural England are greatly depleted – compared, say, with the wilder parts of upland England, Scotland and Wales – that process has been mercifully incomplete. Every farm has its fragment of something that can be protected or better managed; a piece of scrub here which gives shelter to voles (and hence to owls), a filled-in pond there, a piece of unimproved limestone pasture which can be left out of the nitrogen round. And to their credit, since the alarm over intensive agriculture was sounded at the end of the 1970s, many farmers have been willing to do something to protect and encourage wildlife, at least on their marginal land, and have responded to new encouragement to plant farm woods and parkland trees.

Long before he turned his farm over to organic agriculture, Prince Charles tried to do all he could to improve the existing natural habitats of his farm, as any wildlife-minded conventional farmer might do. He was an early client of the Gloucestershire branch of the Farming and Wildlife Advisory Group, the farmer's first stop for practical conservation advice. FWAG, as it is known, run on a shoestring with government and private support, was formed to speak knowledgeably and tactfully about conservation to farmers on their own land. The first requirement imposed upon it is to respect the profitability of farms. The FWAG adviser for Gloucestershire is John Hughes, who has thirty-two years' experience in farming and horticulture behind him, including working as manager of a large fruit and hop farm in Kent.

John Hughes discussing new woodland with the Prince of Wales.

Since he took up the job in May 1979, Hughes has advised on 1,109 farms and smallholdings out of 6,011 in Gloucestershire. He has told farmers how to improve ponds; how to manage hedges to leave birds with food into the winter; how to leave grass hedges and 'beetle banks' in the middle of fields to encourage partridges and natural predators of aphids; how to plant game crops round pylons and other pieces of wasted ground; and how to improve existing woodland. He still finds it exasperating that many farmers and smallholders are unaware that his advice is free.

At Highgrove, Hughes has recommended the reinstatement of ponds and the repair of stone walls, advised against using fertilisers on meadows with wild flowers and tackled the unexpected problem of what to do with hay mixed up with daffodil leaves from the lawns in front of the house. The answer proved to be that the hay should be used for bedding only: daffodils are a lethal purgative for livestock.

Over the past decade, Prince Charles has planted twenty acres of new woods and twelve new hedgerows at the Duchy Home Farm, miles of dry-stone walls have been rebuilt, and half a dozen farm ponds have been dug out, cleared out or rejuvenated, including a former cart-wash beside the main back drive to Highgrove. The Prince has also made environmental and conservation matters a permanent item on the agenda at quarterly farm meetings, before 'any other business'.

A farm walk in summer, with John Hughes as guide, is the best way to see what has been improved or conserved. We set out one day in early August, accompanied by Maurice Tibbles, the *Survival* film-maker, who spent two years making the film that was shot as this book was written. Tibbles grew up on the other side of Tetbury, where he wrote his first book on dew ponds at the age of nine. For him, making a film around Highgrove, after years making natural history films in exotic places, was like a homecoming.

On that hot sunny August day there was an extraordinary profusion of butterflies in the parkland around the house: commas, meadow browns, peacocks, and holly blues. There were also formations of dragonflies, preying on the flies following the beef calves. Was this profusion of butterfly and dragonfly life because of a reduction of sprays in the fields and hedgerows nearby? Or was it simply because the parkland contained plenty of thick hedgerows and patches of woodland with tall undergrowth at their base? There was no way of being sure, but Hughes says he has noticed an increase of butterflies on the farm over the past ten years.

John Hughes introducing frog spawn into the restored pond by the farm buildings at Highgrove. The pond was once a cart-wash. The track down to it, as can be seen from this photograph, was paved so that the horses did not lose their footing.

173

In the parkland he pointed out the signs of grey squirrel damage in some of the young parkland trees. One tree, a sycamore, appeared to have given up after sharp teeth had stripped its bark. Hughes recommends planting a proportion of sycamores, simply because squirrels like them and they keep the hungry rodents off other, more valuable trees. Another discovery in the park was a little owl, sitting watching us in a tree not far from the house. The parkland around Highgrove, though now drilled with a clover mixture to improve fertility as part of the organic regime, still seemed to be providing the necessary habitat for the owl's main diet item: the short-tailed field vole.

Both tawny owls and little owls have been seen regularly around the house by P.C. Tudor Davies, one of the security team, who enlivens his watches in the small hours by recording wildlife on the estate. The proliferation of bird tables and hundreds of bird boxes around the garden and parkland is also his work. Davies has recorded everything he has seen, from the great crested newts in the lily pond, to rare visitors such as the siskin and redwing, to the herring gulls which invade the fields in flocks in the autumn. Few farms can have ever been studied as closely as this.

Tibbles had been preparing for a cherished conservation project for which he had sought the Prince's approval: a carefully staged release of captive-bred barn owls. His theory was that as the ecology of the farm improved with the conversion to an organic regime, the conditions for the short-tailed field vole would improve further. If the land could support several breeding pairs of barn owls, at the top of the food chain, that would be a triumphant signal that the ecology of the farm was working successfully all the way down.

Over the centuries, the barn owl has been traditionally associated with farmland, since it is adapted to hunt only in long tussocky grass and not in woodland. Latterly, however, it has been on the decline – due, it is thought, to a combination of factors: eating rodents contaminated with rat poison, the decline of its long grassland habitat, and the loss of the traditional stone-walled barns in which it was able to nest.

The barn owl is also restricted by its inability to adapt to roads, or the vehicles on them, as readily as other birds of prey, such as the kestrel, have done. It has a habit of swooping, fatally, in front of passing cars and lorries when hunting on roadside verges. This seemingly unalterable trait means that barn owls seldom survive within two miles of motorways or dual carriageways – which write off thousands of barn owls each year and rule out large areas of the country as barn-owl habitat.

A further problem for the barn owl was posed by the fact that, though singularly ill-equipped for twentieth-century living, it does breed prolifically in captivity. Well-meaning releases of barn owls into totally unsuitable habitat had been taking place at a rate of 3,000 a year into a wild population of 5,000 pairs. An unacceptable number of these birds were being found dead from starvation and other causes after failing to adapt to freedom. This had caused great concern among conservation bodies such as the Royal Society for the Protection of Birds, the government's Joint Nature Conservation Committee, the Hawk and Owl Trust and Tibbles's collaborator, Jemima Parry-Jones of the Birds of Prey Centre of Newent, Gloucestershire.

This female barn owl in the loft at Broadfield had a clutch of six eggs.

Five of them hatched.

175

Tibbles and Mrs Parry-Jones planned a high-profile copy-book release scheme as a demonstration of how such releases ought to be carried out. Before they were sure that the owls would be able to support themselves on the Home Farm, a vole-count was arranged in the parkland and at Broadfield to assess the quantities of forage available to the owls. Of the traps put down, 60 per cent were later found to have a live vole inside, indicating, according to the Mammal Society who carried out the test, a healthy source of owl food. The only suggested habitat-improvement, from Jemima Parry-Jones, was that more double hedges should be planted, to enclose lanes between fields which are a favoured barn-owl hunting ground. Ideally every farm would have 'wildlife corridors' on these lines; then the barn owls which presently exist only in island populations would be able to recolonise areas where they are now extinct.

Mrs Parry-Jones provided two breeding pairs of barn owls from the Duke of Devonshire's Chatsworth estate. One pair went to the stable loft at Highgrove, the other to Broadfield Farm. Their young were ringed by the British Trust for Ornithology before release. The idea was that the parents would be released first, and, all being well, return to feed their young. Then when the parents were used to hunting in the wild, the young would go too. In the meantime, both parents and young would continue to be fed with a mixture of brown food, like mice (to remind them of what they were supposed to catch), supplemented by their staple diet of frozen day-old cockerel chicks from a chicken farm.

An early disaster struck, when one of the barn owl parents released at Broadfield was found dead in a cattle trough. Water troughs are one of the commonest causes of death of barn owls, after being hit by cars. One theory was that the owl had decided to fight its reflection and drowned. This was discounted since it was dark at the time. The most likely explanation was that the owl had tried to bathe, but underestimated the depth of the trough. Once in, it was unable to get out. Since then, planks have been placed in all the cattle troughs on the farm to help confused owls who decide to bathe. Mrs Parry-Jones also recommends broken plastic breadbaskets for this purpose, which are slightly easier for cattle to push out of the way with their noses.

At Broadfield, which is quieter and away from the main road, five barn owl offspring were raised in a loft and then released. So far the scheme appears to have been a success, marred only by the death of one of the offspring which, when it was nine months old, flew into a train at Oxford thirty-eight miles away. The others have set up homes in the farmland round about. A pair has set itself up in a tree opposite David Wilson's house and their white, ghostly shapes can be seen at dusk hunting over the newly organic parts of the farm.

The exemplary purpose of the release was overtaken to some extent when the Department of the Environment decided to make it an offence to release barn owls into the wild, except under licence. Releases are advised only after a complete survey of the foraging habitat, backed up by the placing of nesting boxes, and after the birds are ringed so that their progress can be tracked. Licences are likely to be granted rarely, and then only when there is enough habitat and the procedures are followed by experts, as they were on the release scheme at Highgrove.

David Wilson with the barn owl he found dead in the water trough. Water troughs kill more barn owls than anything except roads.

Another habitat re-creation project has been in progress all over the estate with the restoration of many of the dry-stone walls. As John Hughes will show by dismantling part of one of these, stone walls provide almost as good a wildlife refuge as hedges. Small birds nest in them, toads squat in them, slowworms hibernate in them, weasels live in them (as do rabbits, their prey). Tibbles recalls purse-netting dry-stone walls in his youth for rabbits. Mervyn Dart, the farm's dry-stone waller, a retired Concorde engineer, found a whole rabbit warren underneath a partly fallen wall at the entrance to Preston's Wood. Walls are also important for mosses and lichens. The stone for the walls was originally quarried on the farm. Not far away there is an old quarry, by a resident manure heap where grass snakes have been seen. It is not far from the main Cirencester road but the snakes don't appear to mind. They like a muddy puddle to swim in and a warm, undisturbed place to hide and lay their eggs. Broadfield also has a vast badger sett, a metropolis of its kind, where the badgers have thought nothing of tunnelling out under a field of barley from the safety of a new copse planted with oaks.

Hedges do, of course, provide a rich habitat for nesting birds and mammals and when a rough grass strip is left unsprayed and uncultivated beside them they can also provide valuable refuge for insects and wild flowers – as well as barn-owl hunting ground. Prince Charles has left several of these grass rides. Some of the hedges at Westonbirt and Broadfield are hundreds of years old and include a wide range of species. One planted by a crumbling stone wall at Broadfield, pointed out by Hughes, includes wytch-elm, dog rose and black bryony, as well as pollarded ash which once would have been used for the spars and spokes of farm carts. He indicated where a great tit had been nesting in the wall.

Gloucestershire is covered with dry-stone walls in an advanced state of collapse: here Mervyn Dart rebuilds a section by Preston's Wood.

Broadfield Farm has the most interesting surviving habitats on the estate. There, at the back of the wood, is an area of rough grass and hawthorn scrub, of a kind seen over large areas when the Cotswolds were mostly sheep-walks. The full-sized hawthorns provide nesting for birds and cover for woodland species such as bluebells and lords-and-ladies in spring. Nearby, in the margins of Preston's Wood, grows the woolly thistle, a nationally rare plant which is common in this part of Gloucestershire. The thistle flower emerges from a round pompom, the size of a tennis ball, which is defended all around by ferocious spikes.

In a small valley behind the wood is perhaps the best piece of unimproved limestone grassland on the farm. The wild flowers of limestone pasture are acclimatised to growing on poor soils and are easily smothered by grasses when nitrogen fertiliser is applied. Here, though closely grazed by sheep and cattle, the pasture grows ladies' bedstraw, field scabious, rough hawkbit, hairy violet, salad burnet and bird's-foot trefoil. A small cover of conifers had been planted on one end of the pasture, where we found the same flowers growing knee-high, together with yellow rattle and pink convolvulus. A long-term plan of the Prince's is to graze cattle beneath these trees, on the lines of managed medieval forests.

Sixty species of plant were recorded on the open pasture by the county plant recorder, Mrs Sonia Holland, when Prince Charles asked her to survey the field in 1985. Mrs Holland pronounced the wild flowers of Highgrove relatively unremarkable, since on some isolated fragments of limestone pasture like those on the Cotswold escarpment she had recorded nearer 200 species. The amount of such unimproved grassland of any kind left in existence, however, is tiny, so preserving it is a priority for the concerned farmer. This means not enriching it, either by spreading nitrogen on it or by seeding it with fertility-building crops. With the right management, there is the strong chance of something rarer turning up. It is, in any case, part of Prince Charles's philosophy that habitats should be conserved on all farms, and wildlife should not just be confined to a network of tiny ghetto-like reserves.

On Broadfield Farm, Prince Charles had taken a keen interest in the restructuring of Preston's Wood, also known as Preston's Folly. The existing plantation of larch and spruce, planted approximately thirty years ago beside a piece of older woodland, had been under-thinned and was largely valueless. It seemed a pointless use of conifers on soil that could be used to grow better trees. Faced with the choice of clear-felling the larch or thinning them, the Prince decided to thin heavily to make gaps in which broadleaves could be planted. In this way the appearance of the wood was not suddenly altered and pockets of existing ground flora were maintained to colonise the cleared areas. The felled conifers provided useful fencing material and the farm staff used some of the thinnings in a new building for young cattle from the dairy herd. When the broadleaves, now around ten feet high, have grown up, the remaining conifers will be cut down. By another wood, Tidcomb's Gorse, a new area of hazel coppice and widely-spaced oak has been planted. The hazel will provide useful beanpoles and stakes for hedge-laying.

LEFT: *The woolly thistle –
nationally rare – which is
plentiful at Preston's Wood. The
woolly pompoms, with their fierce
spikes, are each the size of a
clenched fist.*

BELOW: *Meadow cranesbill (wild
geranium) in rough pasture
under trees at Preston's Wood.*

Mervyn Dart planting new broad-leaved trees at Preston's Wood.

Forestry is a subject on which the Prince has strong views. When a new wood was to be planted on the 85-acre block at Westonbirt, the Prince told Nick Mould, the Duchy agent, to consult John Makepeace, the furniture designer, on which species were best to plant. Makepeace taught Viscount Linley and other leading furniture-makers at his workshops at Parnham in Dorset. He has created startling pieces out of indigenous timber such as holly – which is ivory-white even when seasoned – and bog oak, the preserved remains of prehistoric oaks dug up in the Fens, which he uses instead of endangered ebony.

Makepeace gave a list of trees to plant which would be useful to furniture craftsmen of the twenty-first century. He recommended white woods such as holly and Scotch laburnum, to be grown in a mixture of cherry, ash, sycamore and alder. Alder, an undervalued wood, grows quickly, thrives in damp places and can be pollarded once it has been used as a nurse crop to stimulate the other trees into faster growth. The Prince of Wales has been heard to observe gloomily: 'It will all look its best in about forty years' time, when I'm dead.'

The question much discussed on our farm walk was whether organic farming made a measurable difference to wildlife and if so by how much. Common sense indicates that a lack of chemical intrusion has preserved the diversity of Britain's wildlife down the centuries, but it is more difficult to separate this from the sheer intensity of cultivation when accounting for the disappearance of so many butterflies, dragonflies, plants and birds since 1945.

John Hughes thought it likely that the removal of spraying regimes at Highgrove was having benefits, principally for the butterflies and the other unseen invertebrates in the crops which provide food for small animals and birds. It was early in the conversion of the farm to tell what the benefits of organic would be. Hughes did not have his heart in intensive chemical farming, and saw the continuation of the trend of farmers reducing pesticide applications as a response to environmental and economic pressures. But he did not personally believe that hair-shirt organic methods were altogether necessary either: they were just more verifiable than any middle way. 'I think,' he gruffly concluded, 'that halfway between the two's where we'll end up.'

What exact benefits organic farming brings to the wildlife of farmland is a question that has never been satisfactorily answered by science. Common sense says that there must be gains, since the ecology of farmland remained relatively stable for thousands of years under organic regimes, but what exactly are these gains – more birds, more insects, more wild plants? And where should organic farming be practised to have the greatest wildlife benefit? The farming and nature conservation establishment has, for not entirely understandable reasons, failed to carry out the studies to find the answers.

Such information that has been assembled is in organic farming's favour. From the few studies that exist in the scientific literature, organic methods appear to result in a greater abundance of insects, birds, wild flowers and earthworms. Only one study in Europe has compared bird populations on organic and conventional farmland. This was a Danish survey which showed that of thirty-nine bird species, thirty-six were more numerous on organic farms.

Even the gaps at Highgrove grow something: here a small greenhouse used by Dennis Brown is surrounded by ox-eye daisies, delphiniums and red roses, mixing the wild and the cultivated.

Dr Nick Carter of Rothamsted laboratories vacuuming bugs from conventional cereals as part of his comparison of conventional and organic farming systems.

A review of organic methods and their environmental benefits by Charles Arden Clarke for the Political Ecology Research Group in Oxford suggests that our present system of 'islands' of nature conservation surrounded by a sea of intensively-farmed crops must ultimately fail as a conservation strategy. In the face of climate change or other unforeseen events, for instance, the protected species in their 'islands' would not survive unless they were able to recolonise the wider countryside through wildlife corridors formed by whole organic farms.

The Nature Conservancy Council's 1990 report 'Nature Conservation and Agricultural Change' also points to the surprising lack of research on the basic question of what the ecological gains from organic methods actually are, but is clearly optimistic that they are considerable:

There have been very few field studies so far which have carried out direct comparisons of the impacts of organic and conventional systems respectively on wildlife, but there are indications that invertebrates, wild plants and birds are present in greater numbers and diversity on organic land. Further research in this area is desirable.

All farming systems necessarily disrupt natural wildlife habitats to some extent. However, organic farming as practised to Soil Association standards clearly provides greater protection for wildlife than do conventional forms of intensive agriculture.

The question of how organic methods benefit the ecology of the countryside is, of course, central to the place of organic farming in European state-supported agriculture. Many instinctively believe that the absence of sprays, the use of organic manures and the reduction of pollution this brings must be significantly better for all wildlife. But to be truly effective in silencing the critics of organic farming and promoting agriculture that is ecologically sustainable, those benefits must be proved and quantified.

It is certainly in the public's interest, but not necessarily that of the agro-chemical industry, that such research is carried out. To this end a joint survey of the insect and bird life on around twenty organic and conventional farms – including Highgrove – is now to be carried out by the British Trust for Ornithology and the Institute for Arable Crops Research laboratory at Rothamsted. This may be a step towards finding an answer.

FARMING INFLUENCES

MOST FARMERS WOULD probably agree that it is more difficult to be a good organic farmer than it is to be a good 'conventional' one. The conventional farmer can make mistakes and get out of them by applying a dose of herbicide to the weeds in his crops or a shot of antibiotic to a sick cow. There is virtually nothing the organic farmer can do to a standing crop full of weeds: he should have timed his weed-strike better the previous autumn. He has to think twice about using antibiotics on his livestock because of the long withdrawal periods the Soil Association demands before meat or milk can be used. Organic farmers need all the resourcefulness and practicality of any successful farmer. But, because they depend on a small unstable, unsubsidised market to sell their goods, they also need what many British farmers, buoyed up since the war by guaranteed farm-gate prices, have often lacked: an aptitude for marketing and self-promotion. One might add to the shopping list of attributes needed by the organic farmer passion, imagination and a skin thick enough to withstand the taunts of his or her chemical neighbours.

Within this Cromwellian breed there is great variety. There are those who became organic farmers as a way of opting out of the consumer society. There are those who believe that they are the future of the consumer society waiting to happen. There are those who lead life styles which are, by and large, very similar to those of consumers like the rest of us. And there are those who are living, often with considerable sacrifice, according to principles they believe the rest of the world has forgotten.

In the course of writing this book I retraced the Prince's steps to two very different farms: Kite's Nest, a spectacularly beautiful farm on the Cotswold escarpment outside Broadway, Worcestershire, and Rushall, Britain's largest organic farm, a couple of hours' drive away in the Vale of Pewsey, Wiltshire. One can scarcely imagine a greater contrast between the Young family, who farm Kite's Nest and Barry Wookey who runs Rushall but both have ways of farming which stimulated or reassured the Prince of Wales at pivotal moments in the development of Highgrove.

Kite's Nest Farm near Broadway: an organic farm managed to provide the maximum benefits for wildlife. In the foreground, some of the permanent pasture where dropwort, pyramid orchids and quaking grass can be found.

185

It seemed important, as well, to visit a farm closely comparable to Highgrove in size and situation which was engaged in converting to organic methods, just to reassure myself that the business of organic conversion could be contemplated without the benefit of a royal bank account – the question that any farmer would want to ask. With this in mind I went to see Helen Browning, a tenant of 1,350 acres on the Wiltshire Downs who I discovered, to the delight of her colleagues in the organic movement and the surprise of many of her farming neighbours, has stayed in profit throughout conversion.

First, I followed in the footsteps of the Prince to Kite's Nest, which lies a mile or so from the antique shops and tourist tea-rooms of Broadway, but it might very well be in another age. Kite's Nest is run by Mary and Harry Young, their son Richard and daughter Rosamund, as an organic farm on inspirational lines. Nature is left to itself as much as possible and domestic animals receive exceptional kindness and consideration. The farm is on the scarp slope of the Cotswolds, and the highest part forms a natural amphitheatre looking out over the Vale of Evesham. Its 470 acres includes 85 acres of woodland, 165 acres permanent pasture and 220 acres on which cereals can be grown in rotation. Much of the permanent pasture is so steep that a tractor driver would risk life and limb to plough it – even if the Youngs wanted him to, which they do not, for nature conservation is important to them. The wild flowers of their unimproved limestone pasture rival any in England.

The richest wildflower meadow at Kite's Nest is a remnant of English flora on a scale that is rare indeed. The Youngs do not cut it for silage or even for hay, in order to allow the wild flowers to reseed. Instead, they allow livestock to graze it in August only after the flowers have seeded. The rarest survival there is Dyer's greenweed, *Genista tinctoria*, a low, fleshy, broom-like plant whose yellow flowers have proliferated with benign management into a series of large clumps on the side of the hill. Rosamund took us to see *Genista tinctoria* on a spectacular late June day when the town of Broadway lay in the valley below largely hidden by trees and heat haze. All around were tormentil, betony, ladies' bedstraw, hawkbit and bird's-foot trefoil flowering among the grasses. Butterflies fluttered about the meadow in profusion: meadow browns, large skippers and a pair of marbled whites. All this diverse activity was in marked contrast to the overgrazed prairie belonging to someone else across the lane. Later, at the top of the escarpment we found other excitements: dropwort, pyramid orchids, quaking grass and clustered bellflower. The Youngs recognise that some forms of nature conservation are essentially incompatible with any kind of farming; certain things just need to be left alone. With this in mind they do not farm all their land: along with the wildflower meadow there is a four- or five-acre area of woodland by a small stream which they abandon altogether to birds, stoats and foxes.

The Prince of Wales visited the Youngs in August 1989, shortly before he took the decision to turn the whole of Highgrove over to organic management. Nobody who visits their farm can fail to react in some way to its special atmosphere. The farm could be called timeless were it not more accurately described as a world apart, a small corner of the country where agriculture has developed along a rocky path that forked off the main highway of conventional practice fifty years ago.

Any visitor to the Youngs' stone farmhouse, rebuilt in 1680, is likely to be introduced first to Mrs Mary Young, a redoubtable lady of radical views and fondness for the *Guardian* newspaper. She will tell you proudly that she does not drink or smoke and – *pace* the Prince – strongly disapproves of fox-hunting. The visitor to Kite's Nest has to have his wits about him. On my visit Mrs Young asked alarmingly: 'Are you a graduate of English literature? They're the only people I have time for.'

I thought hard before conceding that I was, then wished I hadn't, as the riposte was a quotation from *Cymbeline* which I was unable to identify. I recovered, shakily, by trading quotations from *Henry V* and *King Lear* on English wild flowers.

Another of Mrs Young's potential traps begins: 'You must have some of our wonderful food.' I had not eaten all day so was glad to. Rosamund duly brought a plate of home-raised beef on home-made bread and a glass of milk from their cows. 'You can taste the difference,' says Mrs Young. It is not a statement one would dream of contradicting.

It is not every farmer who writes poetry or rushes headlong into arguments about literary criticism. But then the Youngs are not an ordinary family. They mix their literary leanings with the grindingly hard work that virtual self-sufficiency requires. Their two main cash crops are cereals and beef. The beef, which they sell entirely through their own farm shop, comes from the herd of seventy-one breeding Lincoln Red, Shorthorn and Welsh Black cows and their offspring, a herd of around 200 in all. The cattle all have names – there is a Calpurnia, an

Rosamund Young in the hay meadow the Youngs keep for wild flowers. On this June day it was dotted with tormentil, betony, ladies' bedstraw, hawkbit, bird's-foot trefoil and numerous butterflies. Behind Rosamund is a large clump of Dyer's greenweed, with its yellow broom-like flower. Another is beginning near her left foot!

Mrs Mary Young with a young heifer called Calpurnia (after Julius Caesar's wife) because she was born on the Ides of March.

Araminta and an Hippolyta. The cows are allowed to remain in family groups and their names tend to reflect a family connection: Fat Hat, Straw Beret and Bonnet are one such group, and Eleanor, with sons Geoffrey and Plantagenet another. Rosamund explains that you need be reminded of something which makes you smile when you have to watch them calving at 3 a.m. Rosamund and her brother accompany those animals selected for slaughter to the abattoir, comforting them until the bolt strikes so their last moments are not spent in panic, scenting death in a strange place.

Other farmers may scoff or find it embarrassing to see domestic animals cared for with such sympathy and affection. Yet it is an embarrassment which prompts one to ask why all farm animals should not be treated as humanely as this – and whether as many people would be vegetarians if they were. Rosamund argues that it is financial idiocy to make an animal suffer, since stress makes them lose weight and can make the meat tough. She aims to give them a happy life and a quick death. She has lobbied the Government successfully, along with the Humane Slaughter Association, to extend the new EC rules to permit mobile abattoirs which could travel to the livestock instead of the other way around. There appear to be dividends yet to be fully appreciated by all food experts. *A la Carte* magazine's cookery writer, Lynda Brown, ended her search for beautiful beef at Kite's Nest. She wrote: 'The result is beef the best this land can produce, both luscious and yielding plenty of juice, and with the kind of rich, pure beef flavour which once made England's national dish the envy of the world.'

With a total of 200 cattle on 260 acres of grass, Kite's Nest has a low stocking density, compared with some farms. The Youngs are limited by the amount of silage and hay that can be cut from the steepest banks of the farm. The advantages of low stocking and rotating pasture has contributed to the total absence of worm problems, despite the fact that no chemical wormers have been used for twelve years. Wherever possible the cattle are allowed the run of more than one field so that they can decide themselves on the most sheltered spots. The aim is to keep the animals happy and eliminate stress so that they become ill less often. The cows are allowed to decide for themselves when to wean their calves. This produces a gain of an extra hundredweight of live-weight compared to calves that are forcibly weaned at nine months.

Mother and daughter became organic in the 1960s on their previous farm, before the family sold up and moved to Kite's Nest. Richard, then farming his uncle's farm, preferred to go down the chemical route. He was very good at farming with sprays and fertilisers: he won a prize for the best crop of spring barley in Gloucestershire in 1973. Only later in the 1970s did his headaches from spraying begin to persuade him that poisonous chemicals had no part in agriculture. He is now responsible for designing the farm's rotations, a four-year rye-grass and white clover ley followed by two crops of winter wheat and one of winter oats. In recent years this has been very profitable with wheat fetching up to £240 a ton. Richard is the empiricist of the family. Despite being a stalwart of the Soil Association, he is a sceptic about homeopathic medicine, which is one of the touchstones of the organic faith. He recently wrote an article for *Country Life* discussing whether such remedies are successful. He chose to keep an open mind.

The Youngs lead a kind of self-sufficient life which was once universal in the countryside but which is now increasingly rare. The kitchen garden is well stocked. Rosamund mills her own flour, makes her own bread and churns her own butter. Few trips to the supermarket are necessary. The Youngs probably make a better living at the moment, exposed to all the vagaries of the market, than they would by not farming organically. The organic beef commands a premium of 20 per cent and the organic wheat around 100 per cent. Against this is the day-long hard physical work which is needed to support this way of life. They will never be rich, except in the capital value of their beautiful farm. It probably clears each year, after tax, the equivalent of the average industrial wage which then has to be shared between four. But there are few food bills to find and the immense but unquantifiable wealth to be found in living in such spectacular country and enjoying the passage of the seasons. As Richard says: 'It depends what you are in it for.' It does indeed, and Kite's Nest is a place where one catches oneself asking that question.

OVERLEAF: *The beef suckler herd at Kite's Nest: notice some of the cows and bullocks have not been dehorned.*

Barry Wookey, Britain's largest organic farmer, in front of his combined grain store, mill and bakery at Rushall. Note the Soil Association symbol. He was looking unusually formal because he was off to perform his duties as a magistrate.

An organic farmer on a far larger scale is Barry Wookey, who farms 1,650 acres near Upavon on the Wiltshire Downs. His farm, where the two branches of the infant Avon meet a few miles above Salisbury, remains the largest acreage farmed by organic means in the country. Sitting in the yard outside The Manor, Upavon, a homely brick house thatched with tough organic straw from the farm, was a gleaming new charcoal-coloured Japanese four-wheel drive vehicle, a far cry from the Youngs' faithful but decrepit 1970s Range Rover.

Wookey lives in much the same way as other big farmers, except that he farms organically. He is a pillar of the parish council, reads the *Daily Telegraph*, shoots, hunts, fishes for salmon in Norway and for trout in his stretch of the Avon. He has said that his farm is just as profitable as a conventional one. As a living rebuke to the chemical farming fraternity, he is near the knuckle indeed. Prince Charles visited his farm on 5 November 1984, shortly before taking the decision to start organic farming on his own farm. No doubt he was reassured by the scale of Rushall, its sense of prosperous well-being and its well-cared-for thatched estate cottages decked out in their livery of light blue windows and magnolia walls.

The foundation of the Wookey fortunes was Barry's father's and grandfather's good sense in leasing and then buying land, as Barry explains in his book *Rushall: The Story of An Organic Farm*, published in 1987. (As a first-hand account of how an organic farm works in vigorous readable prose this

One of the several thatched cottages on the estate at Rushall. Note the estate livery of light blue windows and magnolia walls.

book should be read by everyone with an interest in organic farming.) Barry's father bought Rushall in 1945. Next door, his son Nigel still farms – conventionally – part of the 3,500 acre Upavon Farms which his father and grandfather first took on as tenants from the War Department in 1928. The Army has now taken back all but 1,000 acres for their training area. Part of the land is on Salisbury Plain and the sound of guns on the ranges can be heard in Upavon throughout the year. Soon, when Barry retires, Nigel is to take on Rushall himself. Nigel will farm Rushall organically if, as Barry puts it pessimistically, organic is still viable by then.

A farmer needs land, but that is only the beginning. The success of Rushall as an organic farm is due to Barry Wookey's own farming and business skills. He was first a successful conventional farmer and still recommends that a young farmer should first learn how to farm conventionally before venturing into organic. Then three things set him thinking about the chemicals he was using, culminating with his beginning to convert to organic in 1970. The first was the decline of the English partridge on the downs, as a result of the spraying of the plants on which its chicks depend for their first few weeks of food.

Traditional baking from the farm shop at Rushall.

The partridges have yet to return to their pre-war levels. The second was the story of the death of the American robins in Rachel Carson's *Silent Spring*: the robins died because of the DDT used to spray elm trees against the beetles that brought Dutch elm disease. When the leaves fell, so did the DDT and formed a layer which was taken into the soil by worms. The DDT built up in the robins from the worms they ate and soon dead robins began to be noticed all over the east coast of the United States. The third case was the Thalidomide scandal which was the subject of a in-depth investigation by the *Sunday Times*.

Wookey had a lot of land and could afford to experiment. Even so, he took from 1970 to 1985 to convert all his farm, an interval which allowed him to develop his business without denting its profitability. The main enterprise at Rushall today is the flour mill, where Wookey stores his own grain, makes his own animal feed, mills and sells his own stone-ground flour and bakes his own bread. Clearly a large part of his business philosophy is to add as much value to his produce as possible before it leaves the farm. The mill manager, David Fuller, is also the baker. He ignores the usual tests that modern bakers use to test the protein content, hardness and machinability of their wheat. He just tests to see if it will bake, which it usually does. The village has no other baker, so one source of income is on the doorstep and people come from many miles around to buy bread. Loads of organic flour go regularly to London bakers. The mill and bakery sells bread, iced buns, cheese scones, sultana bread, garlic croutons and pizza bases, all made with Rushall's stone-ground wholemeal organic flour. The bread has the soft solidity that one somehow expects – but seldom finds – in an organic loaf. The cheese scones are particularly delicious.

Driving round his farm in high summer Mr Wookey pointed contentedly at arable crops miraculously clean of weeds, thanks to his autumn weed-strike techniques. He declined to be photographed in front of one of his fields' rare outcrops of poppies. He grumbles that people always come to his farm looking for weeds. Many conventional farmers have more weeds than he does but always offer the excuse that the sprayer wasn't working properly. An organic farmer has to depend on allowing the weeds to germinate just before drilling his winter wheat in the autumn. The drill has the same effect as a harrow. The only snag is if it is a dry autumn and the weeds fail to germinate. Once the crop is eight inches or so high the weeds become less of a problem.

The grass part of his rotation is turned into profit by beef cattle, Hereford/Friesian crosses bought in and reared on, and the flock of 750 Mule sheep. With the sheep, Wookey avoids complications by entering a joint venture with a professional shepherd, James Oliphant, who provides the sheep. The arrangement pays Wookey a mutually-agreed headage payment and means that he is spared the annual headache of lambing. It also gives a young man who has yet to buy his own farm the chance to get a foot on the farming ladder. It is a characteristic arrangement for a farmer who takes the traditional view that his farm should provide employment and should also house its pensioners and young married couples.

OVERLEAF: *Rushall after cultivation in September, looking out over the Vale of Pewsey.*

The third organic farmer I visited had her first introduction to organic methods at Rushall. Wookey campaigned for years for better treatment for organic farmers from the Ministry of Agriculture and in particular for the Ministry to spend some of its vast research budget on finding answers to simple questions that organic farmers needed answering, such as what is the best wheat variety for growing without bag-nitrogen. A breakthrough came when, after many rebuffs, Mr Wookey persuaded the Agricultural Development and Advisory Service (ADAS) to provide Helen Browning, the bright daughter of a friend of his, with a research 'studentship' to spend time investigating aspects of organic farming at Rushall.

Helen Browning, then in her early twenties and at Harper Adams College in Shropshire, spent a year working with explosive energy on eight projects. These included a study of whether there were more earthworms on organic farms, trials of wheat and grass varieties and an overall assessment of the profitability of organic farms. This showed that Rushall was as profitable as a conventional farm with the same balance of enterprises.

Helen Browning with one of her stripy pigs.

198

Helen developed an enthusiasm for organic methods at college which showed no signs of diminishing when she took over the management of Eastbrook, the family farm, six miles from Swindon on the Wiltshire Downs. She decided to go organic in 1986, prompted by a growing concern about the food quality and animal welfare, and because she saw organic farming as the future. She also recalls a childhood vow to put back the hedges that her father took out in the 1960s. She began when she was still at college experimenting with pigs and chickens on twenty acres lent her by her father. Now nearly half the 1,350-acre farm is wholly organic and by 1995 all of it will be in process of conversion to Soil Association/UKROFS standards.

Perhaps the most remarkable thing about Helen going organic is that she is a tenant farmer. Eastbrook Farm, which has been managed by the Browning family since 1950, is owned by the Church of England. It is one thing to be a substantial farmer who owns his or her own land and another to be a farmer who pays £56 per acre per year in rent. Being a tenant makes the task of conversion a more serious proposition, both in terms of any capital costs necessary for turning the farm organic – fencing, buying livestock, and supplying water if none was already provided – and with the prospect of a decline of income for four or five years while the farm's productive capacity falls and the crops have yet to qualify for an organic premium. It says a lot for her determination that, despite the inevitable slump in profitability, she has managed to stay in profit during the dark days of conversion.

Helen using antibiotics on a sick
beef animal with pneumonia,
aided by the au pair and
daughter Sophie. It is a
misconception that organic
farmers will not use conventional
drugs and only use homeopathic
remedies. However, the
withdrawal periods, before the
animal can be slaughtered or the
milk used, are much longer
under Soil Association rules.

This she has done through a determined effort to market all the farm's produce herself. Helen, a woman of enormous energy, has also found time along the way to acquire a husband, Henry Stoye, and to have Sophie, her first baby.

Helen started with several advantages at Eastbrook Farm. For one, her father had always run two dairy herds so there was no need to buy more livestock. He had also practised a five-year arable and grass rotation so the land was all fenced for livestock, avoiding a potentially huge expense. For the same reasons there was a drinking-water supply for the cattle. Eastbrook Farm is conveniently located at the centre of its land, right in the middle of the attractive Wiltshire village of Bishopstone. At 1,350 acres, it rates as a large farm, which makes for economies of scale and machinery and provides some reserves of fat for the lean years. Most important of all she was not working for the bank. Her father believed in paying off the Inland Revenue and not spending money on expensive machinery which could be offset against tax, as many farmers were advised to do by their accountants in the 1970s and early 1980s.

The two dairy herds continue to produce well from their clover leys and Helen has not experienced the drop in productivity which some farmers have experienced when bag-nitrogen was withdrawn. She puts this down to the amount of farmyard manure traditionally returned to the land. The dairy herds have been very profitable even though their milk has so far been sold to the Milk Marketing Board alongside conventional milk. Organic unpasteurised milk does attract a premium if sold properly but attempts to set up a new organic milk marketing scheme – which she is working on with David Wilson from Highgrove and Oliver Dowding, an established organic dairy farmer – are slow in getting off the ground. Helen, like many other organic farmers, puts a lot of time into the Soil Association and is also on a Ministry regional advisory board. She does wonder occasionally if she might have spent her time better selling her own organic milk, as some farmers have done, and not trying to set up a national marketing scheme first.

Clearly, with the need to maximise the potential of the farm during conversion Helen knew she needed to sell her own produce as well as possible from the outset. The choice of breed was important. To the farm's existing sheep and beef and dairy herds, Helen added seventy free-range British Saddleback sows and free-range hens. British Saddlebacks, the dark pigs with the flesh-coloured stripe round their shoulders, are a rare breed. There were once Essex Saddlebacks and Wessex Saddlebacks but sadly the blood-lines became so few that they had to be combined, like redundant regiments. British Saddlebacks do not reach quite the weight of modern hybrids but they have advantages as free-range pigs as they are good mothers. Their meat also tastes better than faster-growing pigs. Helen chose them because they added to the farm's good-life, good-food image. Outdoor pigs are a low-risk, low-cost system compared to intensive battery pig units. Her stripy pigs are also infinitely more pleasant to look at. The Prince of Wales once saw her at a show. 'Oh, good. You have real pigs,' he said.

LEFT: *The HOF Shop – Helen's Organic Farm Shop – at Shrivenham. Bernard Kift holds up one of Eastbrook Farm's traditional Wiltshire hams.*

OVERLEAF: *Feeding the beef cattle: the demand for organic beef is rising and Eastbrook Farm has just paid off its overdraft.*

Meat from Eastbrook in the HOF Shop's window.

Helen decided early on that the only way to succeed with organic produce was to develop her own markets, and the only way to make a premium for themselves was to do the selling themselves. So, on a shoestring, she started the HOF Shop (Helen's Organic Food Shop) in the nearby village of Shrivenham, Oxfordshire. The shop sells increasing quantities of Eastbrook's own Soil Association-symbol organic produce. Beside the beef, pork and lamb from the farm, the shop sells added-value items such as home-cured hams, bacons and special sausages – Welsh leek, beer and garlic, venison and red wine among others – and traditional farm turkeys at Christmas. Alongside the farm's own produce the shop offers organic rice, baby food, biscuits, pasta, fruit and vegetables. She produces a colour brochure explaining the benefits of supporting organic produce and promoting their flourishing mail-order business.

Helen appears to need few lessons in marketing. She is now expanding the retail side and has taken another shop in Newbury, far enough away to appeal to a different group of customers. The sales are exceeding all expectations: she was not expecting to sell all the meat from the farm, home butchered, for two years or more but she is doing so already. Where she has received an unpleasant shock is on the wholesale side, where a new EC regulation has caught her out severely after she has invested in new facilities. If she is to persist in the wholesale business, she will need a separate curing room, a separate room for unpacking, and a vet on hand all the time while carcasses are cut up. The EC regulation appears to have been concocted with only the largest firms in mind. Helen is sure that she will get round the problem but it is an illustration of how, in the food industry, any business can be thwarted overnight by unexpected regulations.

Helen is proud that she treats all her livestock homeopathically. The farm's medical needs are attended to by Chris Day, one of the few fully-qualified homeopathic vets in the country. Homeopathic remedies combined with competent animal welfare and common sense, such as cold water treatment for mastitis, seem to work well, though at the sight of serious E. coli mastitis she will still pump antibiotics into the cow as fast as possible – and then suffer the lengthy withdrawal periods prescribed by the Soil Association. Her view is that antibiotics have their place but they often tend to suppress, not cure, the real problem.

Eastbrook Farm illustrates not only how many farmers with the right kind of mixed farm *could* go organic without mishap, given sufficient flair, energy and determination, but that marketing and adding value are essential to that result. Here Highgrove is at a disadvantage. It would be difficult to imagine the Prince of Wales running a farm shop, which is the way many successful organic farmers enhance their premiums and keep the profits that would otherwise go to the supermarkets or the middleman.

Helen Browning's farm is not only a case study in how conversion can be done but it is also the most comparable, in many ways, to Highgrove. Eastbrook is – at 1,350 acres – slightly larger than Highgrove's 1,112 acres. The land does not vary widely in quality. The period of conversion runs parallel – through the same recession. When sceptical members of the farming community say: 'Organic farming is all right for the Prince of Wales but how do you expect anyone else to afford it?' I simply venture Eastbrook Farm as an example of what can be done if your heart and soul are in it.

WHOLEMEAL

HIGHGROVE

STONEGROUND

The Duke of Cornwall's
Benevolent Fund benefits from the
sale of this product

THATCHING
AND
BREAD-MAKING

T HE MOST SUCCESSFUL organic farmers obey three rules:
1) convert cheaply;
2) deal with the public direct when possible to keep prices down; and
3) add value.

Not only is adding value good business; it is insurance against the far-off day, which the organic movement hopes for and partly dreads, when organic prices fall because there is a glut of organic produce about. From the moment that Highgrove began producing organic crops, Prince Charles was anxious to try ways of adding value of his own.

The Prince had heard that there was a premium to be paid for organic straw and asked the farm staff to look into it. When he brought up the possibility of selling organic thatching straw at one of the farm meetings the advisers present studied their boots. Terry Summers thought to himself that it would be pretty to watch a binder working again but would it make money? Almost certainly not, he decided.

Thatching straw turned out to be another reversal of the conventional wisdom. The Guild of Master Thatchers was consulted and said, yes, there was indeed a substantial premium for organic thatching straw because it lasted longer than straw that was conventionally grown. Wheat straw grown conventionally sometimes goes rotten in under twenty years because the cell walls have been weakened by fast growth caused by high nitrogen applications. Organic thatching straw, on the other hand, is known to last twice as long: a roof might last as long as forty to fifty years with perhaps the ridge repaired a couple of times. A ready market exists for thatching straw among the surprising number of old houses in central England which still have thatched roofs.

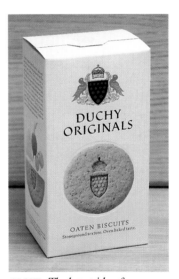

ABOVE: *The latest idea for adding value: an oatmeal biscuit using organic flour from Duchy of Cornwall farms.*

OPPOSITE: *Publicity material taken for the launch of the Highgrove loaf.*

For centuries until the invention of the combine harvester and dwarf varieties of wheat, there was no shortage of thatching straw. Every farm produced the basic raw material. Harvesting, until halfway through this century, was a two-stage process. A binder, drawn by horses or later a tractor, would cut the corn and bind it into sheaves. The sheaves were dried in the sun then piled into a rick, which was expertly thatched. There mice and rats fed on the grain after the autumn ploughing was done. Around November, the wheat grain was threshed from the ear in a threshing drum, leaving long straw which could be used for bedding animals or for thatching. Binding and threshing had their charms but the traditional harvest was highly labour-intensive and wasteful of grain. It is easy to see why someone invented the combine harvester.

In 1989 the Home Farm happened to be using Maris Widgeon, the ideal variety of wheat for thatching. Harvesting it required a binder, which Wilson borrowed from John Hodges, one of the farmers who had share-farmed Highgrove in the early 1980s. Hodges collects vintage tractors and farm machinery.

Wheat for thatching is harvested two or three weeks early, while the grain is still firmly attached to the ear. Once the binder has cut the sheaves and bound them up, the sheaves need to be stooked like the ceremonial wheat-sheaves at Harvest Festival. Stooking entails standing the sheaves up in rows, heads meshed together, which lets the wind dry them. Stooking is a hot and painful business. Each sheaf

Harvesting organic thatching straw: David Wilson takes an unaccustomed turn on the binder. Rupert Cove, driving the tractor, wistfully remembers a time when young men knew how to operate such machinery.

*Getting the hang of stooking:
British Trust for Conservation
volunteers helping with the
harvest of thatching straw, to
allow the farm staff to keep the
harvest going. Still a lot of
practice needed before they pass
the Rupert Cove proficiency test.*

has to be stood up on end by hand and its head meshed with another in one movement, so that the structure stands up on its own.

One of the first days the binder appeared, in hot August weather, almost everyone on the estate, including Prince Charles, turned out to help. Those, including
the Prince, who did not heed Terry Summers's warning to keep their sleeves
rolled down discovered from the wheals on their arms that wheat straw has a
razor-sharp leaf.

It was so dry that year that stooking was necessary only on the headlands
where there were more weeds growing in the crop. The point of stooking is to
dry out the straw and any weeds in the sheaf before they are stored in the rick.
Otherwise a kind of composting takes place, as in wet hay. The rick heats up and,
with ill luck, can spontaneously ignite – taking away the farmer's hard-won crop.
To a farmer in the last century who saw the best part of his year's income go up
in flames, this sight meant probable ruin.

Stacking the sheaves in the barn or, in the early days of this century, in a
thatched rick is an art which farmers have largely forgotten. Wilson discovered

this when his first attempt launched itself out of the barn like a lifeboat. Rupert Cove, an elderly farmer who remembered how it should be done, was enlisted to advise, which he did with polite amusement. He showed how the rick should be built from the outside to the middle, placing the sheaves heads-in. Carting the sheaves and building the rick is a job which requires a lot of manpower and a farm manager with a cool nerve as twelve acres took four men two days to cart and stack when the harvest was at its height. Luckily the first two years it was done, 1989 and 1990, were hot dry summers untroubled by rain.

In November a threshing machine was borrowed, driven by a highly-dangerous transmission belt from a tractor. Threshing the grain from the ear took four men a week with a fifth man working part-time. It was also one of the most unpleasant jobs, Wilson remembers, with chaff and dust filling the air and making everyone sneeze and wheeze. Most of the grinding physical tasks that farm labourers once did have been taken over by machinery. For instance, the harvesting of a comparable twelve acres of wheat would take a man on a combine four hours.

Nevertheless, the result of this hard work was a substantial profit. At first the straw was difficult to sell, but eventually an owner of a thatched house read about the experiment in a newspaper article and bought all fourteen tons to replace her roof which had rotted. Organic thatching straw appears to command a price of around £450 a ton, as opposed to £350 for conventional straw. This boosts the premium for organic wheat by £400 an acre.

Terry Summers feels that harvesting thatching straw is still a complicated job to perform in the middle of a modern harvest on a large farm. He thinks that it is best undertaken on a family farm of a small acreage, where sons and daughters home for the holidays can lend a hand for nothing and boost the profit. Nevertheless, all at the Home Farm agreed that the returns were considerable and they would repeat the exercise.

There was one cause for regret: binding and stacking would have been easier if casual labour were easier to find. Before the Second World War casual labourers would travel for miles to stook and thresh for piece-rates. Ventures to the Tetbury employment exchange to find casual labour proved abortive: the unemployed of Tetbury hadn't heard of stooking and they weren't anxious to learn.

The next project was to find some way of adding value to the food grown on the farm. The market for organic food is small but its size does not make its operation beautiful, in fact quite the reverse. Less than 1 per cent of all food is grown organically in Britain. A small market has meant, for the farmer, expensive distribution and infrequent interest from the supermarket chains. For the consumer, it has meant all too often shockingly high premiums and amateurish quality. Until the late 1980s organic bread looked and weighed like a brick and was largely only available from health food shops.

Prince Charles looked despairingly at the organic movement of which he had become a member. He had a feeling that it had spent the 'green' decade too preoccupied with its internal squabbles and had largely failed to capitalise on the public's growing interest in the environment to market its food. From the time he began to farm at Highgrove, part of what he wanted to do was to help to create

the economies of scale in distribution and marketing to give the consumer the option of buying organic at a not-too-outrageous price. He saw that without the aid of the multiples – the supermarket chains – organic goods would not make their breakthrough into the mass market.

The Highgrove loaf, produced in summer 1990 from the Duchy Home Farm's first organic wheat crop, was a deliberate attempt to do precisely this. A trial run of 41,400 loaves of Highgrove Stoneground Wholemeal Bread was baked by Rank Hovis McDougall and sold in selected Tesco stores in the South-East of England. The loaf cost 59p, about 20p more than a conventional loaf and came sliced and wrapped in plastic like other supermarket bread. It sold well for its allotted twelve weeks. As far as it went, the project was a success. The marketeers learned that organic would sell, at the right price. The Prince and his managers at Highgrove learned about some of the more dubious compromises necessary in the price-sensitive food industry.

Instead of working out how to bake a loaf with the twenty available tonnes of Highgrove wheat, Rank's specialist bakers decided that it would be necessary to blend the Highgrove wheat with organically-grown Canadian wheat. This had the higher protein content 'needed to produce the soft crumb typically required by British bread-eaters' according to the mysterious assumptions of the marketing bumf.

Then there was the price. The loaf had to be priced competitively, including a 3p donation to the Prince's charities. The next discovery was that this meant it was not possible to be wholly organic. A totally-organic sliced wholemeal loaf would have been more expensive to produce because of the rigorous guidelines imposed on ingredients by the Soil Association. For instance, palm oil was required 'to give good loaf volume' said the marketing bumf. And there were no known suppliers of organic palm oil. It was also thought that the Soil Association would not take too kindly to the plastic wrapper. In the end it was decided to describe the product as 'bread made with organic flour'.

So much for principles, even the principles of princes. Prince Charles was forced to make a last-minute decision as to whether the project was worthwhile. He decided a small compromise was worth it to get 'organic' produce on the shelf.

In the late 1980s, the supermarket chains wildly overestimated a slow-growing market. A lot of goods were wasted. But the involvement of the supermarkets in Britain was also partly responsible for one important change: removing the crankiness from organic products and making them familiar to a wide range of people. When opinion polls ask whether the public wants to buy organic produce the answer is now, more often than not, 'Yes, at the right price.'

Yet just as the market for organic goods was getting under way, it was beaten back again by the recession of the early 1990s. When times are hard, people want low prices, not wholesomeness. It is a lesson organic producers are having to relearn, as they did in the recession of the early 1980s. There seems, too, to be an inextricable connection between prosperous times and a concern for the environment. In the meantime, the idealistic businessman must just hold on to what he has got.

So what is the potential size of the market for organic goods? The Soil Association's target for organic produce is 20 per cent of the market by the year 2000. Research by the market organisation, Mintel, in 1991 showed that committed purchasers of organic food represent only 2 per cent of the population. The most likely growth, they say, is 5 to 10 per cent by the year 2000.

John Lister, Highgrove's local miller, understands food markets better than most. From his seventeenth-century mill on the headwaters of the Avon near Tetbury he produces around 70 per cent of all the organic flour produced in Britain. In a former career Lister was a social anthropologist, working with the Yanomami tribe in the Amazon. He bought Shipton Mill in 1980 at a time when many small millers were losing money and getting out. Lister's secret was to buy old milling machinery and run it with modern computers. He thereby saved on machinery and labour and produced a startling £3.5 million a year through-put from an old mill and an ancient relocated barn.

He built a business by selling flour to the craft bakers who distinguished themselves from the supermarkets by moving into quality baking made with first stoneground and then organic flours. By specialising in stoneground flours, Lister undercut the big millers for whom producing stoneground wholemeal flour is, incredibly, more expensive than doing what they do best – producing doctored flour for the cotton-wool supermarket loaf.

The week I visited Shipton Mill, Cranks, the organic and vegetarian restaurant chain, had gone into receivership. Cranks had been sold twice since it was run by the original organic pioneers, Daphne Swann and David Canter, who wrote the famous vegetarian cook books and ran the Cranks restaurant in Carnaby Street in the 1970s. New owners had decided to invest in a £1.5 million cook-chill plant where food was going to be cooked and distributed to a new chain of outlets. Expansion proved to be their undoing as the country slid into recession. For Cranks, the adage that small is beautiful proved to be true.

Lister believes something of the kind remains true for organic products. He has supplied flour for all the supermarkets' own-label plastic wrapped organic breads: Sainsbury, Tesco, Safeway and Waitrose. All were taken off the shelves in the early 1990s, after the first flush of green consumerism, because they were not meeting their selling targets. Since then expectations have become more realistic. Indeed, some loaves have gone back on the market: Sainsbury is selling crusty organic bread again, and at Waitrose organic bread takes a surprisingly large slice of the 'crusty bread' market. Lister sells them his own 'Shipton Mill' brand of *ciabata*, *petits pains* and breakfast rolls.

He thinks that if you ignore both the roller coaster of hype, which has characterised the market for 'greener' products in the past five years, and the crash in organic markets brought about by recession, there is a firm but dedicated group of organic buyers. It is a tiny market, he says, but it is slowly expanding. The fact that the multiples are stocking organic bread at all is significant. Each time there is a food scare or Sainsbury promotes organic bread by giving it favourable spacing on the shelves, sales double, then slip back again.

In the present unfriendly economic climate, he sees the best prospect over the next five years being slow growth. He advises organic producers to stick to what they do well and let people discover the benefits of organic products. The take-off point for organic bread, he believes, is likely to come when some form of subsidy is introduced for organic farming. The average loaf sells at around 45p – when there isn't a price war. Yet there are plenty of people who are prepared to pay around over 80p for crusty, whole-grain or malted loaves. Organic bread, at 20p more, is a step further up the ladder. When the long-awaited conversion grants and organic payments are introduced, it should be possible for the organic loaf to sell at the same price as the average quality loaf. Result: lift-off for the organic market.

Lister is involved in the latest added-value project with the Duchy Home Farm: an oatmeal biscuit, made partly with Highgrove flour, which could pay dividends to Duchy tenants who decide to grow organic oats. The idea began as a deal between Lister and David Wilson to earn some money out of Highgrove's organic oats. The aim has broadened to establishing a high-quality product based on organic ingredients which would act as a standard around which other organic products could gather. As the Highgrove loaf showed, there was no problem selling organic with the royal name attached. The challenge is now to establish organic brand names, which the consumer can recognise as guaranteeing quality, in the wider market.

OVERLEAF: *Shipton Mill: a seventeenth-century mill brought back to life by computer technology and producing high volumes of organic flour.*

DOES ORGANIC FARMING PAY?

So far our organic farming is doing well. With 60 per cent of this country's
organic produce coming from abroad there is clearly substantial scope for
other farmers... There are just two main impediments to success. Firstly
the high prices charged for organic produce continue to put it beyond the
reach of many consumers. Better marketing and liaison with retailers
should eventually lead to an increased market share and therefore to
reduced premiums. Secondly, the conversion period has to be regarded as
an investment, and few farmers have anything left to invest.

Lecture to the Royal Agricultural Society of England,
H.R.H. The Prince of Wales, March 1991.

NEVER MIND THE POTENTIAL WINDFALLS from adding value and the benefits
for the countryside of low-intensity agriculture, the essential question that
working farmers ask is: is organic farming profitable? And if so, how does
it compare with the profits made by a conventional farm? These are questions that
those who work at Highgrove are used to being asked, in a roundabout way or
outright, by visiting farmers who are almost all convinced that going organic
would make them worse off. The conventional farmers are almost certainly right
that the conversion period, an obstacle to all but the most resourceful and dedicated farmers, would squeeze their profits at the beginning dramatically. Later on,
their fears may be misplaced: there is evidence to believe that at present prices, a
fully-converted organic farm can be more profitable than a conventional one.

There is no doubt that converting to organic in the recession of the early
1990s, with no help from the subsidies that support other farmers, has been a
risky and expensive business. The organic farmer can truly be said to be a paragon
of the free market, since he or she operates in a small self-contained market based
on the customer's willingness to pay for healthy food, with almost no contribution from the preposterous £1.5 billion a year which the Common Agricultural
Policy pays out to support Britain's chemical farmers.

It is hard to put a firm figure on the costs of conversion because the capital
investment needed depends on the existing infrastructure of the farm and on the

*Poppies in the organic wheat at
Westonbirt. Barry Wookey avoids
them, the Prince of Wales likes
them and David Wilson seems to
think that they do not eat into the
margins too much.*

217

Eastbrook Farm: the advantage of a few yards of electric pig-fencing is that Helen Browning can easily move her free-range pigs around the farm.

temperament and resources of the farmer. Does the farm have, for instance, fencing around all of its fields to contain livestock? If not, fencing at £2 a yard can be expensive when you need several miles of it. The land bought to form the Duchy Home Farm at Highgrove consisted mostly of grassland with fences too tired to contain sheep and long-term arable land with no fences worth talking about.

A canny farmer will make any changes slowly and without borrowing money. The cost of fencing, for instance, will vary widely. Not everyone lives in Gloucestershire, in Beaufort Hunt country, and can afford the immaculate posts, rails and netting that the Prince of Wales enjoys on his estate. A more ordinary organic farmer might use an old bit of movable electric fencing, push a bit of corrugated iron in the hedge to fill a gap and hope to pay for some proper fencing after the rigours of conversion were ended.

The farms best suited to go organic are family-run, livestock/arable enterprises in the middle to west of the UK. If the farmer already rotates his grazing – as did Helen Browning's father – he will not need to invest in any new fencing on his arable land. He is also likely to have adequate water supplies for his livestock. Laying a new water main is not a task to be undertaken without an understanding bank manager. For the majority of farms, however, organic requires the purchase of more livestock, which can add substantially to capital costs. At Highgrove, livestock numbers had to go up by 20 per cent. Then there were the Soil Association's generous bedding-space requirements which reduce the holding capacity of most buildings by 20 to 30 per cent. This meant new buildings or converting old ones.

An organic farmer needs to buy new implements – a sophisticated muck spreader, able to spread this valuable commodity more thinly than he was accustomed to before. He may also need to acquire a wide modern weeder or harrow because mechanical weeding is the only option available to him in a herbicide-free system. The organic farmer is also likely to need – as did Highgrove – better storage facilities for corn, ideally including different bins to store conventional, organic and specialist wheats, barleys and oats. Farm buildings can cost tens of thousands of pounds. Alternatively a canny farmer with a small budget would borrow or hire additional capacity to tide him over.

There is no doubt that Highgrove has entailed many largely unique capital costs which some people would not have incurred. But David Landale, Secretary of the Duchy, takes the view that the costs of fencing and attractive farm buildings enhance the capital value of the estate. With Highgrove, that capital value is high. This may not be greatly consoling to the average farmer considering conversion. Nevertheless estate agents confirm that the general principle is true that fully-converted organic farms *do* command a small premium above conventional farms – whoever owns them.

Once conversion has begun, there are economic principles which apply to all farms. No one should attempt to disguise the painful shortfall in income of the first three years or so, with low yields and no premiums. This comes at the worst possible time for the farmer, once he has paid out the capital costs of conversion. Around the fourth year, if he is still in business, the viability of the enterprise changes dramatically. A business plan which Terry Summers has conducted for a hypothetical Duchy farm over an eight-year period shows that the farm made a loss for the first three or four years during the conversion to organic. Once the level of premium-grade organic produce had increased, however, the farm became more profitable than it had been under conventional management.

Since the decision to convert the whole farm was taken in 1990, Highgrove is, at the time of writing, still in the three-year trough where the majority of the farm is in conversion. It is a time for a steady nerve. Terry Summers remains cautiously optimistic. 'In ten years' time it could be such a roaring success that we won't be asking whether it will make money. I'm not being too optimistic at present because we're at that stage where the cheque book is coming out pretty much all the time. Much depends on the premiums we can obtain and the support we get from the Government,' he says with agricultural resignation.

In the unsupported free market which has prevailed up to now, the organic farmer has depended for his profitability, as we have seen, on premiums. Premiums are something with which the consumer is wholly familiar when paying for quality products, whether it is Savile Row raincoats, German motor cars, certain American computers, French perfumes, wild salmon, or crusty wholegrain bread. Where organic markets have been successfully established, such as in wheat, barley and oats, the organic farmer may presently expect to gain a premium price for his grain of 40 to 80 per cent above conventional. According to figures prepared for the Duchy by Terry Summers, the organic farmer can bank on gross margins for wheat and oats of £90 an acre above conventional crops on the same land.

Fig. 1 Comparison of profit margins from organic and conventional cereals

	Conventional	Organic
Wheat	2.8 tons per acre at £115/ton	1.5 tons per acre at £225/ton
Total sales	£322	£337
Less: Seed, fertilisers, sprays (seed only for organic)	92	17
Gross margin (per acre)	£230	£320
Oats	2.7 tons at £105/ton	1.7 tons at £188/ton
Total sales	£283	£320
Less: Seed, fertilisers, sprays (seed only for organic)	80	20
Gross margin (per acre)	£203	£300

Figure 1: The Gross Margin system separates the costs of an enterprise which are incurred each time you add one acre or one animal to that enterprise (Variable Costs) from those costs which do not change with such small adjustments (Fixed Costs). Variable costs include seeds, fertiliser, sprays, feed, veterinary bills and medicines. When these costs are deducted from net sales (per acre or per animal) the Gross Margin is the result. Variations in acreage of crops and number of animals can be compared to show the best balance of enterprises for a given level of Fixed Costs – labour, machinery and power, rent and property-repair costs and general overheads (office costs, fees, sundries, etc.).

Markets for organic beef and lamb are less certain. Highgrove has sold organic beef for premiums of around 20 per cent. Premiums are lower because only parts of the animal can be sold in organic markets. (Consumer interest in organic offal or organic dog food was zero at the time of writing.) The market for organic milk is in its infancy and, unless it is made into cheese, it is hard to extract a premium until better methods of distribution are set up. Early attempts foundered in the recession but a cooperative of British organic milk producers (with the memorable acronym, BOMP) is now actively seeking stable markets and added value for organic milk.

A true comparison of profitability between organic and conventional farming can only be attempted properly over a full rotation of seven years. The continually-cropping arable farm can expect to produce a crop off a given field – call it Boggy Bottom – each year. The organic system works by rotation, so the organic farmer has to average out his income over the four years that Boggy Bottom grows cash crops and the three years which it will spend in grass. Figure 2 shows a comparison of average gross margins for conventional and organic systems over a seven-year rotation.

Fig. 2 Comparison of profits from organic and conventional farming systems over a seven-year rotation

Year	Conventional Cropping (per acre) Crop	Gross Margin Average £	High £	Organic Rotation (per acre) Crop	Gross Margin Average £	High £
1	Winter wheat – milling	229	290	Grass ley – sheep	135	150
2	Winter wheat – feed	196	251	Grass ley – beef	150	175
3	Winter barley	158	200	Grass ley – beef/sheep	145	170
4	Oil-seed rape	232	270	Winter wheat	320	400
5	Winter wheat	229	290	Winter oats	300	375
6	Winter barley	158	200	Spring beans	260	300
7	Linseed	190	225	Spring wheat	280	370
Total	Gross margin (£)	1392	1726	Gross margin (£)	1590	1940

Conventional gross margins from Nix's Farm Management Handbook (1991)
Organic gross margins from Duchy Home Farm and *Organic Farming* by Nicolas Lampkin (Farming Press, 1990)
Organic premiums are 40 to 80 per cent above conventional for wheat, 65 per cent for oats, 35 per cent for field beans.

It is reasonable to assume that premiums will continue to be paid for all organic foods. But this, of course, is no more than an assumption. If no premium is paid – and this is the nightmare of conventional farmers looking to convert to organic – it is doubtful that the organic farmer will survive under the rules that have existed up to now, unless he or she has made a business out of adding value, which is an option. As Terry Summers put it in a letter to David Landale: 'I am sure that, provided premiums remain at around 50 per cent for cash crops and 15 per cent for livestock products, organic farming will pay. Without premiums it cannot survive unless the value is added beyond the farm gate. Heaven knows

OVERLEAF: *A fine crop of organic oats: two yards around the edge have been rotavated to prevent incursions of cleavers and sterile brome.*

enough value is added at the moment. Your wheat flakes on the breakfast table cost around £1,500 per ton. The farmer gets £120 – for conventional produce.'

At present the possibility of goods flooding the organic market seems extremely remote. Even in recession, the demand for organic goods far outstrips supply in most sectors and suppliers are importing to keep up. For the next eight to ten years, at least, organic seems likely to attract a premium. What smarts with organic farmers though, is that they are having to compete with growing imports of subsidised organic products from abroad and their products must compete at home beside those of conventional farmers who receive an average subsidy of £135 an acre. What is likely to change is that subsidies for conversion and for the process of organic farming are about to be introduced under the reforms of the Common Agricultural Policy piloted through in spring 1992.

For the majority of sympathetic farmers, conversion has been the sticking point. It has been difficult to see how the average farmer could be persuaded to go organic, without enduring real hardship, unless conversion was subsidised. It has been argued by the organic farming world that government subsidy would be correcting an imbalance caused by subsidies directed for the past forty years towards turning traditional farms into hedgeless, fenceless, arable prairies and encouraging farmers to spray their land as often as possible. Subsidy, it is argued, is also a way of paying farmers for environmental services that the public wants, instead of for food which the market should provide.

An organic conversion grant was promised by John Gummer, the Agriculture Minister, as long ago as 1990. The initial idea was that support for organic farming would be introduced under the EC 'extensification' directive, which aimed to reduce surpluses by reducing chemical inputs. Other countries, Germany and Denmark, introduced conversion grants under this scheme. Germany has 600,000 acres converted to organic compared to Britain's 100,000 acres. The Ministry of Agriculture claimed that help for organic farmers in Britain would have been against EC law, though nobody seems to have taken Germany or Denmark to the European Court for introducing their schemes.

Now the environmental annexe of the deal agreed by Ray MacSharry, called in obligatory Euro-speak the 'agri-environment package', looks as if it will provide the means to impose what organic farmers have long been asking for: the introduction of both conversion grants *and* support for organic farmers who have already converted. The Ministry is, at the time of writing, drawing up a scheme. Mr Gummer has even appeared to concede, in early 1992, that organic farming could play a central part in reducing EC surpluses *and* agricultural pollution. It remains to be seen if that is how it will work out.

If realistic conversion grants were available, and payments comparable to those which keep the rest of Britain's subsidised farmers in business, the economic climate for organic agriculture would be transformed. Many farmers might be persuaded to reconsider the organic route. Prices to the consumer would fall, perhaps even to the magic level where organic goods would compete with conventional goods on an equal footing. It is a fair assumption that there would be a far healthier take-up of organic produce. Subsidies would compensate for the loss of premium as more producers entered the market.

There will be only one speck in the organic milk. The organic farmer, who has until now been exposed to true market forces, is likely to become as dependent on government support as the conventional farmer is today. This will be a shame. Not only will it mean becoming dependent upon that huge, occasionally corrupt, and largely-incomprehensible bureaucratic machine, the Common Agricultural Policy. But it may well mean that, as organic farmers and environmentalists are given a stake in the CAP reforms, true reform of the boundaries of the agricultural market remains as far off as ever.

There are many who believe that instead of, or as well as, supporting organic farming, governments should use 'the polluter pays' principle to encourage more farmers to farm in a more sustainable manner for the atmosphere and the countryside by placing high taxes or restrictions on sprays and inorganic fertilisers. Until the environmental costs of agricultural pollution are 'internalised' within the market, support will always be needed to allow the low-input farmer to compete on the same basis as the spray-mad cereal baron. This would, however, require an application of the 'polluter pays' principle to an industry which has so far been conspicuous for its ability to lobby against it.

The point is surely that society should reward through the market those who reduce pollution by removing pesticides and herbicides from use; who by reducing stocking rates improve the welfare of animals and preserve wildlife habitats; who reduce output and therefore surpluses; and who take care that they build up long-term soil fertility. Society shows every sign of wanting to do just that. Yet for the present, and for the foreseeable future, farmers are being paid large sums of money under the CAP system to continue farming intensively on most of their land and then have to be compensated handsomely for *not* polluting drinking water or *not* damaging wildlife sites. This is both mad and unjust.

A HARVEST
OF WEEDS

THE PERIOD IN WHICH this book was written was a time of upheaval for European agriculture. The cost of buying, storing and disposing of gigantic mountains of surplus food, mostly corn grown because of the historically high subsidies paid to cereal growers, once again threatened to bankrupt Europe's Common Agricultural Policy. The rest of the world was tired of subsidised EC wheat, rape-seed oil, wine and other products being dumped onto their domestic markets. The Uruguay round of world trade talks under the General Agreement on Tariffs and Trade was stalled because of the huge barrier to free trade that the CAP had become. The United States was determined that EC farm prices should be reduced by at least 30 per cent. Reform of the CAP had become a political imperative.

There were many imaginative ways in which the European leviathan could have been tamed, but time was short. So the European Commission's answer to the surpluses that were threatening to bankrupt the Community was to take land out of production. 'Set-aside', and lots more of it, was their barren stratagem to the ever-growing output that was threatening the CAP's survival. The reforms of May 1992 took such Herculean political efforts to stitch together that it is fair to assume that they will be the basis of European agricultural policy for some time to come. At one stroke the Common Agricultural Policy was made more absurd than it has ever been before. However, almost as an afterthought, some welcome opportunities for the environment and for organic farmers were incorporated for the first time – but these, as yet, receive only 1 per cent of the total CAP budget.

The reform package put together by Ray MacSharry, the Irish-born Agriculture Commissioner, contained a momentous shift in policy, away from the principle of subsidising farm prices to a new principle of directly subsidising farmers, which it was hoped would remove part of the incentive to produce ever more crops. Under the package agreed, crop subsidies would be allowed to fall over three

What the countryside could look like but increasingly does not.

227

years, and to protect their livelihoods and compensate for the loss of income, farmers would be paid a sum of up to £84 an acre for all their land, provided that they took 15 per cent of it out of production. This money is social support in all but name.

The labyrinth of European agricultural policy has a habit of breeding monsters. The first of these is the likely size of these direct payments which will be paid to keep farmers farming. The British Government's political objective was to ensure that Britain's farmers, who traditionally farm larger acreages than farmers in the rest of Europe, would not be faced with a smaller slice of the cake than everyone else. The result of a British victory on this principle, however, is that farmers will receive some impressive sums in subsidy. A farmer with 2,000 acres of productive arable land could walk away with £168,000 a year of taxpayers' money in direct subsidy, before adding up the income he makes from his crops. Of that, £142,000 is compensation for receiving lower prices for his crops, and £25,200 for setting aside 15 per cent of his land. Many farming commentators were understandably apprehensive about how this would be received by the public during the deepest recession since the 1930s.

The greatest monster in the labyrinth, of course, is the idea of paying farmers to do nothing – the surrealistic concept of 'set aside'. Once the reforms are under way, the British countryside is going to take on a wholly new appearance as 1.5 million acres of all arable land – an area slightly larger than Lincolnshire – is taken out of production. Fifteen per cent of all arable land on every farm will be growing docks, thistles, cleavers, blackgrass and poppies. The fields will not be ploughed, sprayed, or grazed, just mowed once a year – or else will be cultivated as a 'bare summer fallow'. Around the urban fringe, the sheer redundancy of these fields may catch the eye of developers. The cost to the public of paying farmers to do nothing on this land – the set-aside bill – will be £124 million a year.

There are many people, farmers, environmentalists and organic farmers alike, who can think of many better things that could be done to the countryside with this money. Even Mr Gummer, the Minister of Agriculture who negotiated the deal, conceded that 'set-aside does have many disadvantages'. The set-aside bill, after all, dwarfs every existing present measure for inducing farmers to manage or recreate uneconomic features of the countryside – such as hay meadows, water meadows or dry-stone walls – principal among these being the environmentally sensitive areas (ESAs) which apply in, say, the Somerset Levels and Constable Country. Most people outside government believe set-aside is, at best, a missed opportunity. At worst it could be a public relations disaster for the farming industry. Moreover, the subsidies given as 'social' payments could actually fuel the further intensification of high-input, highly polluting farming on the rest of the land that is farmed. It looks likely that jobs in the countryside will be reduced further and many small farm businesses forced into the arms of bigger neighbours hungry to restore their lost 15 per cent of land area.

The alternative to set-aside that many farmers and environmentalists wanted to see would have entailed paying the farmer to do something active – such as managing uneconomic features like as hay meadows, oak woods, unimproved pasture,

and water meadows outside the small area of the country presently designated as ESAs – instead of paying farmers to do nothing. But this was, bafflingly, not a political option.

There is no doubt that set-aside will have some environmental advantages, depending on how long the land is left unused. But even the Government's own conservation advisers concede these are largely incidental to the principal bureaucratic purpose of set-aside, which is surplus reduction.

There are, to complicate matters, three forms of set-aside. The first that is to be rushed in, because of the desperate urgency of reining-back production, is one-year rotational set-aside. This kind applies to strips at least 20 metres wide and three-quarters of an acre in size which must be mown at least once a year. If cereal stubbles are allowed naturally to regenerate, as will be permitted, there may be advantages for the flora and insects of cereal fields and, as a result, the grey partridge. Set-aside may provide new hunting territory for barn owls. But there will be disadvantages, too. The requirement that the green stubbles or green cover must be mown at least once by 1 July will mean that skylarks, lapwings and partridges which like the undisturbed set-aside fields, are likely to have their nests and young chopped to pieces. If the chosen option is 'bare summer fallow' it will have to be cultivated by 1 June – with the same sterilising effect. The rules for one-year rotational set-aside have been calculated to minimise the potential ecological benefits of neglected land.

Docks, couch grass, hogweed and perhaps the odd thistle: set-aside in all its glory. This field was set aside under the original five-year scheme which had slightly different rules to one-year rotational set-aside introduced in the autumn of 1992. The newer scheme, which offers the option of a summer fallow, has even fewer ecological benefits and is an even greater waste of public money.

An EC grain mountain.
Historically, farmers have been
offered a high subsidised price for
their corn provided that the crop
reached certain minimum
standards. Result: surpluses.
Under EC reforms, farmers will
be paid subsidy direct and the
price will be allowed to sink
nearer to the world market price.

Then there is fixed set-aside, the details of which have yet to be devised at the time of writing, which is likely to be applied to around 20 per cent of the acreage of the farm. Depending on the determination of the Ministry, this kind of set-aside could be used to produce greater environmental benefits. Some of the options are nectar-rich hay meadows, a network of wildlife corridors through the farmed landscape, and buffer-zones beside rivers to stop pollution run-off and collapsed banks through over-grazing. But there is nothing in the regulations to say that this form of set-aside should be an environmental measure, or where it should be targeted. Its benefits will depend on the men from the Ministry having the knowledge and the firmness to tell farmers where these strips should go – in conjunction with a whole-farm management plan, for example. Given the Ministry's shaky record on conservation matters, this seems unlikely to happen.

Thirdly, there is long-term set aside, a twenty-year environmental measure which will attract a higher subsidy and will provide positive environmental measures such as the creation of ponds, farm woodlands and wildlife habitats, with some reductions of surpluses as well. This is an attractive measure. But, under the present Commission rules, farmers will be allowed to use long-term set-aside only *if* they have already taken up the 15 per cent of compulsory set-aside. Given farmers' understandable reluctance to take their land out of production this is unlikely to be very attractive. The same conditions apply to the brand-new organic conversion and payments scheme which will be introduced under the reform package.

Around one of the darker corners in the labyrinth of the CAP reforms is a detail about money. The first two forms of set-aside are funded under the main CAP budget, and therefore farmers have to be paid for them virtually on demand. The environmental measures, such as long-term set-aside and the organic conversion scheme (the measures for which farmers would actually be paid for doing something) exist under what is known as the 'agri-environment programme', a bolt-on annexe to the main reforms. The funding of the 'agri-environment programme' amounts to £285 million a year, little more than 1 per cent of the total CAP budget of about £25 billion. Thus, neither the option of being paid for better countryside management nor the option of turning one's land over to organic farming has been made a real alternative to the absurd system of payments to farmers which compensate for falling prices and for set-aside – even though organic farming could have produced an immediate and quantifiable reduction in surpluses. For the present there is reason to doubt the idea expounded enthusiastically by Mr Gummer – that the environment has been brought 'into the heart of the CAP'.

As to the price-cutting part of the EC reforms, these do begin to introduce some sanity to commodity markets and some tangible benefits for the countryside. Farmers will eventually receive nearer £80 than £120 a ton for a crop of wheat, so there is, theoretically, less incentive towards the 'prophylactic' spraying of land that was seen in the 1970s and 1980s. Farming advisory bodies such as ADAS have been advising farmers to look carefully at the costs of what they are spraying – with lower prices, the efficacy of an extra topping of nitrogen becomes a much more interesting calculation.

Yet the dangers of the current EC reforms look likely to outweigh the benefits. Some agricultural experts predict that set-aside will give farmers an incentive to cheat. It will encourage them to plough up every spare acre to find more land to remain in production. As there are no laws to prevent ploughing this must mean farewell to more permanent pasture, more wild flowers and damp, snipey field-bottoms. In the United States where set-aside has been used in one form or another since the 1930s, surpluses resolutely refused to go down because of fiddling. This was referred to euphemistically as 'slippage'. In the end the US Government was forced to limit the amount that farmers could claim – incidentally, this principle is precisely what the Government has managed to reverse in the EC deal in the interests of equity for British farmers.

Monitoring the new set-aside schemes will certainly be a bureaucratic nightmare. As this book is written, there is talk of the Ministry taking on 40 per cent more staff in its regional offices just to monitor set-aside. All this job-creation will be, ironically, to ensure that the farmers are doing nothing on 15 per cent of their land. Aerial surveys are being carried out, at undisclosed cost, to ensure that farmers don't cheat and satellite monitoring has been suggested.

Yet despite all these efforts there is some doubt whether set-aside will achieve the intended surplus-reductions. Wherever you go, from the corridors of Whitehall to the boulevards of Brussels and from the Farmers' Club to the headquarters of Friends of

Ayrshires on permanent pasture at Broadfield Farm valley – wild flowers of limestone pasture, such as ladies' bedstraw, thrive on constant nibbling and no artificial fertiliser.

LEFT: *Windrows of manure take ten months, turned twice, to compost down into friable matter which is quickly absorbed by the soil.*

the Earth, no one really thinks that the MacSharry reforms will last more than a few years. Large questions remain unanswered, as Sir Leon Brittan, Vice-President of the European Commission, mused in a speech at the 1992 Royal Show: 'Have we really removed the incentive to produce as much as possible? And will it seem wise and acceptable to rely on ever-increasing set-aside to achieve our objectives?'

Ministers and civil servants murmur privately that a few years down the road the whole system will have to be changed. And if 15 per cent set-aside doesn't work, why should 30 per cent? Meanwhile the public, and, no doubt, various House of Commons select committees, are likely to be troubled by all these weeds – and the thought of what they are costing the taxpayer. It is fair to assume that the bureaucratic solution of paying farmers large sums of money for doing nothing will sooner or later become a scandal.

There are many senior people in the agriculture business who believe that we could have reduced surpluses more cheaply, and more reliably, with considerable benefits for the countryside, by other means. One simple expedient would have been to place taxes or quotas on nitrogen fertiliser. This would have created a market in manure – of which there is currently too much in the West of the country – created more mixed farms over time and benefited the soil. As one agricultural economist told me: 'If someone had told me three years ago that a government would have been prepared to spend £84 an acre on the countryside, I would not have believed it. For £84 an acre you could have had a dream countryside – and lower production.'

OVERLEAF: *There is no subsidy or encouragement for farmers to leave wildlife corridors like these, outside a few Environmentally Sensitive Areas which cover perhaps 5 per cent of the country. But all farmers are now to be paid £84 an acre to do nothing on part of their land under the principle of set-aside.*

So the CAP reforms have protected the livelihoods of farmers but they are unlikely to achieve their goal of reducing surpluses. They have also failed to integrate concerns about the countryside and pollution into farm policy – except in a bolt-on programme which will be insufficiently funded to provide a real alternative to paying farmers for doing nothing. Why, one might ask, are such deals struck if, as we often hear, many countries in Europe are so 'green'?

The answer is that the people of Europe may be green but the bureaucrats of Europe do not necessarily feel any pressure to be so – and nor do many European agriculture ministers. To his credit, Mr John Gummer has made it a priority to make environmental concerns a more integrated part of the CAP, but it remains the case that many of his colleagues in Europe are under less pressure from their pressure groups when it comes to the countryside. Oddly, the protection of nature is an environmental issue of greater concern in Britain than in Northern Europe, where much environmental concern is focused on pollution. Another reason for the strange ecological philistinism of the EC is that agricultural agreements are made by *agriculture* ministers, and drawn up by *agricultural* civil servants in the twelve Member States and in the *agriculture* directorate of the European Commission. The agriculture directorate, Directorate-General VI (DGVI), has almost no contact whatsoever with the directorate for the environment, Directorate-General (DGXI).

An illustration of this institutionalised lack of communication happened on an occasion when the Prince of Wales was planning to visit the Commission. The Prince of Wales's Private Secretary, Commander Richard Aylard, told an official in the office of Monsieur Jacques Delors, the President of the Commission, that the Prince would like to attend a joint meeting of EC Directorates VI and XI. The official was perplexed. Not only was this not possible, he explained, but DGVI was responsible for agriculture and DGXI was responsible for the environment. The Prince would have to recognise that the two had no contact with each other. After a considerable amount of discussion such a meeting – a first – *did* prove possible to arrange but it was a year or more before it took place, since by then the Prince had been forced to postpone the visit for other reasons.

People on all sides of the debate over a federal Europe would agree that the difficulties of devising an agricultural policy capable of operating from Aberdeen to Athens are formidable. So, one might ask, why bother? The CAP is really an historic anachronism, dating from the time when there were only six countries in the Common Market and the CAP was the symbol of trade harmonisation. It frequently occurs to many people involved with its Byzantine workings (the *mot juste* to describe the CAP has yet to be invented: its complexities would have boggled even the bureaucrats of Byzantium) how much easier things would be if the majority of decisions about European agriculture were made at national level.

The repatriation of the Common Agricultural Policy is something that is talked about with yearning by its critics. Under a devolved CAP, the Commission would be responsible simply for ensuring fair competition, which is what it does with any other industry, instead of being, as it is now, the holder of the purse-strings for a massive central fund for subsidising agriculture. Countries with vociferous farming minorities could pay social support to their farmers if they wished, as they do now under the CAP, while other perhaps more enlightened (or more ecologically-degraded) countries could pay farmers to carry out environmental tasks in the countryside. The Commission would only be responsible for ensuring that rules were harmonised and the prices for farm produce were not subject to unfair competition. The removal of the Commission's role as the planner of all payments to farmers from Scotland to the Turkish border would give national parliaments responsibility to devise their own more locally-acceptable policies, as they do now in, say, forestry. In fact the Commission's new reforms, based as they are on a move to a world market price for crops plus 'regional' payments might have been devised as the prelude to CAP repatriation.

Wherever the financial heart of British agricultural policy is located, one thing is surely true: common sense dictates that it is desirable for farmers to be paid for real things – whether these are crops, or environmental 'goods', or even verifiable low-intensity systems of farming – rather than to mix them all up with social support in an agricultural policy which continues to subsidise pollution, energy use and the destruction of species.

Mr Gummer's Garden

There are some important similarities between today's situation and the events
that led to the 1947 Agriculture Act...Then, consensus was achieved on the
need to invest in our farming industry to deliver what society needed – large
quantities of relatively cheap, high quality food . . .I believe a similar kind of
consensus is emerging today – this time for a farming enterprise which is
economically viable, responsive to the needs of consumers, socially acceptable,
environmentally friendly and moving towards genuine sustainability.

Lecture to the Royal Agricultural Society of England,
H.R.H. The Prince of Wales, March 1991.

I F INTENSIVE AGRICULTURAL METHODS cause surpluses, pollution, and the erad-
ication of many species from farmland (not to mention occasional risks to
food), is not less intensive farming the answer? It is a question which seems to
come back with renewed force each time the CAP slips back into the red.
Defenders of industrial forms of agriculture insist that farming in Britain must
remain 'competitive' and not seek to isolate itself from technological advances.
What they usually mean is that the present form of agriculture which so often
passes on the cost of its pollution to someone else, or some*thing* else, should continue to get away with it. In fact there are already the early signs that even mainstream agriculture may be moving in a different, more 'sustainable' direction.

As farm prices have fallen farmers have been taking a greater interest in traditional farming methods as a way of solving problems. Some of the things that
organic farmers have been doing for years are beginning to creep back into ordinary farming: rotations, for example, as a way of building up the humus in the
soil; and rearing pigs outdoors, now that animal welfare regulations are making
intensive pig-units more expensive. Many more traditional farming practices will
become attractive as long as farm-gate prices continue to fall and the underlying
subsidy to pollute with a battery of expensive chemicals is reduced. An example
of the greater sanity that reduced subsidy brings to agriculture is provided by

*An arbour covered with
honeysuckle in the walled
garden at Highgrove.*

239

Clover leys have come back and fertiliser use has decreased in countries, such as New Zealand, which do not subsidise farm prices.

New Zealand, which cannot afford to subsidise its farmers and whose goods are sold at the world market price. There, clover leys are widely used as a way of building fertility in grassland and pesticide use is minimised.

In Britain a new initiative called Linking Environment and Farming (LEAF), with a test-bed of twenty farms, has begun to use methods it calls 'integrated crop management' which are midway between conventional continuous cropping systems and organic agriculture. The idea is to reduce the use of fertilisers and chemical pesticides by using rotations and enhancing the habitat of natural predators. This is another intriguing indication that conventional farmers are beginning to think hard about 'sustainability'. Organic farmers are inclined to be sceptical about the environmental gains of these half-way houses, but they may also remember the saying that imitation is one of the sincerest forms of flattery.

Even the Ministry of Agriculture, the home of opposition to low-input farming for so long, has made useful progress in recent years in removing some of the obvious unfairnesses which were holding back organic agriculture. The Ministry still prefers to see organic goods as a market which is not being satisfied rather than as a form of farming which is inherently 'safer'. But in the early 1990s the Ministry has actually begun to carry out the objective research that organic farmers have been demanding to quantify some of the agricultural and environmental benefits of the organic system. This is real progress. Yet only parts of the Ministry are convinced by the case for low-input farming. Some of the most senior civil servants in the Ministry and the majority of the farming establishment still regard organic farmers as a bunch of holy fools.

It is worth summarising the progress since 1985 to see what has changed – very largely as a result of the influence of John Gummer, as Minister of State and then Minister of Agriculture. Until that year, when the first MAFF research project into organic agriculture was commissioned, all state-funded research and advice was channelled into developing the most productive farming systems. Since organic systems were less productive, if also considerably less polluting, this meant that none of the millions of pounds spent each year on research and development were of much help to organic agriculture. ADAS offered the conventional farmer, on the other hand, free (until comparatively recently) instructions on how to grow any crop, down to the recommended sprays, the quantities of nitrogen and the exact profit margin he could expect to get.

Until recently, the Ministry did not accept that it had a responsibility to understand and research alternative farming methods. Asked in 1986 why the Government did not fund organic research, Michael Jopling, then Minister of Agriculture, replied: 'Given competing claims for limited research resources, such a contribution could not be justified at public expense.' When, in 1987, John Gummer decided to visit an organic farm, his civil servants tried to discourage him. Even today, there remains acute scepticism in the Ministry towards both less intensive forms of agriculture, and the need for farmers to be paid for environmental 'goods'. Many civil servants at MAFF appear still to take the view that environmental care is the responsibility of the Department of the Environment.

From 1987 a different theme emerged in the Ministry's dealings. Mr Gummer began to rethink the Ministry's approach to the growing organic market. The time was one of the ascending importance of 'greenery' – the Prime Minister Margaret Thatcher's recognition of the threat of global warming came in a speech to the Royal Society in autumn 1988. Gummer saw that the first problem that organic farming faced was an internal feud over how many 'external inputs' should be allowed. He brought together Britain's organic organisations (the Soil Association on one side and the Organic Farmers and Growers on the other) under UKROFS, the UK Register of Organic Food Standards, chaired by Professor Colin Spedding of Reading University. UKROFS set about evolving a national set of standards, a system of inspectors and a certified registration system for organic farmers. UKROFS published its all-important definition of organic farming in 1989, which described the point of organic farming as 'to produce optimum quantities of food of high nutritional quality by using management practices which aim to avoid the use of agro-chemical inputs and which minimise damage to the environment and wildlife'. In an unusual display of successful British lobbying, the UKROFS definition became the basis for the incoming EC regulation controlling organic food.

In 1990, Gummer decided that MAFF should have an organic strategy, and instructed civil servants in MAFF's Agricultural Resource Policy Division to devise one. This document, when it arrived the following year, signalled an important change in thinking. The strategy said that organic food accounts for only about 1 per cent of food sales in the UK but perhaps as much as 75 per cent of this was met from imports of uncertain organic quality. It argued that the Soil Association's target of a 20 per cent share of the food market by 2000 was optimistic. But an

OVERLEAF: *Harvesting at Babdown. The way ahead – from the conventional farmer's point of view – is to maximise the yield of whatever crops attract the highest price. Only farmers working to Soil Association rules bind themselves to maintaining a flowery species-rich countryside with no financial gain.*

increase to only 10 per cent would, its authors enthused, represent a £1.9 billion share of the food market. This would be a very substantial sector indeed. Yet, the authors mused, unless imports were reduced, the share going to British farmers would be less than £500 million.

At last the case for low-input agriculture was translated into the kind of thinking the Ministry feels comfortable with: British farmers needed to produce more to replace imports. The strategy called for a research programme to assess what methods of organic farming were suited to UK conditions and what the environmental benefits and disbenefits might be. Many of these questions had lain on the table for forty years. A research programme worth £500,000 in the first year, and rising to £1.5 million a year by 1994-5, was announced in autumn 1991. (The Ministry placed its research, cunningly, with its own experimental farms just as they were about to be cut back.) The priorities were cautious: a number of variety trials for organic crops, farm trials to find out how organic farming could be carried out most profitably on a variety of soils, and what organic techniques could show conventional systems. These trials would last up to eight years. MAFF also decided to try to quantify, once and for all, the most potentially polluting part of the organic system, nitrate leaching released by cultivating fertility-building leys. Organic farmers claim that *over the spread of a rotation* they produce only 60 per cent of the pollution of a conventional bag-nitrogen system.

In terms of the £250-million-a-year agriculture research budget the grant was not large. But for the first time it was in proportion to the size of the organic market. The Government had decided to stop ignoring the low-input sector and to start seeing what its potential might be. The message that British farmers were missing out on potential markets was repeated by the Prime Minister, John Major, at the Oxford Farming Conference in early 1992.

The billion-ecu question still to be addressed was whether low-input farming could provide an answer to the gigantic mountains of surplus food troubling the EC. Organic farming provides assured surplus reductions of up to 50 per cent of output for cereals, the most intractable problem, compared with the 15 per cent optimistically expected from set-aside. Given the need for CAP reform, was there not room for an inspired marriage of convenience?

Few would suggest that organic agriculture could feed the country immediately or provide it with the blend of livestock and crops that the market demands – the Prince of Wales certainly has not tried to do so. But he and an increasing number of people have begun to ask whether a flourishing organic sector might not be a preferable option to set-aside. As yet, a take-up of organic as an alternative to set-aside is not an option. Might not the ecological lessons gained in the process exert a powerful influence in guiding mainstream agriculture along more sustainable lines?

Mr Gummer appeared to address this pivotal question in the spring of 1992, when he said that he *was* persuaded that organic methods could help cut EC surpluses and benefit the environment by reducing pollution at the same time. 'Organic farming,' he said, after meeting organic farming leaders, 'can play a central role within the CAP's agri-environment package.' This clearly amounted to a remarkable shift in MAFF thinking.

Thanks to Mr Gummer and his colleagues in Denmark, France and Germany, a small EC support scheme for organic farming is now expected to come about. Organic farming thus stands on the verge of a take-off which could transform the membership of the organic movement as more conventional farmers try their hand at farming without chemicals.

Mr Gummer's support for organic methods would seem to reflect a growing personal conviction that a convergence of organic and conventional agricultural systems is the likely face of the future. Mr Gummer, I understand, has taken to gardening organically on three of the eight acres around his home in Suffolk. That makes him the first organically-minded Minister of Agriculture in history. Gardening is not farming, but it is an indication of how times have changed.

Intellectually speaking, Mr Gummer is not alone. In the universities, too, there are signs of a growing interest in 'sustainable' agriculture and thus in traditional farming methods. The popularity of university courses on sustainable agriculture has meant that even academics who have formerly expressed scepticism about some of the austere principles of the organic movement have rushed to satisfy the demand for the sake of their departments. Certain university departments, such as Wye College, part of London University, offer courses which include teaching on organic and other low-input systems.

Great uncertainty still surrounds the meaning of the term 'sustainability', for the definition was framed in a global context, not a regional or national one. It comes from 'Our Common Future', the report of the World Commission on Environment and Development – generally known as the Brundtland report after Mrs Gro Harlem Brundtland, Prime Minister of Norway, who chaired the working party that wrote it. The definition they used in 1987 was:

> Sustainable development is development that meets the needs of the present without compromising the ability of future generations to meet their own needs.

This definition of sustainability implies a whole range of ethical issues from the use of fossil fuels and other finite resources such as phosphates, to the destruction of animal species. On biological diversity, the Brundtland report makes a point which applies from the timber industries of South America to the tourism industry of the South Downs:

> The loss of plant and animal species can greatly limit the options of future generations; so sustainable development requires the conservation of plant and animal species.

Over 170 countries signed up to the task of promoting 'sustainability', as defined by Brundtland, in the Rio Declaration in June 1992.

The task of establishing what 'sustainability' means for agriculture will provide gainful employment for academics for many years to come. In the meantime, as Professor David Leaver of Wye College, no uncritical supporter of organic agriculture, told me: there is little doubt that the movement in agriculture internationally is towards more sustainable systems, one of which is organic. In the intellectual powerhouses of farming the mission of rethinking agriculture to incorporate a wider definition of food quality and better environmental protection is moving very fast indeed. Britain, though, still lags behind parts of the Continent; the University of Kassel, in Germany, for example, now has four professors of organic agriculture.

Sadly, there are always those who disagree with change, even when that change is the rediscovery of the wisdom of earlier generations. So it was when the Prince of Wales brushed with the farming establishment in 1991. Prince Charles had agreed that year to take on the role of President of the Royal Agricultural Society of England (RASE), the leading body which runs the annual Royal Show, the largest agricultural show in the country. In his presidential speech, he set out his view of the emerging consensus: the need for a new agriculture which was (in the words which begin this chapter) economically viable, responsive to the concerns of consumers, environmentally friendly and moving towards sustainability. He invited the RASE to consult widely with farmers, consumers and environmentalists to improve understanding of what was required.

At his instigation the RASE set up a study group under the chairmanship of Sir Derek (now Lord) Barber, former Chairman of the Countryside Commission, and including Lord Selbourne, a farmer himself and Chairman of the Government's Joint Nature Conservation Committee. The report they produced, 'The State of Agriculture in the United Kingdom', amounted to a robust defence of pesticides, present intensive livestock practices and future biotechnology and contained a loud echo of some of its chairman's known anti-organic views.

Few would disagree with the study group's economic analysis – so far as it went. It advocated a cut in farm prices to more realistic levels. It called for the separation of agricultural payments from social support. It welcomed the idea that farmers should be rewarded instead for environmental services they performed. Where the group perplexed many who believed that their purpose was to achieve consensus was in its refusal to comprehend the word 'sustainable' in anything other than its short-term economic sense. Significantly, it avoided any consideration of the fact that the universally respected 'polluter pays' principle seldom applies to agriculture. It wrote off organic and other low-intensity agriculture as satisfying 'niche markets'. Most perplexingly, the RASE group concluded – against the weight of evidence – that conventional farming practice had not ruined soil, created dangers in food, or despoiled the countryside. Their report reached the surprising conclusion:

> ... Modern farm systems have not degraded soils nor have they been destructive of wildlife on a wholesale basis. There are, however, local instances of insensitive or careless management ... and steps should be taken to protect the erosion of biodiversity in these instances for the cumulative effect of local damage will threaten the overall picture.

We must assume that this statement was written to amuse or out of a sense of mischief, for on the basis of the evidence it is simply not true. It is difficult to see

This area has been set aside as a special reserve and contains a wide variety of habitats: woodland, scrub, old pasture and marsh. Each habitat is managed in order to retain the wide variety of species that are present - 172 species of plants have been recorded in this area alone.

Long-term set-aside holds out hope of recreating some wildlife habitats: but it runs the risk of such land being considered 'waste' and thus becoming vulnerable to development. Surely it is better to set aside synthetic chemicals and fertilisers?

how much more 'wholesale' you can get than the litany of habitat destruction recorded by the Nature Conservancy Council between 1945 and 1984, which I reprise: 95 per cent loss or significant damage to herb-rich hay meadows; 80 per cent loss or damage to lowland grassland on chalk and Jurassic limestone; 40 per cent loss of lowland heaths; 30–50 per cent loss of ancient lowland woods; 140,000 miles of hedges pulled out; 60 per cent of lowland raised mires destroyed; 30 per cent loss or significant damage to upland grasslands, heaths and blanket bogs, through afforestation and hill land 'improvement'. Pesticides are still having an effect on a wholesale basis throughout the country – as can be seen, for example, from the devastating declines of birds of farmland. There is no other industry which is permitted to spread its poisons on the land with such abandon.

Reactionary agricultural 'modernists' of the kind who wrote the RASE report regularly assert that the country could not feed itself if alternative agricultural methods were adopted. There is some doubt as to whether that assertion is true. The evidence comes from part of the American scientific establishment, the National Research Council. Their 1989 report 'Alternative Agriculture' constitutes the most thorough investigation yet of a wide variety of farming practices, from the reduction of inputs in a conventional system to the adoption of a complete organic conversion. They concluded:

247

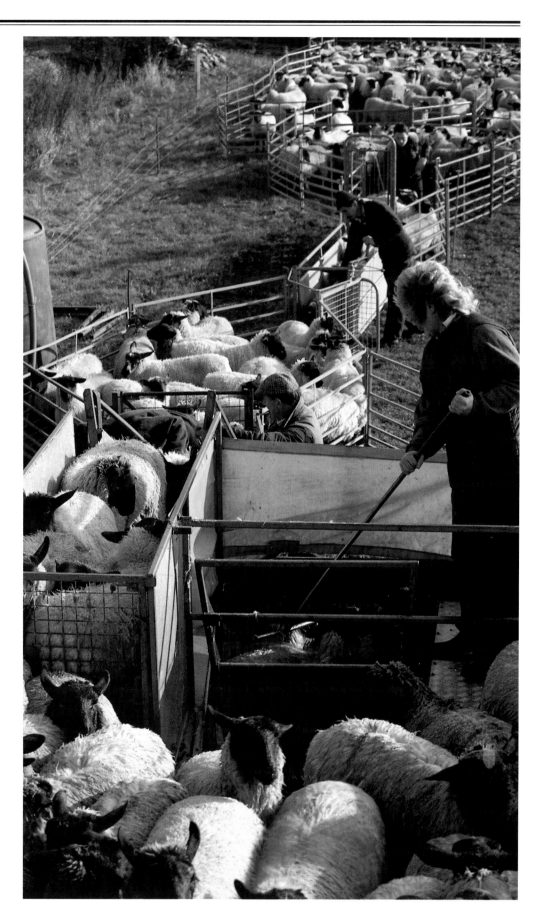

Sheep-dipping: organic farmers are allowed to dip with a non-organophate compound to tackle scab and fly strike. At back, Andrew Baker, middle, Fred Hartles, then John Underhill with a cap. The woman is one of the contract workers.

Well managed alternative farms use less synthetic chemical fertilisers, pesticides and antibiotics without necessarily decreasing – and in some cases increasing – per acre crop yields and the productivity of livestock systems... Wide adoption of proven alternative systems would result in even greater economic benefits to farmers and economic benefits to the nation.

It would be encouraging to think that these benefits might receive a full investigation on this side of the Atlantic. Perhaps they will one day.

The course of farming is changing. It may well be that the RASE report will be seen in the not-too-distant future as the swan song of the last generation of farmers who looked at the present system of chemical farming with total approbation. In the long term, public concerns about pesticide use and animal welfare *do* impinge on public policy. The national policy for agriculture in the Netherlands, the most intensively farmed nation in Europe, is that agriculture should be safe, sustainable and remain competitive. To achieve sustainability, the Government of the Netherlands is aiming for pesticide use to be cut by one-third by 1995 and by half by the year 2000. This is all the more remarkable since remaining competitive internationally is vital to the Dutch because their farming industry exports 70 per cent of what it produces.

The Dutch farming industry thinks it can do it. It is already years ahead in the science of 'alternative' and organic farming. Frank Wijnands, who co-ordinates farming systems research at the Institute for Research in Arable Crops and Field Vegetables at Lelystad told *Farmers Weekly*: 'About five years ago we decided our present system was a dead end road and changed the emphasis at the Institute from being a fire brigade trying to solve last year's problems to looking for better systems which would avoid the problems in the first place.'

Their breakthrough came when, in search of ways of reducing pesticide use, the Institute examined research commissioned for organic farmers (yes, in Holland such science existed twelve years ago). The techniques Wijnands and his colleagues have discovered read like a manual of organic farming. They drill cereals late in the autumn, since they find that these have less disease and fewer aphids. They achieve weed control by a combination of late sowing and mechanical weeding with new harrows imported from Austria and Switzerland. Some fascinating comments from farmers, after a season of using few pesticides, were recorded in the *Farmers Weekly* article by John Burns:

When they successfully grow crops with little or no pesticides they begin to feel in control again. Some have said that they feel they are farmers again. Mr Wijnands comments that it has not always been appreciated how many skills have been lost from farming since 'modern' methods took over, and most younger farmers will have to learn from scratch if they are to break their dependence from pesticides.

Is the Netherlands' pesticides policy the face of the future? Almost certainly it is. What the Dutch do today, particularly on environmental matters, has a habit of becoming European Community policy tomorrow. While Britain's farming establishment remains wedded to 'dirty' methods of farming which may one day be phased out, our European competitors have found ways of performing the same tasks in a cleaner way, thereby seizing the technological and, surely, moral advantage.

SUSTAINING THE SKYLARK

For singing till his heaven fills,
'Tis love of earth that he instils,
And ever winging up and up,
Our valley is his golden cup,
And he the wine which overflows
To lift us with him as he goes:
The woods and brooks, the sheep and kine,
He is, the hills, the human line,
The meadows green, the fallows brown,
The dreams of labour in the town;
He sings the sap, the quickened veins,
The wedding song of sun and rains
He is, the dance of children, thanks
Of sowers, shouts of primrose-banks,
And eye of violets while they breathe;
All these the circling song will wreath,
And you shall hear the herb and tree,
The better heart of men shall see,
Shall feel celestially, as long
As you crave nothing save the song.

From 'The Lark Ascending', George Meredith.

I N DECADES TO COME, what will people make of the story of Highgrove, the estate that Prince Charles bought for himself and developed as an image of his interests in the world? Will it be seen as just a rich man's pleasure garden, a toy irrelevant to the workings of everyday life, or will it be recognised partly as the site of a fascinating experiment, the vehicle of a personal crusade towards making the concept of 'sustainability' a reality? I suspect that people may recognise more clearly than many alive today that Prince Charles was attempting to find answers through Highgrove to a question which others could only ask: how should technological man live so as to leave the smallest possible ecological 'footprint' behind him?

Prince Charles has made his estate a symbol of a changed attitude to the natural world at the highest levels of public life. The influence of the monarchy works

OPPOSITE: *The benefits of habitat protection: dropwort with a burnet moth caterpillar in permanent pasture at Kite's Nest Farm.*

OVERLEAF: *The tractor had to go round: a new spinney on the Westonbirt organic block.*

251

in mysterious ways, but in the case of Highgrove, there are connections which can be traced. When Prince Charles began to farm at Highgrove, for instance, he was aware that his decision to turn his farm organic was a controversial one, not just among conventional farmers but among the public at large. The popular idea of organic agriculture at the time was of a mildly wacky 'alternative' activity practised on Herefordshire communes by ageing hippies in bobble hats, with no hope of changing or influencing the mainstream technological agriculture that was going on around them. The Prince attracted a degree of mockery in some journals for throwing in his lot with such company.

That is not quite how that decision looks now. Organic gardening is the choice of increasing numbers of ordinary people who see no reason why they should use any more toxic chemicals than they absolutely need and practise the 'precautionary principle' in their own gardens. After the food scares of the 1980s and the growing absurdities of food surpluses and set-aside, organic farming has lost its cranky associations. Organic food has a single legal standard across the European Community. There are soon likely to be EC grants to help more farmers to convert to organic methods. It is possible that there could soon be a steady growth in the organic sector. It is an intriguing question how much of all this would have happened without the heir to the throne becoming a figurehead of the organic movement.

It is true that organic goods have yet to make a significant breakthrough into the market, but there is no reason why they should not take a larger share once unfair competition is removed. Prices may also fall to a level that the consumer finds more realistic. Most of us, after all, would prefer to know that our baked potato skins contained no chemical residues and that our breakfast cereals had not been stored with shovelfuls of pesticide. And there are growing numbers of cooks who know that organically-reared meat frequently pays dividends in terms of taste.

For the farmer, whatever he may think of organic methods, Highgrove has its fascination. As Terry Summers wrote recently:

> The change being made to organic farming has taught us that accepted wisdom is not necessarily the only sensible basis for farming. It has taught us that it can be fascinating to face the challenge of a complete change of attitude...Above all we have noticed a genuine interest among many of our visitors which suggests that many farmers are inherently embarrassed by the results of modern agriculture. After all the farming community is, by nature, conservative, and economic necessity has driven them to farm in the modern mode even though the majority (especially the older generation) feel it is wrong.

Many farmers hate to hear it said, but by most common-sense criteria organic methods are the most sustainable, in terms of soils, finite resources and biological diversity. And sustainability is what 180 countries undertook to promote in every area of life at the Earth Summit in Rio de Janeiro in 1992. It would be hypocritical to insist that the agriculture and forestry of the Amazon or Madagascar should be ecologically sustainable and for us in the rich North not to insist upon the sustainability of agriculture at home.

Prince Charles is aware that organic farming may not be the only way to achieve this end, but it poses a challenge to the rest of agriculture to define what other systems can. In the meantime, if the course of mainstream agriculture is to converge with alternative systems, far more research will be needed to explain the benefits of those alternative systems. To this end, Prince Charles has offered Highgrove as the site of a joint research project by the three main Government research councils into how a large estate can move towards sustainable agriculture. The three councils involved will be the Agriculture and Food Research Council, the Natural Environment Research Council and the Economic and Social Research Council. The idea is to show what productivity can be achieved when external inputs are reduced to a minimum, to examine the benefits for soil and water, to examine the economic penalties and benefits of organic farming and to examine the best way of marketing the products. The work will be independent and funded by the research councils but with total co-operation from the estate. The objective of the study, which will run for three years, is to create a model farm for the post-Rio age.

We are still discovering, thirty years after the publication of Rachel Carson's *Silent Spring*, further disturbing effects that modern farming methods are having on the wildlife of the countryside. Contrary to the belief of many farmers and MAFF officials, the story continues; the 'engine of destruction' has not been switched off. Take, for example, the decline of the skylark, the symbol of summer in George Meredith's 'The Lark Ascending' and in Vaughan Williams's music. The skylark appears to be declining because the insects it feeds on in cereal fields have been removed by pesticides. Its nests in grassland have been destroyed by silage making. Present farming methods also account for the decline of dozens of other farmland birds: for example, the partridge, corn bunting, lapwing and stone curlew. Farming leaves just too little room at the margins for these species to thrive. There is a comparable decline to be found in British butterflies and moths, in fungi and in wild flowers. What little remains of permanent pasture, the home of what wild flowers we have left, is still disappearing under the plough. Does the decline of a few hundred species of plants and birds matter when compared with, say, the day-to-day health of the rural economy? I believe it does, for the significance of these living things strikes deep and affects our very sense of nationhood. The countryside of the Cotswolds without skylarks would be like the National Gallery without pictures.

If the Continent were facing war or famine, these ecological losses would be faced with resignation not anger. But in a time of agricultural surpluses, when the farmer is still subsidised to cover the land with chemicals, and when a costly system of agricultural support could have been used to make good some of the damage, the moral perspective of the greens tells us that this is wrong. We are rewarding the farmer for polluting the land and using up scarce resources in ways that he might, in his heart of hearts, be unwilling to do, were he not required to make a living by the incentives he currently receives. By turning his farm organic, the Prince of Wales has hastened the perception that the boundaries of the market in agriculture need to be re-drawn, and that the farmer's role needs to be redefined. Highgrove is his vision of the future.

Future Harvest

I N PLANNING MY ACTIVITIES at Highgrove, I have tried to remember that it is essential for each generation to see itself within a historical perspective, without falling into the trap of thinking, as various individuals have done in the past, that everything worthwhile was being destroyed in their own day and age. Maybe I am falling into this trap myself, but I do believe that in our age we are being confronted with an ever-greater dilemma in the sense of being victims of our own astonishing success. Our technological capabilities are now almost limitless which, in my opinion, places a particular responsibility on all of us as to how we actually employ these capabilities. Just because, technically, we can perform some remarkable feats of harnessing Nature to our will, or subjugating Her altogether, does not necessarily mean we have to carry out those feats if, in the process, we damage the long-term stability of those natural systems on which our descendants will ultimately rely.

An important component of natural systems, and something which I hope my activities at Highgrove will promote, is biological diversity. It is fashionable (and correct) to point out the importance of maintaining biological diversity, on a global scale, to provide the broadest possible gene bank for future medicines and sources of food. But, when transformed from a rather dull and abstract concept into the reality of a myriad of living forms it is also, I believe, a source of great joy in our lives – to be treasured for more than purely utilitarian reasons.

None of what I am saying is very original. Some people would say that the argument has, to all intents and purposes, already been accepted – as evidenced by what took place at the UN Environment and Development Conference in Rio de Janeiro in June 1992. Progress is certainly being made in various quarters, but I still maintain that the greatest threat we face stems from our contemporary inability to contemplate taking a long-term view. We find it much easier and more 'cost-effective' to choose the cheaper option, with the quickest return, only to find that it costs us even more to rectify the damage in the long run. Many countries fall into this trap and it is only when the damage becomes glaringly

ABOVE: *Listening to, but not necessarily taking, advice.*

OPPOSITE: *Rampant may blossom and a wide field margin by one of the best dry-stone walls on the Duchy Home Farm.*

OVERLEAF: *Planting oak trees near the woolly thistles in Preston's Wood.*

257

obvious that people start to make a fuss in order to try to preserve the last remaining examples of whatever it is that has been swept away, damaged, or brought to the verge of extinction. It is, I suppose, ultimately a measure of the true worth of human civilisations as to how they cope with such fundamental questions.

Can those of us living in the richer countries, in all conscience, call ourselves civilised societies if we allow our unbalanced obsession with industrial systems, with cost-effectiveness, with 'efficiency' and competitiveness to cloud our sense of proportion? Can we call ourselves civilised if we fail to see that such a lack of balance in the way we conduct our affairs, in the way we view the natural world as a mechanical process that can be analysed, synthesised, categorised and compartmentalised, can only lead to the ultimate destruction of all the things which have allowed us to claim we are civilised?

Is it the hallmark of a civilised society to educate people into believing that sentiment and efficiency are incompatible, to the extent that we are in severe danger of removing the last vestiges of our cultural foundations in Britain by driving the smaller farmers off the land – the land which has been nurtured by generations of their forefathers as a way of life, as a veritable form of art? And why are we doing this? Because, we are told, it is in the interests of efficiency, cost-effectiveness and competitiveness. Machines may function perfectly satisfactorily in accordance with such imperatives, but human beings, and human societies, do not. They may appear to do so, but it is an illusion engendered by our inability to take a long-term view.

Perhaps what we are witnessing in our age – albeit over a long time-scale – is the inevitable earthly process of decay, death and ultimately rebirth. Perhaps it will be necessary for human societies to experience environmental or ecological catastrophes of one kind or another, as has happened in the past, before we appreciate the wisdom of adopting a longer-term perspective? Perhaps, tragically, it will be necessary to witness the extinction of many more species of animals, birds, fish, insects and plants, let alone, God forbid, of human communities caught up in a nightmare world of rapidly diminishing vital natural resources and burgeoning population growth before we alter our 'conventional' attitudes? This is such a gloomy subject that I will undoubtedly be told I am being needlessly pessimistic and that there are many signs which give rise to optimism. However, I am one of those people who believes in the precautionary principle, especially in view of all the evidence available and the warnings expressed by increasing numbers of reputable scientists and field workers whose own observations fuel their anxiety.

You could be forgiven for wondering how all this relates to Highgrove! It may sound odd to say this, but I infinitely prefer action to words, which is one of the reasons why I decided that conversion to a fully organic/traditional system at Highgrove was essentially right, and perhaps action can speak louder than words.

The truth is that, in a very modest way, I am searching for the most successful – and mildly profitable – way of adopting a longer-term perspective in terms of management of the land, enhancement of wildlife, adding value to the primary products we produce, developing better energy efficiency and more effective

A bee seeking nectar in a foxglove in the garden at Highgrove.

waste utilisation. In this way I hope we can, perhaps, over time develop a model which could be used to explain in a practical way how it might be possible to live more effectively off the 'income' produced from Nature's 'capital assets', rather than exploiting those capital assets in the short term.

Apart from many other considerations, I also happen to believe that somehow we need to show those millions of people living in the materially-poorer parts of the world (though they may be much richer in spirit) that we are making serious attempts in the North to limit the rate at which we consume so many of the world's resources and to find better ways of harnessing our technological ingenuity to this end. There are already some very interesting developments in this field and what I am trying to do at Highgrove is, of course, very small and very domestic by comparison.

This book shows that the conversion process to an organic system is not an easy one; nor is it cheap. The Duchy of Cornwall is certainly in a more fortunate position to undertake such a conversion than most, but when I think of those farmers who have taken the decision to farm organically and to accept the inevitable loss of income for the first two or three years, my admiration knows no bounds.

Expensive it may be, especially if the farm is spread out in parcels of land and there are few existing buildings which can accommodate the increased numbers of stock associated with an organic or, more appropriately, a traditional mixed

There are some farmers who seek to put their profits back into the land by repairing traditional buildings. Here, a restored thatched barn at Rushall.

Organic wheat: Maris Widgeon, a long-strawed wheat, at Highgrove.

farm, but, nevertheless, I believe that it is part of the duty of the Duchy of Cornwall to utilise its Home Farm to experiment, pioneer and set an example. It is as important in farming as it is in any other area of human activity to meet the challenge of our times, which it seems to me is to integrate a concern for sustainability and the preservation of biological diversity into economic activity.

There is still a need for modern technology – but as slave, not master. At Highgrove we use modern strains of clover, grass, wheat, oats and beans to optimise our yields. We use a state-of-the-art harrow-comb as an additional arm to enable us to control weeds and to aerate the soil. We have also recently purchased the most modern manure spreader for the main reason that it produces a higher quality spread which makes it possible to utilise this valuable renewable resource to greatest effect.

To me, one of the most interesting and challenging aspects of organic farming is the development of products which add value to what we grow or produce. In my view, the marketing of a quality product is an essential feature of an organic system, whether the product stems from meat, milk, cereals, fruit, vegetables or herbs. Nowadays it is no good expecting official agencies to buy your primary produce at guaranteed prices. In order to have some possibility of long-term survival in a very changed agricultural world it seems to me essential that we should rise to the challenge of forming marketing cooperatives and developing outlets for the kinds of

Fred Hartles feeding ewes at Highgrove.

food which have been grown or reared in less artificial and industrially-orientated circumstances. Already in the UK, we import around two-thirds of the organic produce sold in supermarkets or shops, so there is room for improvement. . .

Perhaps we could learn something useful from the experience of other countries, in this case Japan which, after all, is the world's most industrialised nation. Japanese agriculture has endured massive restructuring since the Second World War, but despite this – or perhaps because of it – a fascinating example of successful closer cooperation between the farmer and the consumer has been established over the past twenty-five years in the form of a purchasing cooperative, known as the Seikatsu Club. With some 200,000 members, the club buys *directly* from farmers and primary producers. In return for asking farmers to use organic fertiliser and fewer chemicals, members buy a contracted amount of produce and agree to overlook physical imperfections if they exist. Members also assist the farmers in the harvest when their labour is necessary. However 'unconventional' this may seem to many people in this country who have only known one way of doing things, it is hard to dismiss the club's annual spending budget of £160 million. I am not saying that such a scheme is necessarily replicable in an exactly similar form in the United Kingdom, but it represents a possible way forward in achieving one of the elements of an integrated approach to farming and the countryside which, in a very small way, I am trying to explore at Highgrove.

Now that the conversion to an organic system is well under way, I am keen to look at other areas of our operations at Highgrove, with a view to establishing as self-contained and sustainable a model as possible.

The reed-bed sewage-treatment system is a good example of the kind of thing I have in mind. It has no connection with the farming operations, and is therefore not covered by the Soil Association standards for organic production – but it does help to make the estate operate on a sustainable basis. As Charles Clover described earlier, the system produces compostable material from the bark-filled pits, the willows produce a crop for basket-weaving or biomass energy and the reeds themselves can be composted. The only input (apart from the sewage!) is electricity. Since the site is flat, pumps are required to make the system operate. It may be that we can harness solar power to drive them and I am trying to find out how large a solar panel would be required – quite large I suspect, under habitually grey Gloucestershire skies!

Water conservation is another priority area for research. Our local company, Wessex Water, have an enviable record of maintaining supply throughout drought conditions which cause problems further East, but water is an infinitely precious resource, to be husbanded carefully. We do not use sprinklers on the lawns – if the grass sometimes goes a bit brown that is just part of a natural cycle as far as I am concerned – and only water those plants which really need help.

A pollution-treatment system with a difference – it does not pass on its pollution to someone else for disposal.

Ideally, water for this purpose could be collected from the large expanse of roof, and stored underground until needed. There are the remains of an underground storage system which dates back to the days before a mains supply and I am looking to see if this can be put back into use.

Energy efficiency is a particularly important subject. Cutting down on energy use has three main environmental benefits. It preserves resources of fossil fuels which will be increasingly valuable in the future, it reduces the amount of carbon dioxide released into the atmosphere to contribute to global warming, and it reduces the amount of atmospheric pollutants which cause acid rain.

A couple of years ago I asked a firm of consulting engineers to have a look at all aspects of energy use at Highgrove and they came up with some interesting recommendations – which have saved money too!

There are practical limits to what can be done to improve the insulation of an eighteenth-century house, but even things like blocking up disused chimney flues and putting draught-proof seals on windows make a difference.

I would like to have installed a straw-fired central heating system, but it was pointed out that there is little surplus straw in the area, and it would not make sense to import it from miles away. In addition, such systems need a steady load to be efficient and the load at Highgrove is anything but steady as people come and go at irregular intervals.

I am interested, too, in what is known (rather confusingly, in my opinion) as biomass production. This involves planting fast-growing tree species, usually willows or poplars, and then harvesting them on a short rotation coppice system. The wood which is harvested is then chipped and used for fuel. The theory is well developed, but all the research I have seen suggests that the biomass is produced on a short rotation from an intensively-grown monoculture. I find it hard to believe that this would be sustainable in the longer term without considerable use of artificial fertilisers, not to mention herbicides in the early years to get crops established. I would much prefer to see unfertilised coppice, of a mixture of species, and in a series of strips or copses, rather than the field-scale blocks of willow monoculture which others are currently recommending.

It may be that we shall end up planting shelter belts on the edges of fields, using a mixture of species but including a high proportion of alder which is leguminous and fixes nitrogen in the ground to the benefit of adjacent trees, in the same way that clover does. In one copse planted some time ago we have noticed that the ash, sycamore and cherry have established particularly well in the presence of an interplanting of alder (which also happens to be a good habitat for siskins and redpolls).

LEFT: *Biomass crops, in liquefied form, are likely to provide fuel for propulsion when fossil fuels run out.*

Elsewhere in Europe, I know that experiments are proceeding well in producing a fuel from rapeseed. This is an interesting idea, but not one which I shall be pursuing because the production of rape requires the application of large amounts of nitrogenous fertiliser, which in turn can only be produced by a large input of energy. Over the whole process, the ratio of energy in to energy out simply does not appear to stand up to detailed examination. This is something of a relief because growing rape seems to lead inevitably to smelly honey, a plague of little black pollen beetles on the roses and children suffering from hay fever!

OVERLEAF: *Sycamore for the squirrels, and alder, an undervalued wood, in a new spinney at Westonbirt.*

I am told that the energy efficiency of large modern tractors is actually much better than their smaller predecessors and that recent improvements in tyre technology have helped in making better use of the available energy, as well as reducing soil compaction. Smaller and lighter tractors and farm machinery appear to be an attractive option in reducing energy use, but whilst organic production reduces the number of passes of machinery, it also puts a premium on the timing of operations. Larger equipment can cover the ground much more swiftly and allow the all-important cultivations to take place at the best possible time. Even so, an instinctive distrust of some of the more ludicrous hi-tech practices has led me to ask the Intermediate Technology Development Group (of which I am Patron and who do such excellent work in developing countries) to take a look at the farming operations at Highgrove and see if there are any possible applications for the kind of simple and straightforward equipment more commonly encountered in the Third World.

Achieving the maximum bio-diversity requires some thought, even in an organic regime. Maximum bio-diversity would almost certainly be achieved through the encouragement of low fertility (as found in those old, unimproved meadows which look so wonderful and provide an ideal habitat for butterflies, small mammals, barn owls, wild flowers and rare fungi). However, the key to productive grassland under an organic regime is achieving high fertility through the introduction of clover, a balanced stocking regime and the use of farmyard manure.

This conundrum of bio-diversity versus optimum organic production highlights the need for a set of environmental objectives for the farming operations. Having gained a bit of experience of some of the many factors involved, I believe we are now in a position to undertake an exercise of this sort. I am aware, too, of the need to prove that, at least after the conversion period, the kinds of farming systems I have been talking about can be shown to be profitable if we are to set any kind of example which others will wish to attempt to follow.

There will undoubtedly continue to be a large element of trial and error in the way we go about things – mistakes will be made and lessons will be learned. This process may be accelerated, and made rather more public, by the suggestion which was put to me recently that our operations at Highgrove provide an interesting test bed for the study of the full effects of a transfer to a more sustainable form of agriculture.

An independent, objective, scientific study is an exciting, if rather daunting, prospect but what better way could there be to attempt to prove that at least some of what I believe in so strongly is also both practical and sensible in the long run?

It is, perhaps, worth noting one interesting feature of the Highgrove experience so far – and that is that after six years along the organic path the farm staff have all been surprised by the results and have become very supportive in all aspects of the operations. I leave it to you to judge whether this is significant (you may, of course, think that along with everyone else they just agree with everything I say. I used to have a member of my staff who would pull my leg by saying 'When His Royal Highness laughs, we all laugh . . .'!), but I can only say that if the organic movement was (as some people would have us believe) a total confidence trick, then with their level of involvement they would be the first to see through it. None of them seems to feel we are taking a backward step.

It is only too easy for other people, especially the expert proponents of 'agricultural industrialism', to pour scorn on such attempts to create a balanced system of farming. They will say that it cannot possibly meet the challenge of providing adequate quantities of food for the growing population of the world and is relevant only in very marginal terms as a response to a niche market in richer countries. They will say that it is going 'backwards', 'reverting' to the 'peasant' agriculture of our grandfathers (I hear this comment all the time and it reveals, yet again, the extent to which our educational system has brainwashed us into viewing the world in linear terms). But is it really going 'backwards', as those farmers who were shown round the Duchy Home Farm in 1986–7 clearly thought it was, if we try to establish a natural or biological system in which waste does not occur and in which the inherent cyclic nature of 'traditional' farming is capable of regeneration and reproducing itself indefinitely?

Is it really going 'backwards' to treat animals, not as machines or units of production from which ever-higher yields can be extracted in an intensive, factory environment, but as biological entities that perform far more satisfactorily under less stressful conditions, present fewer diseases when their numbers are kept at a reasonable balance, and ultimately ensure a better quality product? (Ask the butcher who purchases the lambs and the steers from the Duchy Home Farm what he thinks of the end product from this system of farming.)

Is it really going 'backwards' to limit, or even cease, the use of inorganic fertiliser and instead to 'fix' nitrogen naturally by the use of clover-based leys in a 'traditional' rotation, or to abandon the use of pesticides and herbicides?

As a result of adopting this approach and of utilising 'older-fashioned' varieties of cereals (which may be lower yielding, but are also often more resistant to disease) we have found that the fields are not overrun by weeds. Arable weeds associated with conventional farming use artificial nitrogen to their advantage, making extra growth which allows them to compete with the crop. By not using nitrogen we have found that the crop will still grow to the same height. However, weeds like cleavers, field pansy and chickweed stay close to the ground where they do not compete but provide a diversity of plant types that is beneficial to herbivorous insects, which in turn support a reservoir of predatory species. A further benefit is that crops which do not receive artificial nitrogen are not forced. The plants are less lush and sappy, with a stronger cell wall which is less vulnerable to fungal attack.

Is it really going 'backwards', for instance, to re-establish a mixed system of farming in which stock play a vital part in the overall, self-contained cycle and in which their 'waste' is returned to the soil in order to maintain its 'living' *long-term* fertility? Many agencies – in particular the National Rivers Authority in England and Wales – now recognise that 'waste' from farms which have responded to the modern industrial imperatives of farming and have increased the numbers of cattle beyond the natural carrying capacity of the land is a major cause of river pollution.

OVERLEAF: *Maintaining biodiversity requires, paradoxically, the maintenance of low fertility in species-rich permanent pasture.*

The organic garden showing Lady Salisbury's crab-apple crowns. Note also (centre) the leaves of a variety of purple Brussels sprouts.

I have written rather a lot about the farming and conservation activities at Highgrove, but one of the projects which has provided me with enormous pleasure and satisfaction has been the development of the kitchen garden. At the time I completed the creation of the new design in the walled garden I had no knowledge of growing vegetables and fruit (I am still pretty ignorant, I can assure you!), but by a gradual process of experimentation and performance and of meeting and talking with interesting, knowledgeable people, I have learnt more and more about growing fruit and vegetables in a chemical-free environment. I have also, as I said in the introductory chapter, discovered at first hand the magical powers of good, old-fashioned muck! There is, of course, a problem with various pests and diseases which, if I were growing vegetables and fruit on a commercial basis, I would perhaps find awkward. But through my association with the Henry Doubleday Research Association I have begun to discover the possibilities of dealing with pests and diseases through biological and 'natural' means.

One of the problems we have created for ourselves, through an entirely 'industrial' approach to growing things, is the susceptibility of monocultures of cereal crops or trees to pests and diseases. A diversity of species, on the other hand, whereby various crops are grown in association with other, complementary plants or trees, can have a beneficial effect by reducing or eliminating the need for ever more powerful chemical sprays. Another problem, of which you only become aware when you start to grow things yourself, is the extent to which modern varieties of seed are almost totally dependent on certain chemical sprays to produce the kinds of yields the industrial process demands.

What has decidedly depressed me is to discover in recent years just how close we are to losing a very large number of traditional, but less high-yielding varieties of fruit and vegetables – not to mention the difficulty of preserving the rare breeds of sheep, cattle and pigs whose very genetic diversity (as in the case of fruit and vegetables) will doubtless prove to be of enormous importance in a future made increasingly dangerous and uncertain by climate change and by the more unscrupulous forms of commercial genetic manipulation and engineering.

I often wonder how many people realise what they are in danger of losing, or how much poorer our lives would be without the infinite variety that Nature offers? Perhaps only a very small number of people actually care about these things we all take so much for granted, and as long as the supermarkets are stuffed with totally unblemished produce of a standard size and appearance there seems to be no particular problem. And yet there are a number of dedicated bands of remarkable people – like the Henry Doubleday Research Association – who battle every day of the week against a rising tide of European Community directives aimed at standardising everything in our lives which, ultimately, despite the inevitable bureaucratic protestations to the contrary, and unless we are careful, will destroy some of the more enjoyable foundations on which our European civilisation and culture has been laboriously and lovingly constructed over thousands of years.

One of the reasons I grow the rarer varieties of vegetables and fruit at Highgrove is not only because I actually enjoy eating them, since they invariably taste much better and look much more interesting – if, perhaps, more 'blemished' than those in a supermarket! – but because I am also *determined* to find a way to preserve these varieties for future generations. Fashion and novelty play a

Unusual varieties often taste better.

surprisingly dominant role in our lives, but fashions change and what was once considered irrelevant and decried as too traditional can frequently become interesting and even essential to another generation.

In the introductory chapter to this book I mentioned the positions adopted by a large majority of the professional colleges in this country. It is perhaps illuminating, and somewhat demoralising, to note that only a tiny handful of university departments of agriculture or agricultural colleges now teach agricultural history. References to the past are usually to confirm the superiority of modern over former methods. This contrasts with the experience of the current Director of the Institute of Agricultural History and the Museum of English Rural Life at Reading University who finds that many of the older farmers testify to the intrinsic interest of 'old' farming systems with their internal logic, sustainability and 'balance'. Likewise, in the older farming families, the collective memory tends to be a reminder of the cyclical nature of farming, with its booms, slumps and changing fashions, and this acts as something of a brake on their wilder ambitions, especially those involving new technology. Many of these families would ascribe to the view, born of experience, that survival *in the long run* is best achieved through sound, rather than 'progressive', farming.

I am afraid that the arguments over agricultural and environmental policy will continue to rage furiously for many years. The 'high-pitched buzz' farmers, favouring a twin-track approach to farming and the environment and preferring to opt for hi-tech, intensive systems of agriculture on ever bigger farms, will accuse the organic farmers, and those who believe that farming, the environment and wider cultural considerations have to be pursued through an integrated approach, of being out-dated, 'muck-and-magic' eccentrics, not living in the 'real' world and simultaneously conducting a green confidence trick on the gullible consumer! One of the counter arguments from the eccentrics will be that surely no one in their right mind would want to see a pattern emerge in the United Kingdom which is similar to the history of the restructuring of American agriculture since the Second World War, whereby the policy adopted successfully reduced the farm population by 56 per cent between 1950 and 1970 and saw the replacement of a substantial proportion of the medium-sized family farms by a small number of huge 'super farms', aligned with agribusiness interests and whose highly intensive operating methods have had, and are very likely to have, a negative impact on the ecological balance in the countryside.

I realise that to express concern about these crucial questions lays one open to the inevitable charge of being anti-technology and anti-'progress'. However, to my mind, the overriding challenge we face is to develop the most *appropriate* technology, bearing in mind the goals we want to achieve. After all, it should be possible to encourage the development of alternative forms of technology through incentives and other mechanisms. And, surely, these goals should be part of an *integrated* approach to the life and long-term health of our countryside? These goals incorporate not only the commercial process of producing a crop, but also the quality of life and employment of *people*, the quality of the end product, the maintenance of soil fertility, and of water quality, the conservation of flora and fauna through the skilful management of habitat – in other words, that subtle blend of private interest and public good which, when all is said and done, must surely amount to what we describe as the 'cultural' life of a nation.

Such eighteenth- and nineteenth-century travellers and writers as Defoe, Johnson, Young and Cobbett clearly saw agriculture as the heart of culture; as a diverse and multi-faceted activity involving not just food production, but land and culture management. Even William Cobbett, in his day, was commenting on the cereal lands, saying that there were 'no hedges, no ditches, no commons, no grassy lawns. . . All the rest is bare of trees and the wretched labourer has not a stick of wood, and has not a place for a pig or cow to graze, or even to lie down upon. . .'

Managing the countryside in the interests of food production, wildlife, natural resources, public amenity and landscape value is a delicate task requiring particular skills and commitment. It is infinitely more complex than managing an industrial concern. The people best suited to carrying out this task of enlightened stewardship are, I feel sure, the farmers themselves. I also believe that many of them have become profoundly uneasy in recent years about the path they have been encouraged to follow and are looking for a different approach which echoes their better instincts about true husbandry. But to enable farmers to put their stewardship skills to best use there needs to be a change in the accepted, official thinking which for the last fifty years has dominated the direction taken by the agricultural sector.

For all our sakes, and particularly our children's, we must ensure that it is possible, somehow, to farm and manage the countryside in such a way that our instinctive feeling for nature and the natural cycle is not totally subsumed by 'commercial' considerations.

As far as I am concerned, I felt it right in my heart to attempt to pursue this course and I must remain true to this conviction. (When all is said and done, I would like to emphasise that although it takes two years, a considerable degree of extra planning, extra costs and an initially reduced income to convert to an organic regime, it is perfectly possible to convert back to a conventional system virtually overnight – simply by the purchase of artificial inputs.)

Only history will judge whether I took the right decision. In the meantime, I will continue striving to develop a model of sustainable, natural farming that is more appropriate for the twenty-first century, in the same way that I will fight with all my might and main to find ways to preserve the cultural aspects of agriculture and to ensure the survival of the smaller farmer as the veritable backbone of our country. For without them we will have no true culture, no real values and a future that may be industrially and economically 'correct', but deprived of those elements which invest human life with true meaning and inspiration.

Appendix

The Prince of Wales's mixture

This is the basis of the wildflower mixture recommended by Miriam Rothschild for planting along the drive at Highgrove: a more elaborate version of her decorative mixture called 'The Farmer's Nightmare', a blend of cornfield annuals and meadow perennials, which was sown with a mixture of short grasses.

CORNFIELD ANNUALS

25g *Agrostemma githago*: Corn cockle
65g *Centaurea cyanus*: Cornflower
35g *Chrysanthemum segetum*: Corn marigold
35g *Matricaria maritima*: Scentless mayweed
25g *Papaver rhoeas*: Field poppy

MEADOW PERENNIALS

50g *Anthyllis vulnoraria*: Kidney vetch
20g *Agrimonia eupatoria*: Common agrimony
25g *Chicorium intybus*: Chicory
70g *Centaurea nigra*: Lesser knapweed
40g *Centaurea scabiosa*: Greater knapweed
21g *Daucus carota*: Wild carrot
21g *Galium verum*: Ladies' bedstraw
35g *Geranium pratense*: Meadow cranesbill
10g *Knautia arvensis*: Field scabious
10g *Leontondon hispidus*: Rough hawkbit
40g *Leucanthemum vulgare*: Ox-eye daisy
21g *Linaria vulgaris*: Toadflax
30g *Lotus corniculatus*: Bird's-foot trefoil
70g *Melilotus officinalis*: Yellow melilot
60g *Onobrychnis viciifolia*: Sainfoin
40g *Plantago media*: Hoary plantain
70g *Primula veris*: Cowslip
21g *Prunella vulgaris*: Selfheal
40g *Ranunculus acris*: Meadow buttercup
21g *Rhinanthus minor*: Yellow rattle
21g *Silene alba*: White campion
30g *Silene dioica*: Red campion

SOWING RATE: 150g/100 sq. yards.

Aquatic plants known to attract dragonflies

A list supplied by Miriam Rothschild as a basis for planting the pond and its immediate surroundings in the sewage garden.

Juncus inflexus: Rush
Iris pseudacorus: Yellow iris
Potamogeton natans: Broad-leaved pondweed
Callitriche stagnalis: Starwort
Lythrum salicaria: Purple loosestrife
Phragmites australis: Common reed
Veronica beccabunga: Brooklime
Mentha aquatica: Water mint
Lysimachia vulgaris: Yellow loosestrife
Myosotis laxa: Tufted forget-me-not
Polygonus amphibum: Amphibious bistort
Sparganium erectum: Branched bur reed
Menyanthes trifoliata: Bog bean
Nasturtium officinale: Watercress
Nymphaea alba: White water lily
Chara: Stonewort
Elodea canadensis: Common pondweed
Hydrocharis morsus-ranae: Frogbit
Stratiotes: Water soldier
Utricularia: Bladderwort
Nymphoides peltata: Fringed water lily
Nuphar lutea: Yellow water lily
Typha latifolia: Reed mace
Scirpus lacustris: Club rush
Ranunculus peltatus: Water crowfoot
Ceratophyllum demersum: Hornwort
Myriophyllum spicatum: Spiked water milfoil
Equisetum fluviatile: Water horsetail
Butomus umbellatus: Flowering rush
Carex: Sedge
Caltha palustris: Marsh marigold
Eleocharis palustris: Common spike-rush
Alisma plantago: Water plantain
Potamogeton crispus: Curled pondweed

Miriam Rothschild notes that some of these plants may temporarily become dominant. It would be well to consult English Nature, the Countryside Council for Wales or Scottish Natural Heritage regarding the suitability of the region for planting any of these species. The environment differs from place to place and professional advice is useful.

Selected Sources and Further Reading

Balfour, E. B., *The Living Soil and the Haughley Experiment*. Universe Books, 1943, 1975.

Barber, Sir Derek (study group chairman), *The State of Agriculture in the United Kingdom: A Report to the Royal Agricultural Society of England*. RASE, 1991.

Body, Richard, *Agriculture: The Triumph and the Shame*. M. T. Smith, 1982.
  Our Food, Our Land: Why Contemporary Farming Practices Must Change. Rider Books, 1991.

British Medical Association, *Pesticides, Chemicals and Health*. Edward Arnold, 1990.

British Organic Farmers and the Organic Growers Association, *Organic Farming: An Option for the Nineties*. British Organic Farmers and the Organic Growers Association, 86 Colston Street Bristol, 1990.

Carson, Rachel, *Silent Spring*. Hamish Hamilton, 1963.

Clarke, C. Arden, *The Environmental Effects of Conventional and Organic/Biological Farming Systems* (a review funded by the World Wide Fund for Nature). Political Ecology Research Group, Oxford, 1988.

Conway, Gordon R. and Pretty, Jules N., *Unwelcome Harvest: Agriculture and Pollution*. Earthscan, 1991.

Council for the Protection of Rural England and the World Wide Fund for Nature, *Future Harvests. The Economics of Farming and the Environment: Proposals for Action*. 1990.

Countryside Commission, *The Cotswold Landscape: A Landscape Assessment of an Area of Outstanding Natural Beauty*. Prepared by Cobham Resource Consultants, 1990.

Dudley, Nigel, *The Soil Association Handbook*. Optima, 1991.

Friends of the Earth, *Off the Treadmill: A Way Forward for Farmers and the Countryside*. FoE, 1991.

Hills, Lawrence D., *Organic Gardening*. Penguin, 1977.

Hoskins, W. G., *The Making of the English Landscape*. Penguin, 1955.

Kingsley, Nicholas, 'Modelling in the Provinces: The Work of Anthony Keck – Part I', *Country Life*, 20 October 1988; 'A Vision of Villas: The Work of Anthony Keck – Part II', *Country Life*, 27 October 1988.

Lampkin, Nicolas, *Organic Farming*. Farming Press, 1990.

Lang, Tim and Clutterbuck, Charlie, *P is for Pesticides*. Ebury Press in Association with the Pesticides Trust, 1991.

Leopold, Aldo, *A Sand County Almanac*. Oxford University Press, 1949, 1987.

Mabey, David and Gear, Alan and Jackie (eds), *Thorson's Organic Consumer Guide* (foreword by HRH The Prince of Wales. Thorsons, 1990.

Martin, W. Keble, *The Concise British Flora in Colour*. Mermaid Books, 1965.

Nature Conservancy Council, *Nature Conservation in Great Britain*. NCC, 1984.
  Nature Conservation and Agricultural Change (Focus on Nature Conservation, no. 25). NCC, 1990.

Rackham, Oliver, *A History of the Countryside*. J. M. Dent, 1987.

Robbins, Christopher, *Poisoned Harvest: A Consumer's Guide to Pesticide Use and Abuse*. Gollancz, 1991.

Sanders, Geoffrey and Verey, David, *Royal Homes in Gloucestershire*. A. J. Sutton, 1991.

Shoard, Marion, *The Theft of the Countryside*. M. T. Smith, 1980.

Thomas, Keith, *Man and the Natural World: Changing Attitudes in England 1500 – 1800*. Penguin, 1983.

U. S. National Research Council, *Alternative Agriculture*. National Academy Press, Washington D. C; John Wiley and Sons, 1989.

Wookey, Barry, *Rushall: The Story of an Organic Farm*. Blackwell, 1987.

World Commission on Environment and Development, *Our Common Future* (the Brundtland report). Oxford University Press, 1987.

Journals and Pamphlets

The Ecologist. Agriculture House, Sturminster Newton, Dorset, published monthly.

Henry Doubleday Research Association, *Step by Step Organic Gardening* (a series of leaflets), 1990.

New Farmer and Grower. British Organic Farmers and Organic Growers Association, 86 Colston Street Bristol, published quarterly.

Index

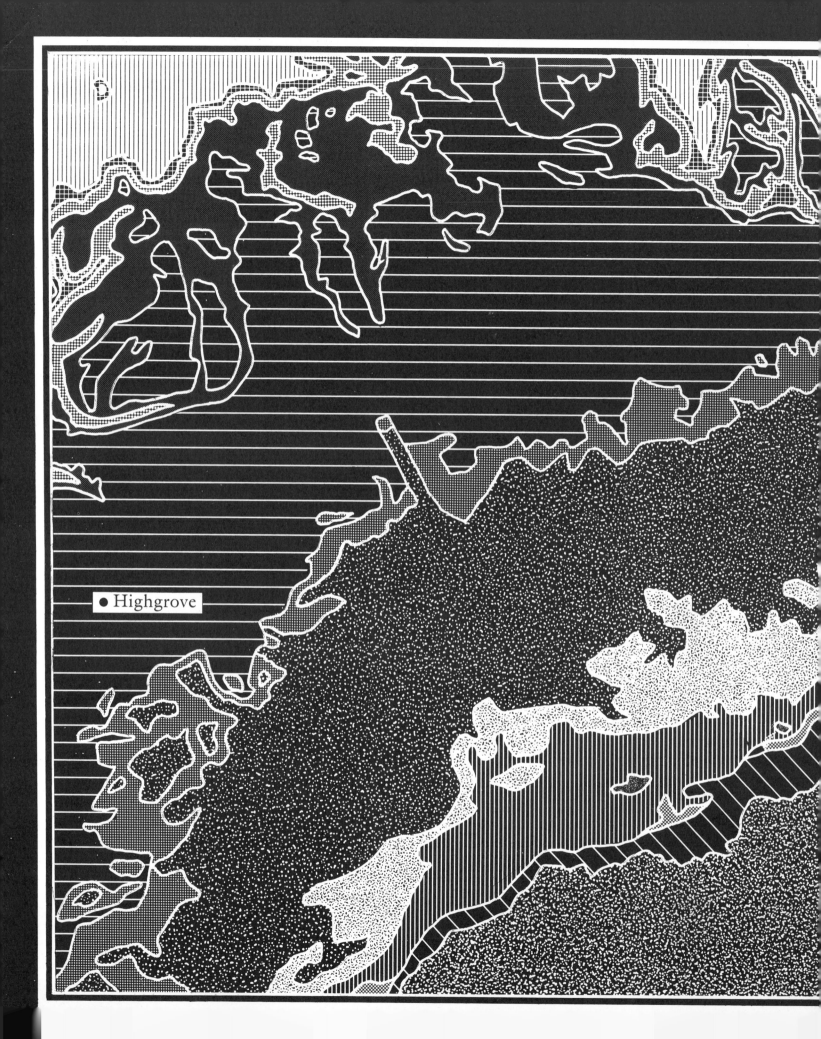